THE DESPAIRING DEVELOPER

THE DESPAIRING DEVELOPER

Diary of an Aid Worker in the Middle East

TIMOTHY MORRIS

I.B.Tauris & Co Ltd
Publishers
London · New York

Published in 1991 by
I.B.Tauris & Co Ltd
110 Gloucester Avenue
London NW1 8JA

175 Fifth Avenue
New York
NY 10010

Published in the United States of America
and Canada by
St Martin's Press
175 Fifth Avenue
New York
NY 10010

A CIP record for this book is available from the British Library
ISBN 1–85043–347–X cased
ISBN 1–85043–322–4 paper
70–009–060
Library of Congress Cataloging in Publication Data
ISBN 1–85043–486–7 cased
ISBN 1–85043–350–X paper

Printed and Bound in Great Britain by
Hartnolls Limited, Bodmin, Cornwall.

CONTENTS

1 Developmentalism   1

2 The Making of an 'Expert'   10

3 Sojourn in Sana'a   16

4 Into the Field   32

5 A Junket of Discovery   58

6 What to Facilitate?   88

7 Glimmers of Hope?   135

8 Battling for Health   162

9 Facing Frustration   189

10 Things Fall Apart   217

11 Packing It In   248

Glossary   287

1

DEVELOPMENTALISM

Developmentalism is a beguiling creed, to be a developer of backward lands an attractive vocation. We all want to see ourselves as bearers of aid, rectifiers of past injustice. To be sent far away to a distant nation as a conveyer of progress can only make one feel good. It assuages the collective guilt induced by the legacy of our colonial predecessors. It invites admiration from those left behind. It boosts self-esteem. It is to regain certainty and purpose, to cast away the ennui and despair of decaying industrial society and to restore bracing faith in the goodness and charity of one's fellow men and women.

For those of us sent as 'volunteers' the moral buzz is further enhanced. We unshakably hold the moral high ground. Our success is guaranteed. Laudatory stories are written in local rags as we depart. On arrival we have a licence to cloak ourselves in sanctity, to revel in rural discomfort far from the amenities enjoyed by tainted sybaritic fellow expatriates in the capital. By subtle remarks guilt can be induced in those not experiencing the pain of proximity to the 'real' natives. Modern communications, regular holidays and constant ego-boosting from 'desk persons' in the departed metropolis spare these modern missionaries the moral morass into which their predecessors may have sunk. On return, we may be written up as saints who have lived without water, electricity or nutritious food.

This book is a chronicle of my career in 'development', its delusions, frustrations, achievements and abrupt termination. Inevitably, these pages bear the scars of autobiography. It is an account of working as a promoter of primary health care for a small British project in the northern coastal plain of what was at the time the Yemen Arab Republic, a small country in the south-western corner of Arabia which in May 1990 merged with the People's Democratic Republic of Yemen to form the Republic of Yemen.

This is primarily a work of self-examination, a narrative of the sheer frustration of trying to influence change in a culture so different from one's own, in a manner not desired by the locals and resolutely opposed by powerful interests. It recreates the circumstances which caused suffering, anger and disappointment to a handful of ill-assorted, unqualified, underprepared individuals sent to the ends of Arabia. It describes the uncomfortable predicament of an anthropologist, a cultural interpreter trying to bridge the gulf between Yemeni and British perceptions of good health and its maintenance. It is about the progressive unmasking of illusions, those held by myself, my colleagues and the Yemenis with whom we worked. It traces our very different ways of coming to terms with doubt and the slow realization that we had been set almost surrealistically absurd goals by those who had sent us.

I believe it contains general truths about the development industry. It questions the wisdom of imposed development which answers no felt needs and is incapable of inducing changes in perceived needs. It argues that aid agencies delude themselves if they talk of fostering self-reliance while excluding beneficiaries from the most vital stage of any development programme – the determination of aims and plans. It suggests that it would be both more cost-effective, and more conducive to success, if those aid agencies who now concentrate on sending 'experts' to the developing world stopped routinely doing so. More support should be given to ongoing locally-initiated schemes which have shown both a potential to persuade beneficiaries of the relevance of the change they are seeking, and a proven ability to co-exist with opponents threatened by such change.

In any development game there is a large and unwieldy set of players: permanent officials of the aid organizations, the providers of their funding, the general public in the West, the aid workers sent abroad for two or three years, various factions of westernized bureaucrats in high positions in the capital of the recipient country, local business interests, traditional community leaders and last, and often least considered, the local people arbitrarily designated as beneficiaries. The interests of the players are not identical and the images they wish to project not congruent.

I have found this to be insufficiently appreciated by development organizations. They are often unequipped to cope with contradiction and ambiguity and take refuge in a perennial assumption that the goodness of the developers' motives and the relevance of their objectives will be accepted. The good will of counterparts, the recipients of aid, is taken for granted. There is a sociological blindness which takes the rhetoric of equality and justice espoused by leaders as a signifier of social reality in emerging nation states. There is a, perhaps peculiarly Christian, insistence on the ultimate triumph of altruism. This belief that the foreign developer can lead by moral example and bring about profound changes in another country is strangely at odds with the modest realization that little influence can be brought to bear on the wielders of political power at home.

Developmentalism may legitimize itself with scientific pretensions. Complex systems of project evaluation are contrived and quantifiable variables identified. Meeting after meeting is held to further hone the precision of the evaluative system. This 'meetingitis' and the related obsession with planning may be a symptom of shock, of the inability of those who wish to be in charge and who believe work is in itself ennobling, to sit round passively and await developments. Little effort is made to justify such apparently time-consuming and diversionary procedures to the understandably impatient recipients of aid.

The academic world may support the scientific pretensions of developmentalism by turning out postgraduates in development studies whose training may have been so general that they actually know little of the history, geography, language, social structure or political conflicts of any particular developing country, background without which they cannot begin to judge any nation's development prospects. Yet, despite such lacunae they are thought to be able to fly in to a new country and in the course of a brief visit provide an assessment of a particular area of development. Often their report is more highly regarded by the officials at home than the first-hand accounts of those of their employees who have actually lived in that country and toiled at the developmental coal-face.

For the aid workers sent abroad for a few years, those who are more than development tourists, a destructive cycle repeats itself again and again. Imbued with hope prior to departure, told little of conflicts or the controversial nature of the changes they are to bring about, poorly trained in the language or dialect they are supposed to use, they are unequipped to cope with the discrepancy between image and reality. For those whose technical training has not accustomed them to controversy, what could seem less likely to provoke conflict than to bring health services, catch and store rain-water, provide houses or build roads? When they fail to achieve the goals set them they may become consumed by guilt, attempt to disguise their enforced idleness by a charade of hard work, immerse themselves manically in diversionary activities, hoard information in order to inflate their own importance, project their guilt at non-success onto others, backbite about their colleagues and/or become cynical or racist about the 'natives' they are working with. A grim development shock troop ambience may emerge in which each expatriate aid worker vies to outdo the asceticism of colleagues. There is, in short, a developmental scapegoatism which can scar individuals for years after their return to the West.

While the team has, in reality, ceased to exist a stubborn *esprit de corps* desperately continues. The project develops a life of its own as its expatriates become mere developmental cannon fodder. So much has been invested in terms of money and the energies of colleagues and their predecessors that to suggest pulling out becomes disloyal. No one dares do so. Projectismo, a conviction of the rightness of one's cause, takes hold. In each project there may be a pendulum swing from despair towards flights of fantasy, from abject frustration to belief in the omnipotence of the developers and the inevitability of their success. Usually, however, only one end of the swing of mood is reported back to the home country.

Frank feedback from those in the field may not be welcomed by those who stay behind. A rigid format for reports may force aid workers into assigning numerical value to variables they find meaningless and allow little scope for free expression of opinion. As reports from the field circulate upwards through the hierarchies of aid agencies they can become shorn of even the most veiled disquiet. Iconoclasm is not welcomed. At some level, whether conscious or not, the notion of closing down unviable projects may not be entertained because of the job losses which would result for desk persons, those in the various western capitals administering projects from afar. Discordant reports, rejecting the jargon and the conventional mould, may be buried at the bottom of filing cabinets, dismissed as 'non-objective' pique, and not shown to new recruits. An 'expert' at evaluation from outside the organization is hired, visits the country for a fortnight and comes up with the recommendation he or she has been employed to produce – the show must go on, everything is not as bad as some disgruntled people have said. Rivalry between agencies and between different western nations means that reports from other agencies on developments in the same country are hardly ever read. Thus desk persons and fund raisers feel themselves able, in all conscience, to solicit further funding by projecting an image of complete success. Another glossy brochure is produced and is favourably compared with those published by rival development agencies. Further volunteers are recruited and the cycle goes on.

Being a recipient of aid is equally traumatic. Officials of a new state, especially one like Yemen which has to contend to establish its legitimacy against entrenched traditional leaders, may exhibit apparently schizophrenic behaviour. Gratitude is constantly mixed with resentment. Forced, given the paucity of the state's financial resources, to solicit aid from foreigners, they yet resist the authority foreign organizations inevitably claim. They are angered by the implication that foreigners need to oversee the distributive process to ensure aid reaches the earmarked recipients. Any weak Third World government is understandably eager to be seen by the citizens it has taken under its wing as the source of all improvement in their lives. The jargon of development-speak, talk of securing local co-operation and encouraging self-reliance, does not necessarily boost the benevolent image the state wishes to project. The aid organizations, whose philosophy of growth is shaped by the experiences of late industrial society, new-found conservationist enthusiasms and a nostalgic reaction against materialism are simply not speaking the same language as any of their counterparts. The messages they convey are constantly being contradicted by salesmen for the goods produced in the industrialized world who are more readily seen as purveyors of modernism.

The emphases of the aid agencies thus seem curiously old-fashioned and inappropriate to both the impatient modernizing bureaucrats and a bewildered citizenry beginning to doubt the validity of their former achievements. Is it possible in today's shrunken world to convince either the citizens or the leaders of understandably proud new nation states of the virtues of a preventive health system when they are determined not to be fobbed off with second-best barefoot doctors, but to leap straight to the high-tech medicine so loudly and efficiently publicized by western interests? Advocating the benefits of intermediate technology is easily interpreted as insulting by those who have yet to perceive the limits of progress, the finite nature of energy resources. What is an ordinary illiterate person to think when an aid worker comes along talking of the benefits of breast milk when equally plausible westerners have appeared on television promoting milk powders? When herbal medicine and traditional curative techniques have been condemned as 'superstition' by westernized local doctors how is a foreigner to be taken seriously who pops up in one's village and argues it is vital that such knowledge be recorded before it is irretrievably lost? Just as a peasantry accrues wealth, copies emerging urban elites and switches to a 'superior' western diet of processed food and white flour, a foreigner arrives to argue that the traditional diet was wholesome after all. Who can give credence to such anachronistic nonsense?

The Yemen Arab Republic, North Yemen, may have been an extreme case, a country which during the cold war was regarded by the Arab oil states, and by East and West as so strategically important that it probably received more aid per capita than any country in the Middle East apart from Israel. After the YAR emerged into the modern world in the early 1970s aid money became by far the greatest source of revenue available to successive governments. North Yemen's leaders showed the greatest skill in exploiting their country's buffer position between Marxist South Yemen and feudalist Saudi Arabia to solicit aid from China, Russia, America and a host of the superpowers' clients and allies.

The sheer scale of the aid circus in a small, chronically underdeveloped, country such as Yemen brings issues to light. All the areas of the new nation firmly under the control of the state are apportioned as spheres of influence among the various foreign organizations competing for influence. For reasons of national prestige or commercial gain the aid enterprises hold determinedly onto the slices of the development action granted them. Members of the aid community have an extremely visible profile. The foreign *khubaraa* (experts) are pandered to. They are seen to earn high salaries, to distort the property market in the capital and provide employment. Because almost all parts of the country can now be reached within a day from the capital, the air-conditioned vehicles of the experts have been seen by almost everybody.

No matter how isolated or ill-educated they may be, all Yemenis have come to develop expectations about *khubaraa*. The YAR's foreign policy was almost totally directed to maximizing the input of aid monies and the state-controlled media are concerned to lavish nothing but praise on foreigners. In private, whether amongst sophisticated urbanites or the scattered peasantry, there is now a continued debate about the value of such aid, part of a wider uncertainty whether to take pride in Yemeni traditions, social relations and material products or to wholeheartedly embrace those arriving from abroad. Inflated expectations of wealth from newly-discovered oil and gas are encouraging Yemenis to think foreign assistance can soon be dispensed with. I have met few expatriates, and even fewer Yemenis, who would argue that the vast influx of foreign assistance has been wisely invested or produced lasting benefits. The confusions and contradictions wrought by the aid community, the muddle, naïvety and waste described in this account are, without doubt, replicated throughout the developing world.

This book would not serve its purpose if it deterred anybody from contributing to the work of aid agencies or led them to conclude that the developing world is so riddled with apathy, incompetence or corruption that its peoples should be left to stew in their own juices. Nor would I wish Yemen to be written off as undeserving of assistance. The great majority of its citizens and civil servants are unfailingly hospitable to foreigners. Considering its legacy of tyranny, isolation and underdevelopment and the painful geo-political circumstances which caused it to be unnaturally divided for so long, the Yemeni government has a great deal to be proud of.

Anthropologists, as iconoclasts, have written scathingly of the short-comings of aid projects. I trust that this account, uneasy reading though it might be for those of my colleagues whose names I have changed, is more than a simple hatchet job. My hope is that those in authority in the proliferating aid agencies become more accountable to the millions of well-disposed people who have made possible the recent rapid growth of the development industry and whose money has provided jobs for the growing ranks of aid administrators. The current rivalry between agencies, the scrabble for funds and the carving up of regional, class and party-based donor con-stituencies is unedifying. Agencies who promulgate complete success in glossy promotional materials are in danger of becoming morally indistinguishable from the advertising agencies whose methods they are increasingly adopting. Aid agencies are promoting a vital product – understanding the causes of inequality and underdevelopment and methods of overcoming them. They do themselves a grave injustice, and insult the intelligence of the public, by projecting the kind of fictional image of success chronicled in this book. From our daily lives we all know the world is full of disappointments, frustrated hopes, petty rivalries, jealousies and institutional conflicts. Plans fail to come to fruition and money and energies are wasted. The world 'out there' needs to be seen in the same light, peopled with energetic men and women struggling to improve their lives, often succeeding, but also making grave errors. Cock-ups should not be hidden for they have much to teach us.

It should be noted that the agency for whom I worked, the real name of which I have not given, takes a different approach to development in other countries where it is involved.

Sending volunteers abroad is not the agency's sole activity. It collects and disseminates information on issues of injustice and human rights in areas of the world where it has acquired more expertise than would appear possible reading this tale of misunderstanding of Yemeni society and its needs. The agency deserves its reputation. It has done much to bring about Christian engagement with the problems of the developing world. Though it is inevitably enmeshed in rivalry with other aid agencies the general tone of relations with its competitors (and especially with the major British agency which I refer to as Action for Justice and Development) is not as petulant and confrontational as the tensions I describe below would suggest.

Only in Yemen is the organization in intricate, and ultimately constricting, collaboration with a state and only in Yemen do its employees lead such materially pampered lives. Elsewhere it is involved in providing technical assistance to non-governmental community organizations who have requested relevant help. Volunteers go as individuals not as part of an expatriate team running projects and defining priorities.

2

THE MAKING OF AN 'EXPERT'

I first visited North Yemen in 1978. I returned in 1981 and spent twenty enjoyable months living as an anthropologist in a mountain community. By the spring of 1985 I had almost finished the doctoral thesis which was my reward for the patently unequal relationship with 'my' Yemenis whose generosity and hospitality I had not been able to return. Though quite glad to leave Yemen and return to home comforts, running water and electricity, I had, through prolonged exposure to the coldness of London, become nostalgic for the ebullience, generosity, tolerance and egalitarian assertiveness of Yemenis which had earlier fascinated me. Just as I was beginning to fret about my future lack of prospects I saw an advertisement. An aid organization, one of the four British volunteer-sending agencies, was looking for a social researcher, preferably female, for a health project on the Red Sea coastal plain in Yemen. Surprised that ability in Arabic was not indicated as a prerequisite for such employment, and agonizing, given the religious affiliation of the organization, over how honest to be about my own lack of faith, I sent off my application form.

I was invited to a weekend to choose candidates for projects as far apart, ideologically and geographically, as Ecuador and Zimbabwe, Yemen and Nicaragua. I found myself amongst a score of fellow *Guardian*-readers. We were each given a copy of the agency's glossy annual report and read of its success in three continents. We were shown a well-put-together audio-visual presentation of a project improbably based high on a mountain top in North Yemen and wowed by scenes of villages clinging precariously to cliffs and selfless health

10

workers trudging between them. I was as awed by the stunning scenery of the Yemeni mountains as those who had never been there. Clearly this was a show-piece health project of which the agency was justifiably proud.

The selection procedure was explained to us. I would have three separate hour-long one-to-one interviews to determine my professional competence, mental and moral stability and political soundness. On returning the following day, I was a little daunted to see a fellow candidate reduced to tears by the rigours of his first interview. My fears abated as it became clear that my first interrogator, an ex-volunteer in Yemen, had never interviewed anyone before. As she determined how much I knew of health and other development problems in North Yemen she was more flustered than I was. In the end she overran the time allotted for the interview by an hour. The person in charge of the Yemen desk then grilled me, albeit in a sympathetic manner, about my personal circumstances before I was sent to a third person, a senior apparatchik of the organization. Her task was to assess my level of political sophistication. She started out asking me if I did not feel ashamed of myself, wanting to run away from Britain instead of joining the fight-back against Tory misrule. The meeting was not as congenial as my previous chats and broke up before the hour was over. The three interviewers went into conclave to discuss me.

When I got to Yemen the interview notes were made available. I learned that my refusal during the political vetting interview to be needlessly loquacious, except on the subject of Yemen, was interpreted as potential hostility to the interview process. I was awarded a lowly 'C' grade for what was perceived as my ignorance of world and development affairs, but had more impressed my other interviewers and their majority opinion held sway. The desk person informed me that I could not become a researcher as, given the extreme segregation of the sexes in Yemen, the organization preferred a woman and had found one. However, my skills would be highly desirable for the Yemen programme and a job would be found for me. It all seemed rather amateurish to find a job for the person, rather than vice versa, but I thought no more of it, went away to finish my thesis and was glad to have my future resolved.

I subsequently discovered how the desk person set about securing a niche for me in his Yemen team. Enthusing greatly about my abilities, as apparently he did about every candidate who had successfully passed the agency's initiation ritual, he pressed for me to be given a research role based in the capital, Sana'a. I was to monitor the ravages caused by the inappropriate and unnecessary food aid given to North Yemen and the machinations of the pharmaceutical multinationals flogging dubious drugs to vulnerable peasants. Collecting such important information to feed back to international organizations campaigning on behalf of the developing world was supposed to be part of the brief of the man co-ordinating the ten-person team in Yemen. There was a danger this task would be taken over by our rivals, the agency I call Action for Justice and Development (AFJAD) – one of the largest and longest-established British aid agencies. AFJAD provided all the funding for our projects in Yemen. Given the rivalry between us and the much better-known AFJAD, this was clearly not a good thing.

However, this job, apparently suited to my abilities and experience as a researcher, was, for reasons I never fully determined, not offered me. The desk person pushed for the post to be created but met with opposition. When, a few months later, the desk person rang me back he had another proposition. Was I interested in becoming a primary health care training facilitator in a place called Ahad? The unwieldy job title looked no friendlier when phrased as a PHC T/F, the first of many acronyms, the in-house jargon of developmentalism, I would have to get to grips with. The woman who had been recruited to work as a researcher in Ahad had withdrawn for reasons not explained to me. I was to promote training of PHCWs (primary health care workers) and construction of PHCUs (primary health care units) and do whatever research my unfortunate gender would allow me. My ignorance of matters medical was not considered a problem. I wondered if I would be able to cope with working in one of the hottest, most humid, places in the world. Failing to emulate the example of the woman who had come to her senses in time, I expressed an interest in doing whatever was entailed in 'facilitating'. I was invited along for a fortnight of 'orientation'.

Being a volunteer has its rituals. One does not just slip away to the 'field' and return from it. Rites of passage must be observed. Thus I was 'oriented' in the London office of the organization about a country I had already spent two years in, in the company of Susan, a midwife also destined for Ahad who had never been outside Europe. As I already spoke Arabic and Susan did not, would I mind teaching her the Arabic alphabet? Remembering my fitful attempts over many years to learn the alphabet, I was quite uncertain how to proceed in explaining this fearsome script. I had not claimed to read and write the language with any degree of proficiency. London is full of qualified Arabic teachers. Surely one could have been hired? In any case, what was the point of teaching her to read and write when she was going to work amongst illiterate women? I could have helped her practise Yemeni conversational Arabic but was not asked to do so. For a few hours every morning I did my best to teach the alphabet.

Afternoons were spent in the organization's library reading about the goals of primary health care and progress in implementing them in various countries. Some of the reports written by previous volunteers in Ahad were put in front of me and I learned the history of the project I was to work for. It was attached to a government hospital built twenty years previously by the Egyptian army which at the time was supporting republican insurgents who had just overthrown the ruling Imam. Our goal was 'by 1991 to have created a health service which will have a greater preventive orientation, be less mystified, be more empathetic, have more female staff employed, be reasonably priced and have a greater degree of community financing'. Success depended on training male and female health workers who would be accepted and supported by their communities, by doctors and by relevant arms of the North Yemeni government.

Because it was a felt need of local people – and therefore essential to establishing our credibility in the community – we had provided, as a purely temporary measure, British midwives, nurses and doctors who worked in a clinical capacity in the hospital. It was also stressed to me that the local people and their elected representatives had expressed a desire to begin training programmes for men and women. My appointment as a promoter of community health who did not have a medical qualification was indicative of the progress which had been achieved. As trained Yemenis were brought forward we would work ourselves out of a job and the project would reach a natural end. The continuation of our presence for ten years was dependent on demonstrable progress being made towards the ultimate goal. At regular intervals success was to be measured. If the signals were not promising, then we would leave Ahad.

My preparation was completed by being sent to have the basics of car maintenance explained by the father of a volunteer working in Yemen. After a potted account of the workings of the internal combustion engine, we were introduced to two cars of a kind probably never encountered anywhere in Arabia. As all the cars used by the organization's three projects in Yemen are powerful four-wheel drive Toyotas should we not, I wondered, be told about traction, how to get out of sand, clean dust from air filters, remove impurities from petrol filters, change tyre pressures according to terrain and other aspects of motoring life needed for the tracks of Yemen?

A week later, fully jabbed and thoroughly 'oriented', I met Susan at Heathrow. A fawning letter we had been given to present to Egypt Air asking them to overlook our excess baggage because we were engaged in good works in a sister Arab nation, cut no ice. The last of my bank account disappeared to pay the charges demanded. I boarded the plane, impatient for a chance to show Susan that though I may be confused about some of the letters in its alphabet, I could speak Arabic. A great disappointment – our stewardess did not know any.

Landed in Cairo, and faced with a seven-hour wait in the transit lounge, Arabic speakers were everywhere at hand. We found ourselves at a table with young Saudi drinkers, on their way home and quite happy to buy expensive miniature whiskies for strangers. Why should we not accept? Were we not about to leave booze behind us for two years in dry North Yemen? The *bonhomie* dissipated when the Saudis burst out laughing on hearing that our destination was Yemen. Who would want to go to such a backward place when there was good money to be earned in their go-ahead country? Bemused, they staggered off to catch a flight to Jeddah, leaving us to watch the improbable spectacle of Madonna cavorting on the airport video. By the early hours of the morning, the airport clocks had all stopped working and the indicator board become catatonic, yet the video remorselessly replayed the same tape of the beautiful people of America 'Saving the World'. Smug in my drunken conviction that we were off to do the real thing in a country resolutely turning its back on such hypocrisy and decadence, I departed for Arabia.

3

SOJOURN IN SANA'A

The sight of the mountains of Yemen in the early morning light brought back pleasant memories. After seeming to weave and dodge over highland Yemen's broken terrain, our plane straightened up over the wide plain of Sana'a, flew in over the wreckage thoughtlessly left scattered at the end of the runway and touched down. We whizzed past MIG jets and a complex housing Soviet advisers and slowed down abreast a zone of the airport given over to rival Americans and their weapons of war. The air at 7,500 feet early on a fine autumn morning was bracing, and immediately evocative.

The Yemen Arab Republic had progressed. Its gateway to the world had become Sana'a International Airport and the terminal had been enlarged. The President, Commander-in-Chief of the Armed Forces and Secretary-General of the People's Popular Congress, looking as benign as a bemedalled military ruler can, cast a beneficent eye over the arrival concourse, his picture flanked by advertisements for the large number of brands of locally-produced soft drinks, biscuits and confectionery that his compatriots now consumed.

The Yemen programme co-ordinator, a Scottish ex-religious studies teacher, stood out amongst the crowd of short men wearing daggers and skirts. Talking his way into the customs hall, he tried in vain to persuade the officials that my computer did not represent a threat to national security nor Susan's drugs imperil the national economy. The remainder of our luggage was heaped into the Landrover provided by the United Kingdom Overseas Development Administration and we set off. Olfactory sensations, seemingly heightened by the altitude, revived a flood of memories so intense that the two years since my previous visit seemed to vanish.

16

We drove past the Passport Office where I had spent many hours waiting in queues and arguing my case first for the right to reside in Yemen and then for the privilege of an exit visa to leave it. We passed the heavily fortified complex of the United States Agency for International Development (USAID) and the shell of a luxury hotel abandoned when the insufficiency of its foundations had become apparent. We came to the headquarters of the national airline, the country's highest building whose glass façade had, according to an apocryphal tale of the kind always circulating in Yemen, provoked an unfortunate argument between puzzled *qabiilis* (tribesmen) new to the capital. Their debate about the fabric of the incongruous building was only resolved when one of them had determined its consistency by riddling it with his Kalashnikov.

We passed the headquarters of the emigrants' association representing the interests of those whose labour in Saudi Arabia earns what little wealth North Yemen has. Past the headquarters of the state-controlled co-operative movement, the impressive edifice known as the Central Planning Organization and on to the even more ironically entitled Ministry of Civil Service and Administrative Reform. Through this familiar landscape the co-ordinator of the Yemen programme fought the jungle of Sana'a traffic like a demented *qabiili*, conceding an inch to no one, tooting his horn at the slightest provocation and joining with relish the contest of badinage and impromptu jest which is a constant, and endearing, preoccupation of Yemeni men. I began to wonder about the co-ordinator. Had he been in Yemen too long, 'gone native'? Little did I realize how quickly I would also come to love the thrill of this exhilarating style of motoring.

The large house we were taken to in the former Jewish quarter of Sana'a was surprisingly welcoming and comfortable. I was to have my own room. Clearly being a volunteer did not entail suffering. The programme co-ordinator disappeared to his own house to be replaced by another colleague who introduced herself as 'doctor'. I imagined she had a medical qualification and racked my brains trying to place her. I learned that she was a fellow anthropologist and co-ordinator of the project in an area called Kahima the success of which had been exhibited to would-be volunteers on the recruitment weekend in London. She told us that a third administrator, responsible for co-ordinating the project in Ahad, would arrive in Sana'a that evening to direct our 'in-country orientation'. She explained the rules of the house to us. In passing, she told us that she also did not live in what was strangely called the transit house but had her own accommodation.

I wondered whether my new colleagues were avoiding each other. Why was the Kahima co-ordinator not in the country-side co-ordinating? Why did we need a programme co-ordinator, two project co-ordinators, a Yemeni administrative assistant and a part-time Yemeni 'fixer' to 'administer' the work of only seven people 'in the field'? Overwhelmed by renewed impressions and new puzzles, but thoroughly exhausted, I fell asleep, oblivious to the smell of sewage wafting into my window.

That afternoon formal briefings began. I learned that in deference to Muslim sensibilities the organization dropped all mention of its Christian affiliation and styled itself in Yemen as the British Social Development Agency (BSDA). I thought the 'social development' bit had a menacing ring to it in Arabic, rather too redolent of Marxism for the determinedly non-communist government we were working with. Financially, the news was good. Whenever we needed money all we had to do was to get the key, open the safe and help ourselves. I was struck by the carelessness with which money was handled.

I was informed that all BSDA employees earned 2,400 Yemeni rials – £240 tax free a month – with free rent, water, electricity and transport. We could take salary in advance if needed. Though entitled to a month's paid holiday a year, we were at liberty, it was implied, to take more if we so desired. Some colleagues, I later learned, were absent from Yemen for three months a year. Our salaries would, unlike those of our Yemeni counterparts, rise in accordance with the high rate of inflation. There was no shortage of transport – the organization ran six cars, one for every two employees – and they could be used for private purposes if we paid for the petrol.

It all sounded rather decadent. How could we new recruits be 'volunteers', our remuneration in all conscience be described to funders of our organization as 'based on local rates'? Susan was to be better off than on her meagre National Health

Service salary. I calculated that my salary, even discounting the perks of free housing, furnishings, water, gas and electricity, was five times that of the Yemeni health workers I was to work alongside.

In the days to come I soon found my BSDA colleagues were the poor cousins of Sana'a's high-profile 'development community'. Only the Peace Corps earned less, but their hidden rewards on return home made comparison difficult. Our colleagues in the adjoining office rented by AFJAD, our sister British agency, earned three times our salaries. Each had a new model Toyota, comfortable accommodation and the prospect of an annual conference in a Cypriot resort in addition to their holidays. German and Dutch 'volunteers' working in Yemen were also earning three times our salaries, fifteen times the salary paid to the Yemeni state employees with whom they worked. In turn, this was chicken-feed compared to the wealth to be made working as 'experts' for agencies funded by the United Nations or western governments. People with fewer qualifications than myself were earning fifteen times my salary. Indeed, there is money to be made in the hills of Yemen.

That evening a drawn and haggard young woman was sitting in our transit house. To our horror, Susan and I learned she was one of the two midwives finishing their service in Ahad. She had just come up to Sana'a and was due to leave Yemen in a few days. It had been planned that she and Susan would overlap by several weeks so that she could brief Susan on her work. But she was burned out and eager to leave the country. She spoke disjointedly and in a whisper. Her confidence and physical and mental well-being improved over the following days as her departure drew near. However, the impression of the rigours of life and work in Ahad remained with us.

The next day the Ahad project co-ordinator continued our orientation. Our relations were immediately unclear, for while Graham earned the same amount as us and in London the organization had vaguely intimated it had non-hierarchical principles, the co-ordinator clearly thought himself our boss. He certainly encouraged Yemenis to do so by his constant use of the first person when describing our plans and hopes. 'Co-ordinator' does not translate well into Arabic and always puzzled those we misleadingly dubbed as 'counterparts'. From our first contact with Yemenis in a Sana'a restaurant I realized the difficulty of my position. After a year in Yemen, spent mostly in expatriate circles in the capital, Graham spoke hardly any Arabic. Yemenis turned to me as the person they could most readily understand and assumed I was the holder of greater authority.

More secrets of our sect of developmentalism were revealed. For an hour Graham explained the mysteries of an arcane 'systematic evaluation procedure' known as 'Eze-Vu'. We learned how to define a 'project problem', set a 'project objective', 'establish a criterion for success in achieving the objective', 'evaluate the fit, adequacy and side-effects' of each objective against the international ideals of the agency, the BSDA programme in Yemen and each particular project. We were told how to define an activity to reach the strategy, how to produce a timetable sheet for each activity, how 'to timetable a strategy review', how to 'identify an indicator', 'to compartmentalize tasks' and to quantify the extent to which each individual project worker was to be involved in each particular objective and strategy. We were presented with Eze-Vu sheets of many kinds and exhorted to diligence in regularly completing summary sheets, activity review sheets, project objective review sheets, project strategy review sheets, check-lists of constraints, checklists of resources and six-monthly reports whose strict format detailed and quantified how individuals had been involved in particular objectives, strategies and activities. This evaluative system, especially in its refined forms which we novices could not yet appreciate, would, so Graham assured us, help to keep us on our developmental toes, ever aware of the viability of the objectives we were seeking.

Eze-Vu immediately had an Orwellian ring to it. I understood not a jot of this new magic and was relieved when Susan confessed to her own bewilderment. The next week we were obliged to sit through a three-day ordeal known as 'the six-monthly conference' when there was much mention of this evaluative tool. I began to suspect that planning could be a symptom of shock, a psychological defence of the impotent to deny their inability to bring about desired change. I realized that the process of assigning values to variables, of rendering order out of chaos and convincing ourselves of the rationality of our plans, found greatest favour with colleagues like Graham whose education had been purely scientific. It became clear that Eze-Vu abhorred negativity and lack of success. It had a built-in success mechanism, for failure could always be explained away as a lack of 'baseline data'. At times during the conference when a positive assessment of an activity could not be reached a believer came to the rescue. It was argued that a particular vital variable had, for reasons of lack of time, not yet been accurately measured. Only when all the data was to hand could conclusions be reached.

Because we worked directly with the state we would have to spend much time liaising with the Ministry of Health. To acquaint us with the Byzantine procedures of North Yemeni bureaucracy we were taken to visit the ministry which is situated in the heart of modern Sana'a, Tahrir (Liberation) Square. The centrepiece of Tahrir is the Russian tank which on 26 September 1962 shelled the palace of the last of the Imams who had ruled Yemen for a thousand years. The unskilled tank crew destroyed only the top floor, allowing the Imam to flee Sana'a, join his tribal supporters and harry the republican forces during eight years of civil war. The ministry adjoins the Military Museum which inexplicably remained about to open throughout my time in the country. To get into the ministry we picked our way between groups of forlorn Egyptian, Somali and Sudanese doctors and nurses sitting on the entry steps waiting, we learned, for their long overdue salaries.

It was soon apparent that the Ahad project co-ordinator, like other Sana'a-based *khubaraa* ('experts'), felt at home only amongst the relatively small number of officials who spoke English. A number of foreigners were spotted in the office of the congenial man heading the International Affairs Department of the ministry. All these lost souls were waiting, with various degrees of impatience, for the supreme accolade bestowed on visitors to the ministry, permission to pass the portals of the office of His Excellency the Deputy Minister. (The minister, an almost mythical creature, was rarely glimpsed in his ministry.) We did not linger, as Graham had papers to chase round the labyrinth of corridors. He made a desultory effort to find the wielders of relevant stamps or those whose signatures were needed to authorize the wielding.

Working hours in Yemen, officially from 8 a.m. to 2 p.m., are kept by no one, much less by those in senior positions whose signatures are required for any kind of executive act. I soon found that received wisdom among the expatriate community took this to be clinching proof of the inherent indolence of the 'Yems', a ruse to free them for dissolute afternoons chewing *qat*, the popular local stimulant. In fact, the minimal hours seemed to indicate a fairly brave tacit recognition by a resource-starved government that the salaries paid to its employees, frozen since the late 1970s despite persistent inflation, were inadequate and that civil servants had to be freed to look for more gainful employment elsewhere. As almost all food is imported and transport costs are prohibitive, the cost of living in North Yemen is extremely high. It was a constant mystery to me how civil servants manage to make ends meet.

As we searched through the ministry a negative correlation between position in the hierarchy and amount of time spent at work became apparent. Kindly pen-pushers, interrupted in their reading of *Al Thawra*, 'The Revolution', the nation's only daily paper, seemed very eager to reassure us and other busy and important-looking foreigners that we were not wasting our time. If we would only sit down and 'relax' or pop out for a late breakfast we would be sure, 'after a little while', to find the particular official we wanted at his desk.

For days on end we reported to the ministry without achieving anything. I had been told of 'institution building programmes' financed by the World Bank and the United States Agency for International Development, yet it was clear little had changed since my previous sojourn in Yemen: there was still no real demarcation of authority between different departments. I realized that individuals were constantly renegotiating their position in the hierarchy. Chains of command were obviously cross-cut by alliances of tribe, natal status, sect of Islam, military regiment, regional affiliation and kinship. Permanent flux is the norm of such bureaucracies. We were forever either being sent elsewhere by officials keen to shuffle responsibility onto others, or told that colleagues in other departments had had no right to do what they had done.

I wondered whether my BSDA colleagues understood the nature of power in Yemen. They pointed out certain low-ranking civil servants who wielded influence disproportionate to their position but at the same time gave me a copy of an administrative flow-chart prepared by the programme co-ordinator. This listed various ministry departments and sub-agencies and their directors and invested the daily disorder of power relations with a comforting illusion of stability. I began to see parallels with earlier colonial endeavours in the Middle East. Foreign administrators, faced with the constant flux of authority and allegiance inherent in tribal society, were once more trying to ossify boundaries and relations of power in this fashion.

A haven of tranquillity amidst the warren of offices crowded with men brandishing pieces of paper, was the suite of rooms given over to the World Health Organization. This was the domain of the WHO expert, an exiled Iranian, who like so many of the United Nations personnel I was to meet had not learnt Arabic despite spending years in the country. Our visit seemed a welcome diversion in his uncrowded day. For a quarter of an hour he lectured us on the principles of primary health care and his achievements in the good old days under the Shah. The primary health care worker was an integral part of the state's health system. Because the North Yemeni population was so scattered, and because there were 50,000 villages with an average population of little more than 100, a system of barefoot doctors was the only way to deal with health problems. The YAR was fully committed to expanding the network of health posts and training men and women to work in them. Hospital-based nurses and doctors were sympathetic to the aims of primary health care and liaised closely with local health workers. An initial kit of basic drugs would be supplied by UNICEF after which the ministry would assume the full burden of supplying drugs. Salaries would be paid to all primary health care workers. Each was to serve a community of exactly 3,500 people, an optimum size determined with scientific precision. The proportion of the worker's time devoted to attendance in the health post, vaccinating children and home visiting was set out. He concluded that there was every reason to believe that the YAR was doing its best to implement WHO's global strategy of 'Health For All By 2000'.

We asked about progress in achieving these laudable aims in North Yemen, how many health workers were working and being paid and whether the ministry was assuming the burden of supplying drugs for health posts. We had no success, for the expert simply did not know. I was later to realize that this avuncular figurehead rarely set foot in the countryside and had little idea of the demography, topography or social structure of the country he was pontificating about.

As we were leaving the ministry we ran into a vital personage, guardian of the doorway to the deputy minister's office and, so I later found, the unqualified owner of one of the pharmacies lining Tahrir Square. Recognizing the co-ordinator, he playfully wrenched his arm behind his back, released him and went on his way, oblivious to Graham's calls for assistance. This seemed a ritual of subordination and humiliation, but Graham, despite holding a postgraduate degree in primatology, good-naturedly took it as evidence of his acceptance.

Papers needed to obtain a residence permit necessitated a visit to the Central Planning Organization (CPO), a neo-Stalinist monstrosity staffed by hundreds of people with indeterminate overlapping functions. For a markedly *laissez-faire* government this edifice, and other trappings of a Marxist command economy, seems a curiously inappropriate monument to national vanity, an attempt to project a level of control over the nation and its destiny which the North Yemeni state did not yet have. The sheer size of the building serves to belie what the humblest, least educated Yemeni knows – that his government cannot plan with any accuracy, or even gather economic data. Except for aid donations, and levies on imports, all the wealth of the country is in the form of cash and gold carried back by those who go to the oil states to sell their labour. Hardly any of it is in the banking system and controlled by the state, a curious reversal of the typical developing world scenario of a cash-starved peasantry. Supposedly the CPO has a vanguard role overseeing all other ministries. Because foreigners share the delusion of some Yemeni bureaucrats that the five-year plans prepared by the CPO are objective scientific documents, rather than a list of aspirations, foreign organizations compete to plant their men inside CPO. I was reminded of my previous visit to the building in 1982 when working for a West German company funded by the German aid agency GTZ. I had been taken to visit Bonn's man in CPO. I found him poring over statistics engaged in a task of vital importance – extrapolation from fictitious data to reach a fictitious figure for Yemeni per capita GNP in the year 2000.

Equally bizarre was a visit paid by the whole BSDA team to the UNICEF headquarters. We had been invited for a briefing about the mass vaccination campaign due to coincide with the twenty-fifth anniversary of the 1962 revolution. The Yemeni director of the campaign told us of his plans and how they had been worked out with UNICEF officials in the United States. He stressed that state-of-the-art technology had been used to prepare the plan. Ninety-five per cent of all Yemeni children under five would be vaccinated, and all in the space of a few weeks. We were told that funds and transport had been pledged to deliver sufficient quantities of vaccine to hospitals. After that it was up to the local development associations to get children to the vaccine or vaccine to the children.

This was obviously the weak point of the plan. A colleague asked how difficulties of transport and shortage of trained vaccinators could be overcome. When our high-ranking host stated that every Yemeni lives within a two-hour walk of a hospital our astonishment could not be contained. Another colleague began describing the eight-hour journey on foot to one health post and problems he had faced obtaining funds to hire transport donkeys. The Yemeni official continued to insist that all his compatriots lived within easy reach of a hospital. If he really believed this, it was not up to us to challenge his notions of Yemeni topography. None of us dared voice our fears that the campaign had been planned for political, rather than medical, reasons and could not succeed as envisaged.

For Susan and me a further bureaucratic hurdle had yet to be overcome – the acquisition of Yemeni driving licences. Oddly, this paper chase began in the Ministry of Health. Our

organization's 'fixer' obtained the necessary letter from the
deputy minister to his 'brother', the deputy director of the
traffic police, allowing us to begin our quest. Susan and I
presented ourselves at the traffic police headquarters, unad-
visedly arriving at 8.30 a.m. to find the building virtually
deserted. After two hours of soliciting stamps and signatures
we were sent off to the Al Thawra (Revolution) Hospital, to
have our physical and mental soundness determined.

The lobby of the Al Thawra was crowded with outpatients.
Their male relatives were pressed up against a guichet trying to
hand over money, without which no consultation could be
obtained. Despite its name the 'Revolution' was obviously a
private hospital. I shamelessly exploited my height and weight
advantage over Yemenis and was able, after a mere quarter of
an hour, to hand over money to the cashier and have more
paperwork thrust into my hands. Scrutiny of these forms, and
welcome assistance from patient and friendly fellow scrim-
magers, showed we had to be examined by no less than five
specialists and that they had to be visited in a particular order.
Finding the relevant rooms was no easy task given that the
services of the specialists, all of them Eastern Europeans, were
greatly in demand. A large crowd of Yemenis was jostling
outside the consultants' rooms, rushing forward to be repulsed
by Indian and Filipino nurses whenever doors were opened.
How were we to be seen to and, indeed, why should we be
seen to when there were genuinely ill Yemenis requiring the
services of the very few specialists in their country? We were
pondering this dilemma, shyly waiting at the back of the
crowd when a door was briefly opened to expel a patient. The
nurse must have spotted us for the door was immediately re-
opened and we were beckoned to press forward through those
struggling for medical attention. Still reluctant to accept this
privilege, we tarried too long with the result that a dozen
people tried to enter the room. The nurse called a policeman
who used a broom handle to repel the sick and propel us into
the room.

A harassed Hungarian accepted our statements that we were
healthy people, scrawled his signature and passed us back to
the kindly Filipino nurse who advised us which other rooms

we needed to visit. The same process was repeated outside the opthalmologist's room as the colour of our skins again facilitated progress. With all the pandemonium, pushing and shoving, Susan had developed a migraine, was suffering the associated disturbances of vision and failed to identify half the letters on the eye chart she was put in front of. No one seemed concerned about this apparent drawback to successful motoring and we both obtained another signature. Eventually we came to the door of an East German psychiatrist where, curiously, there were no clamouring patients. Earnestly staring into my eyes, he asked me if all was well. I nodded and received my last signature.

A urine sample had to be tested which required leaving the outpatient section and passing through an administration block to the laboratory. A soldier was adamant we had no right to pass and we spent ten minutes obtaining a chit of paper permitting him to relax his vigilance. My sample was tested, whereupon I inquired about the blood test also demanded by my papers. The hospital, though the best equipped in the country, lacked the facilities to determine my blood group so I was sent out to one of the nearby private laboratories set up to compensate for such shortcomings of the state health system. We had now passed all the mandatory tests and only required a final stamp and the signature of the hospital's director. By now, however, it was well after one o'clock. Though the crowd of Yemenis pursuing the Eastern Europeans had not diminished, the hospital bureaucrats had finished their working day. Despite our pleas, we were told we would have to come back for the final stamp.

That afternoon we practised some of the difficult manoeuvres possibly required by the pernickety driving testers. I had already had experience of driving without the handbrake, a piece of equipment scorned as wimpish by Yemeni drivers and allowed to fall into disrepair. Susan, however, needed practice in making reverse hill starts without the handbrake as the regulations required. We tested each other on the mass of road signs we needed to know.

The next day we were ready to actually get into a car and be tested. I went back through the rooms in the traffic police building we had earlier passed through and finally learned we had to go outside and look for a certain 'Ahmad'. Finding a likely individual, I asked, in Arabic, if I was speaking to 'the brother Ahmad'. When he haughtily replied in English, 'No. I am Captain Ahmad', I thought all my efforts to get a licence had been in vain. However, my fears proved groundless as the captain seemed intent on quickly getting through my test so he could enjoy the far more riveting experience of driving with a foreign woman. I had only driven 100 metres when I was ordered to turn round and come back. Susan then went off for a ten-minute drive.

We had heard that many people came so far only to fail the final hurdle – the traffic sign identification test. The tester seemed inscrutable. I easily identified his first sign – the prohibition on needless use of the horn which is disobeyed by every Yemeni driver. With an expectant grin, a more difficult puzzle – a sign indicating an untended level crossing with gates – was pulled out. There has not been a railway in Arabia since T.E. Lawrence blew up the Hejaz railway but I had been forewarned and had my answer ready. My success could not continue and, sure enough, I failed to recognize the next sign indicating how I should exit from a motorway should Yemen ever get round to building one. All was not lost, honour had been satisfied, the foreigner had been shown to be fallible. I was earnestly told to go home and further study the road signs but that I knew enough to be allowed on the roads. Only later did I hear that I should not have been so vain and tried to answer the questions in Arabic. Other expatriates reported getting through simply by saying whatever came into their heads but with great confidence, secure in the knowledge that the testers would not reveal their lack of English.

A further delay ensued. So demanding is the licence procedure, it is not surprising that only a handful of people each week manage to pass it. Thus the man whose job it was to take the official photograph of successful licence-holders did not stay at his post when not required. This was explained to us by a Yemeni who had been waiting five days to have his photograph taken. Once more, however, we were in luck as friendly officials made exceptions for us and speeded up the process. After an hour the photographer was found, our licence was laminated, given a final stamp and we were permitted to drive. For the privilege we had each paid £100 – a month's salary for a Yemeni civil servant.

I was less successful in my attempts to become familiar with the structure of rural primary health care. I had been told in London that I was to spend a number of weeks at the hospital in Mocha, the decayed medieval port in the south of the Tihama coastal plain, which was once the conduit for all the coffee reaching the markets of Europe. This was to acquaint me both with the peculiarities of the Tihami dialect of Arabic and the problems of implementing North Yemen's primary health care (PHC) plan. I had been assured the Yemeni driving force behind this project was very fond of BSDA, a confirmed Anglophile. As days passed and he failed to answer our messages my doubts grew. For the next twenty months I was to hear of the keen support of a great number of Yemeni officials. Undoubtedly our Dutch, American, German, Scandinavian and Russian rivals suffered the same delusion about their 'friendlies'.

A crisis had arisen in Mocha. The French agency financing the project had reviewed the effectiveness of their aid and decided that North Yemen was not as deprived as it appears. In order to maximize aid revenue the North Yemenis were insisting their country be classified as one of the twenty-eight least developed countries. In fact, though the state is strapped for cash, its citizens are far from destitute. The absence of reliable statistics, and the inability of the banking system to monitor the flow of remittances into the country from abroad, make Yemen's relative deprivation hard to determine. If the probable per capita GNP of Yemen is regarded as a suitable measure of development Yemen is relatively fortunate. If, however, the rate of infant mortality is taken as the benchmark, the country is among the half dozen least developed countries in the world.

The French had decided their money would more profitably be spent elsewhere on behalf of a government more demonstrably interested in setting up a primary health care system. They had abruptly withdrawn their backing. Now, in pique against all *nasraanis* (Nazarenes, the less than complimentary term used for Christians in Yemen) the invitation for me to spend several weeks in Mocha had been withdrawn. This distressing development was not immediately made plain to me, perhaps because BSDA was reluctant to have to admit that friendship with the 'Anglophile' was so shallow.

Thus I hung around Sana'a for no apparent purpose than to have two hours Arabic every afternoon with an incompetent teacher insistent on teaching the pure classical Arabic, the unchanged language in which the Koran was revealed fourteen centuries ago. Much sensitivity was to be called for in this field. In a society where there was next to no formal education before the overthrow of the Imam in 1962, the illiteracy rate is understandably much higher than elsewhere in the Arab world, and knowledge of literary Arabic the least widespread. In such circumstances, the acquisition of skill in reading and writing classical Arabic, akin to the value once placed on proficiency in Latin in our culture, is not an accomplishment to be hidden. Important bureaucrats imperiously reject letters which have the slightest grammatical errors or use collo-quialisms. Those who teach foreigners are also keen to show off their knowledge and to deny the existence of a variety of almost mutually incomprehensible dialects in rural districts. Yemen's intelligentsia has not yet appreciated, as the Syrians, Lebanese and Egyptians began to do fifty years ago, that there can be any merit in the vernacular. This is especially true of the dialect of the Tihama coastal plain, the tongue of the 'uncivilized', 'non-Arab' 'blacks' which is interleaved with words from Ethiopian languages and is often very hard for highlanders to understand.

Fortunately I was able to distinguish classical Arabic and deter my teacher from inflicting too much of it on me. I found he knew nothing of the dialect of the north Tihama and did my best to deflect the lessons towards the language of administration and bureaucracy which I imagined I would need for my work. Susan, knowing nothing of Arabic, was thoroughly confused by inappropriate instruction and ill prepared for the work she was to do amongst illiterate women quite unconversant with classical Arabic. Over time it became clear this was a general problem, that hardly any of the 'volunteers' and 'experts' had been properly taught. I was to find that none of my new colleagues in Ahad knew the Arabic phrase 'primary health care', and that one of the departing midwives, after two years in the town, did not know the most commonly used word for 'midwife'. Very few aid workers I met could begin to converse with their Yemeni counterparts. Some, like the director of the US Agency for International Development (USAID) health assistance programme, made no bones about this. There was no need to learn Arabic, she assured me. Far better if Yemenis all learned English like the charming high-up officials whose trips to America for 'training' and 'language' courses she arranged.

Unlike her, officials of our organization seemed to be aware that hardly any Yemenis outside the capital knew even a smattering of English. The absence of an education system prior to 1962, combined with the shortcomings of the English language teaching being inflicted by Egyptian schoolteachers, meant that we had to learn Arabic. Despite this, people in BSDA seemed as thoroughly complacent, and generally British as many anthropologists I had known. One would, it was intimated, somehow 'muddle through' and 'pick up' this very difficult language, and the exotic strains found in the countryside. When, time after time, it became apparent that, however determined they were to acquire Arabic, new volunteers had barely picked up enough language to do their job properly by the time their two-year contracts had finished, odd excuses were advanced. I even heard it being seriously argued that it might be better for those conveying health messages to have a limited, purely health-related, vocabulary to avoid being side-tracked from their main tasks. Our counterparts were constantly exasperated by the lack of interest BSDA showed in helping its workers acquire proficiency. AFJAD, our rival British agency, by comparison, took the language issue sufficiently seriously to begin holding their team meetings in Arabic.

4

INTO THE FIELD

In the meantime, Susan and I were taken, within a week of our arrival in Yemen, on a three-day visit to Ahad, our future home. To our disappointment Graham, our co-ordinator, did not leave Sana'a sufficiently early to complete the six-hour journey in daylight. After four hours on the road, enjoying neither the constant bumping due to the corrugations of the unsealed road nor the heat, I asked to stop for a drink to wash down the dust lining my throat. In a dimly lit corrugated iron roadside shop I was first exposed to the kind of people I was to work amongst. It was hard to believe they shared a common nationality with the proud, olive-skinned, relatively prosperous, gregarious, dagger-bearing highlanders with whom I was familiar. In the shadows cast by a flickering oil lamp were rather bedraggled, dark-skinned, weaponless men who, much as I tried to suppress the thought, were incurious and unwelcoming in comparison with their highland compatriots. Trying to speak to them was disturbing. Though they could understand my rather posh Arabic I could barely catch one word in ten of their lowland dialect. I was horror struck. Had I perpetrated a fraud? Not only did I know next to nothing about medicine, but also I did not speak the same language as the people I was an 'expert' on. How could I 'facilitate' anything without language? It would only be a question of time before I was exposed and sent home in ignominy.

We arrived in Ahad at 9 p.m., having seen nothing of the Tihama because of the early tropical sunset. A chilly reception – insofar as it was possible with everybody dripping sweat in the clammy 35° (95°F) heat – awaited us as we met our three colleagues: Simon and Elizabeth, a young married couple, both doctors, and Irene, a midwife in her sixties. They were obviously annoyed at our failure to arrive when expected. I wondered why this relatively minor irritation provoked such a prickly reaction from my new colleagues.

The supper prepared for us was hastily reheated and served al fresco under the glare of the solitary naked bulb dimly lighting the doctors' tiny walled compound. A variety of insects played gaily round the light and occasionally darted into our plates. A ring of glowing mosquito coils failed to add romance to the occasion. The meal being completed, and it apparently being already well after normal bedtimes, I was taken away to Graham's house. His was a typical featureless Tihama compound enclosed by a high wall. A single high-ceilinged room stood alone in the middle of a dusty yard. An airless kitchen and adjoining toilet with pit latrine lay in the corner. There was, in contrast with the doctors' dwelling, not a trace of vegetation to be seen. Rusty tins and rotting rubbish bags lay everywhere. Graham threw open the door to his room revealing unwashed clothes and surfaces covered with dust.

I was instantly depressed. What sort of example was this setting to Yemenis? We preached personal cleanliness, and I had dutifully mugged up the Islamic phrases enjoining it, and yet a colleague lived like this. How soon would it be before I too succumbed to the pressures of working here and resigned myself to the squalor? I scooped some water from the limited amount left in his tank and carried it into the toilet. While pouring it over myself I wondered what my colleagues' apparent lack of interest in harmonizing their living conditions suggested about the difficulties of living in Ahad. It was such a close, humid night, and the toilet so poorly ventilated, that no sooner had I towelled myself dry than I began sweating all over again. Over the next few days I realized the pointlessness of washing too frequently. However extensive the precautions, the stench of body odour could not be staunched for long.

My host helped me string a mosquito net above the tall, wood-framed woven bed common amongst the Tihamis, but unknown in the mountains. I perched miserably on it, tucking the net into the thin mattress to prevent nightlife reaching me. In vain – I soon found the net had many holes. I lay sweating, swatting insects, searching for sleep. As I am a foot taller than the average Tihami, the bed was uncomfortably short. The atmosphere was not conducive to sleep.

I had imagined I would be coming to a somnolent rural town whose inhabitants would follow nature's rhythms, retiring early and rising at dawn. Not a bit of it. Half the youths of the town seemed to be racing up and down the alleyway outside on their motorbikes. Several Toyota pick-ups pulled up, blaring their horns and revving their engines to shake off the dust after their long journey from the foothills in search of drugs from the nearby pharmacy. The hubbub of domino players from the café across the alleyway, each histrionically clacking their tiles and thumping them down with gusto, was deafening. Later the government was to crack down on these rowdy youths and outlawed dominoes after 10 p.m. Half a dozen televisions from neighbouring compounds blared out the raucous sounds of an Egyptian soap opera.

It was well after midnight. Surely these people would have to go to bed soon? The guttural tones of Egyptian Arabic were improbably replaced by excited English. It was time for the American wrestling programme, broadcast twice a week from Saudi Arabia, which I was to learn was by far the most popular programme. I wished myself back in the agreeable climate of Sana'a and away from the range of Saudi transmitters. Once more I admired the North Yemenis for their refusal to broadcast any western television programmes.

Clearly I would need fortitude to live in such a place, would somehow have to summon hitherto unknown reserves of character. Mental preparations for the ordeal had to begin at once. As soon as I awoke I would mark out a chart from one to seven hundred and thirty indicating the number of days remaining of my sentence.

Resolution faded in the dazzling morning light. The heat of the sun on my body awakened me and the buzzing of flies prevented further sleep. I was taken to a third house rented by our project. It contained one of the largest compounds in the town with two separate concrete buildings containing rooms being used as bedrooms, kitchen, office and a dusty store-room. The store was crammed with boxes of contraceptive pills and condoms long past their date of expiry, bags of

UNICEF midwifery equipment, a broken-down cine projector, a decrepit slide projector, a non-functioning generator,
numerous old car parts and other detritus collected by the
project since its inception three years previously. I learned that
this compound had once housed the entire BSDA team,
disregarding local sensitivities that unrelated men and women
should not live together. Now, due to friction between the
team members, only Irene, the departing midwife who had
stayed behind in Ahad to orientate Susan, lived in it.

A stairway led to a flat concrete roof, protruding from
which were metal rods allowing the possibility of the addition
of another storey. The roof afforded a fine view over the town
and into neighbouring compounds. Despite the early hour a
dust haze reduced visibility to a few kilometres. The
atmosphere was muggy and oppressive. As an urban landscape
it was unprepossessing. Plastic bags were everywhere to be
seen – caught in the thornbushes corralling the sheep and goats
which are the mainstay of Tihamis' livelihood, trapped in the
thatch of their conical huts, lying in the narrow alleyways
between compounds, attached to the television aerials sprout-
ing from every compound. Later I was to become so used to
this litter culture that I found beauty in the welcome touch of
colour the plastic provided. Compounds were fairly spacious,
typically comprising a walled-off open-air pit latrine, an open-
air kitchen, a small pen for the animals, several huts and one or
two more fashionable nondescript concrete buildings identical
to Graham's and used by the men for receiving guests.

I found the town to be on the extremity of the Tihama plain
up against the first of the desolate black foothills which
gradually give way to the lush mountains of the 'real' Yemen.
Above the town I noticed a small fort used to monitor the flow
of traffic from Saudi Arabia and spot smugglers seeking to
bypass the customs and security checkpoint to the north of the
town. Two hundred metres away ran the best highway in the
country, the first sealed road linking Yemen and Saudi Arabia,
financed by Saudi Arabia and completed by South Koreans
four years previously. Across the highway from the town a
helicopter was taking off from the army base, relic of the years
of civil war in the 1960s when the Egyptian army had
maintained a large garrison to prevent the Saudis sending
supplies down the Tihama to their royalist allies.

We were taken on our first visit to the Ahad health centre.
The hospital was only a quarter of a mile distant but as the
shade temperature had, according to Irene's thermometer,
already reached 42° (108°F), the walk was an ordeal. We passed
three prosperous, freshly-painted private pharmacies immediately outside the gate and walked into the dusty hospital
compound. Our first sight was of a rusting ambulance donated
by a long-forgotten aid donor. I later learned that this eyesore
had been lying around for five years but had not been removed
in case some *khubaraa* (foreign experts) might arrive to repair
it. The hospital consisted of two rows of crudely built rooms
facing each other. Each had a narrow verandah crammed with
patients seeking shade. There were no seats for those forced to
wait and the whole place was in dire need of a coat of paint.
Rusting beds on the flat roofs belonged to the expatriate
Sudanese and Somali hospital staff who, unlike the Tihamis,
climb to rooftops to catch whatever breeze is to be found
during the oppressively hot nights.

A solitary tree between the two buildings afforded some
shade to the patients hanging about the hospital. I was struck
by the slightness of the Tihami physique, the improbable
thinness of the wiry men and women surrounding us. Most
men wore the typical all-white Tihami costume – grubby
head-dress, Chinese-made T-shirt and a length of cloth
wrapped round the waist and held up by a broad canvas belt.
Women, in contrast to their highland sisters, were not veiled,
and were brightly clad in layers of nylon. Those from the
town itself were recognizable from their distinctive flowing red
outer garments. Both sexes were wearing Chinese flip-flops.
The patients stared at us newcomers, but were not so bold as
to try to speak. Their mien was one of resigned, almost
morose, patience.

We entered the office of the septuagenarian hospital director.
The young men clustering under the ceiling fan for fresh air
seemed to constitute a wholly different class of sartorially-
aware Tihami. Some were wearing climatically inappropriate,
but decidedly chic, jeans. Others were wearing colourful
Indonesian-made sarongs wrapped so tightly that they accen-
tuated their improbably slender hips and made walking
difficult. Care had been taken in the choice of Taiwanese sports
shirts.

Our arrival caused consternation. The startled old *mudiir* (director), the owner of the smartest of the private pharmacies we had passed on the way into the hospital, was especially taken aback. I later learned that somehow we had not announced that a new midwife and a nondescript 'facilitator' were about to arrive. Later that day there was recrimination between Graham, the co-ordinator, and Simon, the doctor 'facilitator' of primary health care, each suggesting the other had been negligent in not informing the hospital management of our arrival.

The old man ushered us forward into his crowded office, displacing the youths who had been lounging and chatting on his desk. Did we want a *kanada* (the generic word for soft drink whether bottled by Canada Dry or not)? I knew that presentation of these luridly-coloured concoctions has become a rite of hospitality at least as important as the more traditional offerings of tea and coffee and nodded acceptance. A boy was dispatched to a nearby shop and returned laden not only with soft drinks, but also with bottles of mineral water which are consumed by prestige-conscious men throughout Yemen. I thought the *mudiir* was being particularly generous but was to learn that the money he handed the boy was not his own but came from the hospital's hospitality allowance most of which went on receiving important people such as ourselves, visitors from Sana'a or the local prefect or security chief. A bottle opener could not be found and none of those milling about to see the new *nasraanis* (Christians) happened to be carrying a Kalashnikov – the magazine clip of which makes an excellent opener. The bottles were passed to a handsome young man called Ali Ahmad who, it became apparent, was the real motivator of the bureaucracy whose somnolent rhythms we had disturbed. He opened them with his teeth.

A desultory conversation ensued which, to my great relief, I was able to follow as Ali Ahmad and the other young men switched away from their local dialect for my benefit. As I listened to the manner in which they spoke to Graham I was impressed yet again with the skill of Yemenis at communicating across barriers of language and dialect. Graham, who had been badly instructed in Arabic by the Peace Corps, had a strictly limited vocabulary. The locals had absorbed the idiosyncracies of the co-ordinator's pidgin Arabic and spoke to him as if to a child, destroying grammar and syntax and, of course, in the process reinforcing his errors.

The relationship between the *mudiir* and Graham struck me as oddly symbiotic. They greeted each other with warmth but were unable to converse. Over the next few days I learned that the old man, self-taught, with no medical training and dependent on others to draft correspondence in proper literary Arabic, had no contacts in arenas of power beyond Ahad. Like other elderly Tihami men, he was so terrified of the 'cold' weather to be braved in the mountains and the ridicule which his strange accent and appearance would provoke in Sana'a that he had not visited the Ministry of Health for eight years. Directors of the other two hospitals with which BSDA was associated were always in and out of the ministry fighting to secure funding, but the old man in Ahad relied totally on Graham. The *mudiir* was upset to hear the hospital budget had not yet been approved although the accounting year was already three months old. Graham promised to return to Sana'a to lobby further. Somehow, Graham's impression of bustling confidence could not conceal his inability to do the strange job foisted on him. For reassurance he clutched the briefcase – the only one in the town – which he carried everywhere. It looked rather incongruous borne by a European wearing a *futa* (sarong) and a distinctly non-Yemeni panama hat.

After a while, photocopies of various impressively stamped documents were produced from the depths of Graham's briefcase. He seemed to have little idea of what they were about and did not welcome my proffered help in reading them or facilitating conversation with the *mudiir*. Similarly, the old man did not immediately realize what the documents referred to and passed them across to the eager Ali Ahmad to be quickly read and summarized.

It became apparent that the documents related to problems surrounding a hospital annexe which had been under construction for three years. We were taken by a roundabout route to visit the new building. Though the extension lay alongside the compound enclosing the old buildings, there was no direct access between them. Ali Ahmad told me the *mudiir* was reluctant to knock a hole in the wall without receiving permission from the provincial office. He also told me the new building had been paid for by the British Embassy in Sana'a, the Canadian Embassy in Saudi Arabia, AFJAD (who funded our project), the local development association (LDA) and the national organization co-ordinating the LDA movement. Liaison between these scattered parties had not been good. For more than a year the building designed for use as a mother and child health (MCH) facility had, to all intents and purposes, been finished.

The building, designed by an American, makes allowance for the torrid climate – unlike most modern public buildings in the Tihama. It consists of eight well-ventilated rooms each with an overhead fan and wash basin. Each has two doors, one leading to a very wide shaded verandah, the other to a part of the town which, it was at once clear, was used by men for defecating and urinating. The fabric of the building was already deteriorating as termites munched their way through the unprotected doors and window frames. Simon, the doctor, and Graham talked enthusiastically of how the building would be utilized. There would be a store for primary health care equipment and drugs, a centre for training health workers, a delivery room, an ante-natal clinic, a vaccination room, a room for a paediatrician, a room in which to register and weigh children and a room for demonstrating and cooking sample infant meals. Ali Ahmad listened attentively but, when asked if he understood English, said he understood nothing. It was not clear if he or our other Yemeni colleagues shared our thoughts on the planned allocation of rooms.

A number of men were resting on beds arranged on the spacious verandah. They turned out to be visitors from the malaria prevention project who stayed in Ahad for a few days each year. I stopped to chat and to ask about their work. The men, all educated highlanders, seemed surprised that I should think that educating Tihamis about malaria, its prevention and its treatment, should be any concern of theirs. Their job was to spray insecticide.

I learned that the extension had remained unused because there was no wall around the building nor were the rooms tiled as the specifications had dictated. Each party to the agreement seemed to be blaming the others and, in the meantime, the contractor had used his connections to powerful people in the provincial administration to receive full payment for his work. I innocently asked Graham and Simon, my fellow facilitator of primary health care, why we did not put up the relatively small amount of money required to open at least some of the rooms in order to provide services vital to improving the health and life prospects of the children of the area. They both looked shocked. Did I not realize this would be 'interventionist'? In the religion of developmentalism this was, I had learnt, the cardinal sin.

Suitably abashed, I remained silent as we returned to the old building and peered in at Elizabeth, the only member of our team actually doing anything to try to change the circumstances which cause about one child in three to die in the first year of life. She was working with two untrained Yemeni assistants, Nuriya and Amina, in a room only 3 metres by 5 but encumbered by several tables, cupboards, and a score of adults pressing forward to have their children seen to. There was one small window and no fan. No order, no patient flow was to be discerned. It was truly survival of the fittest or, rather, of those whose parents were fittest. Some were brandishing money in the quite mistaken belief this would persuade the *doktuura* to attend to them more quickly. Elizabeth barely had time to glance up and acknowledge the visit of her colleagues. I was glad to leave the stifling atmosphere.

Near her room was the hospital pharmacy where we were greeted by an obviously highland Yemeni. Proffering my hand was foolish, an invitation to be humiliated. My wrist was wrenched and my weakness commented on. He announced to the world that I must have drained myself sleeping with local women. I learned that this unsavoury man, possessor of a primary school graduation certificate and owner of a pharmacy on the highway, was one of the richest men in the town, had the grandest house in Ahad, was regularly able to afford new wives and divorce old ones and was protected by his patron, the director of health in the province. His white coat and stethoscope, the props to persuade the gullible of his status as 'doctor', looked odd worn over a grubby caftan and flip-flops.

The contents of the hospital pharmacy were quickly examined because they were so sparse. While the shelves of private pharmacies groaned with the weight of hundreds of kinds of drugs, the hospital had only a dozen. Curiously, there were large quantities of valium and largactyl but no vital drugs such as chloroquine or paracetamol and no antibiotics of any kind. Obviously it was against the financial interests of both the director and the pharmacist to ensure that the institution they worked for received regular drug supplies. Why had no one so much as hinted at this to me beforehand when it was so clearly apparent? Why did we put up with it?

We visited the dusty vaccination room and were told that the roof leaked. I learned that since our project had arrived in Ahad the number of children being brought in for vaccination each day had risen from about half a dozen to thirty or forty. Pleasing, if modest, progress; but a drop in the ocean considering that upwards of half a million people lived in the hospital's catchment area. Our hopes of seeing the two vaccinators in action were dashed. Both were studying, it being very common for government employees to combine a job with attendance at school. One of the vaccinators, after fifteen months in the job, had not started receiving a salary. I naïvely thought it was noble of him to work as a volunteer and report to work at all. Ali Ahmad, who himself was still a student but found it beneath his dignity to actually attend classes, could not criticize his colleagues. There was no point in their staying at their posts. Supplies of vaccine had run out two days previously. No, he had no idea when the official in charge of supply, the nephew of the provincial health director, would see fit to come down to Ahad with new vaccine. Simon told me that on several occasions he had gone up to Nakhwa, the provincial capital, to fetch supplies. Surely, I thought, this was 'back-stopping', another of those sins against our developmentalist creed which I had been warned against: assuming a responsibility which by rights belonged to the Ministry of Health.

Still to be seen was the delivery room, Susan's future workplace. Such was the priority that the hospital administration had allocated to the safe delivery of children, that Irene had been given the worst room in the hospital – the only toilet.

As with all toilets in public buildings in Yemen only staff used it for its intended purpose lest patients and the general public should foul it. From this windowless room Irene had somehow worked for almost two years delivering the relatively small number of expectant women who voluntarily came to hospital, dealing with the emergency cases brought in from the town and its surrounds, as well as managing to encourage the training of traditional birth attendants (TBAs), illiterate local midwives. Considering the conditions she had laboured under, Irene seemed remarkably well balanced. She told me she had worked in other developing countries but never in such poor conditions. The hospital not only lacked running water but the metal water tank in the compound, from which water had to be carried, was often allowed to run dry before anybody got round to ordering a water truck.

An atypically outgoing local woman, wearing a bizarre Chinese plastic hat, bustled up to greet us. I learned that in theory she is only a hospital cleaner but is, in fact, one of the major practitioners in the town. Because of her age and lowly natal status, no shame attaches to her entrepreneurial activities, foremost of which is injecting women. In some cases this is because the male doctors and nurses prescribe injections but, being barred by custom from touching female patients, cannot themselves administer them. In other cases the cleaner herself decides what kind of injection would be appropriate. She uses the privacy of the toilet to inject patients and receive appropriate remuneration free from prying eyes.

The nearby X-ray room was being operated by a genial Sudanese technician eager to practise his English. No disturbance was caused by our chat as the technician could do no work – his machine had been broken for three months. Inquiries revealed that it was the responsibility of a West German aid project to maintain equipment in this and other hospitals. A German had paid a quick visit some time previously but no one knew when the machine would be working again. As it turned out, the equipment was never repaired during my time in Ahad. In fact this proved a blessing for such is the magic supposedly wrought by technology that many Yemenis believe that standing in front of an X-ray machine is, in itself, curative. This belief is fostered by charlatans allowed to import such machinery and display neon signs advertising 'curative X-rays'. I learned that one 'doctor' offering this service was the medically unqualified deputy director of the provincial health administration. Later I was often to be shown blurred X-rays and assured the patient had felt much better after travelling to obtain one in Hodeidah, Yemen's main port a 150 km. to the south, or going north across the Saudi border to the ethnically Yemeni city of Jizan.

Such knowledge was yet to come. In the meantime I was glad to be taken back to the house to escape the heat and recover under the fan. Elizabeth staggered home from her hectic morning and, in dire need of rehydration, drank glass after glass of water. It was so hot in the closed room where she was forced to work that she regularly shed over a kilogram in the course of her morning clinic.

After lunch we were taken to inspect the town. Ahad was bursting at its seams as the weekly market, one of the most important in the north Tihama, was at its height. A haze of dust lay over the town raised by the tramp of thousands of feet and the procession of laden Toyota pick-ups over its unsealed roads. We soon became lost in the maze of pedestrian-only alleyways but recovered our bearings on finding the only multi-storey structure in the old town, the house of the sheikh. Clearly the inhabitants of this area of the town put great store by privacy as each compound was flanked by a high mud wall topped with thorns or – notwithstanding the complete ban on alcohol in Yemen – with broken Johnny Walker bottles. The brightly dressed women scurried past, modestly averting their gaze.

We paused to look in on a corrugated iron shed. Inside were six strapping, virtually naked, black men, members of the *abiid* slave caste manumitted only shortly before the 1962 revolution. I had seen no *abiid* in the hospital and learnt they rarely came to be treated because they are too poor and knew they would be made to wait even longer than other patients. The men were seated on the bare earth floor using their legs to grip stone mills which they were turning to grind tobacco. Supervising them was a much shorter, slighter and more stereotypically Yemeni, overseer. We were shown how this tobacco, strengthened with saltpetre, is placed under the tongue, producing a violent buzz, glazed eyes and rotten teeth among the many men, women and children who habitually use it. Would I like to 'see my country', 'spin my head' and try some? The result was a fit of sneezing, watering eyes and much merriment as I rushed outside to spit out. If more Yemenis lived into their sixties and seventies than is now the case the incidence of mouth cancer would probably be horrendous.

We were in the *madina*, the part of Ahad which by custom belongs to the *qabiilis* (tribesmen), men whose warrior self-image is belied by their sedentary lives. Being a tribesman in Yemen has no connotations of belonging to a marginal ethnic group (as it may elsewhere) for tribesmen regard themselves as occupying the apex of the caste-like hierarchy of Yemen. Though the tribesmen of the town insist that they belong to the *qabiili* caste of Yemeni society, they are racially different from the true highland tribesmen who do not, for the most part, permit their women to marry lowlanders.

We found ourselves in the heart of the labyrinth of Ahad, the original part of the town, the *Haara al Hinood* (Indian quarter), containing the most important of the ten mosques in the town. A youth told us the origins of the name. The original inhabitants had lived, for reasons of security, on the bare rocks to the east of the town overlooking what was then a forest. A group of Indian wanderers had appeared on the plain below and, in the course of exchanging goods, the local sheikh had been impressed by the morality of the Indians, despite the fact they were infidels. If only they would convert to Islam and go on the *haj* to Mecca, they could settle in the area and be given wives. This they eventually did, the original settlement was abandoned, both peoples interbred and the forest was steadily cut down to meet the fuel needs of the growing town. Today the surrounding plain is treeless.

I later heard other settlement legends linking the town with the pre-Islamic warrior Antar bin Shadad who is famous throughout the Arab world. But this account, with its stress upon the openness and hospitality of the locals, gave me heart, for the initial evidence had been otherwise. As yet no one had stopped to greet us or invite us into their homes as invariably happens when strangers visit communities in the highlands of

Yemen. When I had arrived in my mountain community I had been deluged by hospitality and for weeks had no privacy. In contrast, my presence in Ahad seemed not to excite the slightest interest. Maybe I was paying the price for the aloofness my predecessors had cultivated. Hopefully social interaction would come.

Moving on, we suddenly came across a blindfolded camel trudging around a firmly-rooted sesame oil press. I learned that most of the sesame now comes from Sudan as locally grown sesame cannot compete in price. The oil is used to cure a number of ailments. By now we had left the *madina* and reached the *suq* (market), home of the *abiid* (slaves) and the slightly paler *akhdaam* (those who serve). These non-semites of supposedly Ethiopian ancestry traditionally provided demeaning services to their tribal betters. They live cheek by jowl, their most intimate activities completely exposed to passers-by for their huts have no concealing compound walls.

Market day is the *akhdaam*'s only real opportunity to earn money and their living space was a mass of humanity. Tribal customers, lounging on Tihama beds placed under makeshift thatched awnings, were impatiently shouting orders as they prepared to chew leaves of *qat*. *Akhdaam* men were rushing backwards and forwards serving tea, soft drinks and new bowls of tobacco to replenish water-pipes. Their children, despite their poor circumstances, seemed relatively healthy in comparison with those we had just seen, perhaps because they had grown up with breast-milk, not been subjected to dangerous, but fashionable, powdered milk products. Older girls and their mothers were clearing away lunches they had served their customers. Other non-tribal women, squatting wherever they could squeeze themselves and find shade, were selling bread, charcoal, henna, strings of jasmine, bunches of basil to be worn as head decoration, clay pots, camel muzzles, woven prayer mats and basketware. A web of tarpaulins had been set up for the day. Marketgoers, all much shorter than myself, laughed good-naturedly as I kept running into the ropes holding the tarpaulins in place.

On the outskirts of the market area were the butchers, another despised caste, neither tribesmen nor *akhdaam*. Men were carrying in carcasses of animals they had slaughtered beside the rubbish dumps outside the town. Flies were swarming everywhere. Huddles of men were noisily competing to buy the best cuts while wild dogs fought over the entrails. By comparison, the fish market was orderly and relatively hygienic and the cats, competing for the fish heads, were models of decorum.

We passed through the grain *suq*. The consequences of the devastation wrought on Yemeni agriculture by the twin processes of labour migration and food aid were immediately apparent. Again I was struck by the irony of seeing, in a supposedly agricultural country which had just enjoyed a year of above-average rains, large groups of farmers buying grain in bulk for their own consumption. Sacks of Yemeni-produced sorghum, maize, wheat and barley were available, but at a high price. Much cheaper, and far more plentiful, were the stacked sacks of European, American and Australian wheat, white flour and Sudanese sorghum. Much of the foreign grain appeared to be aid and, though marked in English and Arabic as a gift from the United States, the EEC or the World Food Programme, was being sold. Other illicit grain had been smuggled from Saudi Arabia where, thanks to generous state subsidies to encourage wheat production in a totally inappropriate environment, flour is cheaper than it is in Yemen.

We came to the two streets of permanent concrete shops, all owned and run by tribal Yemenis. The press of bodies was intense, the heat in the heart of the *suq* dreadful. I wondered why in such a torrid climate the people did not begin the market early and close down before the heat of the day.

Most crowded of all was the *qat suq* where hundreds of men, but no women, were engaged in inspecting the produce. Prices were high as there had been little rain the previous month in the nearby mountains where the *qat* bushes grow. *Qat*'s bitter unappetizing leaves are placed in the mouth and after a few hours the active chemicals are absorbed through the mucous membranes and induce a mildly euphoric state. Many market-goers seemed to have come simply to watch. They shook their heads ruefully at the price and their inability to buy. Later in the day they would be at a loose end, deprived of the social occasion chewing provides. Nor would they be able to proclaim their wealth to the world by strolling through the town with a bunch of twigs under their arms and returning, hours later, proudly displaying the characteristic bulge of masticated leaves wedged into a cheek. But they would suffer no physical distress for *qat* is in no sense addictive.

The more prosperous market-goers and leading merchants – most of them true highland *qabiilis* – were carrying Kalashnikovs but there were no signs of the gun-merchants and ammunition sellers frequently found in Yemeni *suqs*. As Ahad is a *markaz*, a government centre, gun dealers do not openly ply their wares. I later found that this is not the case in another nearby *suq* where government soldiers do not intrude.

The *hakuuma* (government), an imposing collection of stone buildings dating from the time of the Ottoman occupation of Yemen which ended in 1918, lay in front of us. As is often the case in Yemeni settlements, the *hakuuma* lies on a hillside separated from the town, a physical expression of the uneasy relationship between central and traditional authority. Hordes of petitioners were coming and going in the hope of catching the ear of the centrally-appointed prefect, the security chief or the *haakim* (judge). Large numbers of ambulatory prisoners, fettered on the orders of the prefect or the security director, were to be seen hobbling round the *hakuuma*, dragging chains attached to their ankles. More favoured were those who were carrying their chains in plastic bags, ready to hurriedly put them on should an important official pass by. Other prisoners were sheltering in the shade provided by a large concrete water supply tank. I heard that for a brief period in 1984 it had provided water to a distribution network which reached several points in the town before being over-extended and breaking down. At the bottom of the hill lay a rusting Egyptian tank, a relic of the civil war. One of the dozens of sheep and goat traders had tethered his animals to it and strung a tarpaulin alongside to escape the sun. Purchased sheep were bleating their protests as they tottered away on their back legs, their new owners grasping them by their tethered front feet. Some were wearing muzzles ingeniously contrived out of the used plastic water bottles strewn everywhere around the town.

By now thoroughly exhausted, I was glad to return to our dusty office, turn the overhead fan to its maximum setting, and have a nap. That evening we dined out. I was told the

Ahad eating places served only tinned beans or tinned peas, typical evening fare for Yemenis whose appetites have been suppressed by an afternoon spent chewing *qat*. For a wider range of food we drove a kilometre up the road to eat in Khamis, a Wild West boom town which had grown up following the completion of the highway to Saudi Arabia. The town is at the junction of a poorly-maintained track leading to Nafaq, a prosperous *qat*-growing region renowned throughout Yemen for the quality of its produce. The people of Nafaq are also famed for their reckless driving and the feckless individuality which makes it impossible for them to pool resources to build such amenities as a properly graded road down from their mountain. As a result, their four-wheel drive Toyotas rarely last for more than a year.

The growth of Khamis is characteristic of the unchecked ribbon development common throughout North Yemen. Car repair workshops, car part shops, restaurants, hotels, photo studios and general stores stretch along the highway. Due to the housing boom there are many hardware stores and welding shops making water tanks and gaudily-painted metal doors embossed with the eagle emblem of republican Yemen. As elsewhere in Yemen, a line of unused shop premises, built for speculative purposes, snaked out of the town in both directions and grew appreciably longer during my stay.

By day the place is fly-infested and unprepossessing. Most lorry drivers and those who ferry migrants backwards and forwards to Saudi Arabia prefer not to drive in the heat of the day. By night the excitement at this crowded truck stop on Yemen's main outlet to the world is electrifying. We sat at a table outside a large restaurant watching a constant procession of vehicles pull up and disgorge an improbable number of passengers. On the other side of the road someone had draped a North Yemeni flag over the sign indicating the number of kilometres remaining to Jizan: a none too subtle reminder that though the Yemenis are glad the Saudis have built such a good highway to facilitate their journey to work, they are far from resigned to the conquest of Jizan and other former Yemeni territories by Ibn Saud in the 1930s. I had realized the strength of Yemeni irredentism on a visit to the Interior Ministry in Sana'a in an attempt to buy one of the first proper maps of North Yemen. I had seen a copy of the glossily presented map, but was told none were available. I learned that Swiss cartographers had infuriated the North Yemeni government by accepting the status quo and drawing the Saudi–Yemeni border in the 'wrong' place. A roomful of clerks were busily 'correcting' the map and Tippexing out the frontier.

The excitement of those coming from the north, returning from labour for the despised Saudis, was in marked contrast to the drawn faces of those on their way to the kingdom. In Saudi Arabia Yemenis are an undifferentiated proletarian mass, shorn of the weaponry and distinctive dress which sets them apart from all other Arabs. Egyptians, Palestinians, Lebanese and other Arabs employed in Saudi Arabia mostly share the Saudi prejudice that Yemenis are argumentative, backward, ignorant of Islam and dishonest. To counter such discrimination, and the attention of police looking for illegal immigrants, Yemenis often try to dress as Saudis.

On this, their first stop back inside Yemen, many were eager to restore the tokens of their Yemeniness. Brightly-lit shops displayed a range of the gaily coloured *futas* (sarongs) worn in many parts of Yemen. Vendors moved from table to table selling the prominent curved daggers and colourful belts, formerly exclusive to tribesmen, but now worn by all social groups in Yemen as an egalitarian symbol of their revolution. Other hawkers were trying to sell *kufiiyas*, expensive woven fez-shaped hats. More successful were those wandering round proffering bunches of *qat*, the chewing of which, though a relatively harmless pastime, is prohibited in Saudi Arabia with even more vigour than alcohol. A blind beggar being led by a young boy stumbled between tables. Malnourished black children and their mothers waited to snatch food left on tables. A better equipped mendicant, accompanied by a grave-looking group of kinsmen, was using a megaphone to elicit sympathy for his plight – several passengers he had been driving had been killed in an accident and he had been ordered to find bloodmoney equivalent to about £30,000 or face the vengeance of the victims' relatives.

It was good to be back in a bustling Yemeni restaurant sitting outside on a warm, and now more bearable, tropical

night. As street theatre it was fascinating. Interaction between
customer and waiter lacked western politesse but was just as
stylized. Within seconds of a new car load plonking themselves
down, the ever-vigilant head waiter, known as Al Tawiil (the
tall one), would be beside them.

'What do you want, brothers?'

'What do you have, tall one?'

'Everything!'; feigning surprise and impatience at such a
stupid question.

'What?'.

'Peas, beans, eggs, liver and fish', snapped Tawiil, his
cleaning cloth flicking across the table.

'Is the liver *baladi* (indigenous, i.e. not from an imported
beast)?'

'We serve nothing but *baladi*', replied Tawiil haughtily.

'Give us five livers and make sure they are *baladi*. Bring
them quickly!'

'You are welcome, youth of the future', replied Tawiil,
ironically.

Tawiil returned to his perch next to the till from where he
could survey the restaurant. With his sergeant-major's lungs he
bellowed the order across the crowded restaurant to the cooks
dripping sweat in the bowels of the building. The kitchen was
a vision of hell, flames leaping a foot or more into the air from
half a dozen gas burners. Yemenis have, as yet, no conception
of the need to conserve finite resources, and the kitchens of
busy restaurants are always profligate in using up cylinders of
gas. Cooking by blowtorch is, however, quick. Within
minutes five livers, undoubtedly of Somali or Sudanese origin,
were dropped unceremoniously onto the tables by the boys
under Tawiil's stern command. Service was fast, furious and
efficient, one Yemeni doing tasks which in other Arab nations
would be done by half a dozen.

Yemenis, though a gregarious and talkative people, put no
store by lingering over a meal and always wolf their food.
They have other times for conviviality and their convention is
to get on with their meals. Some parties were resuming their
journey down the highway within minutes. Others, intent on
chewing *qat*, summoned waterpipes and spittoons and settled
down on the raised beds surrounding the tables. Many would

eventually sleep on the same beds though those wanting to be away from the road would pay a few rials more for a bed under a fan in an upstairs dormitory. We got up to pay, and became involved in a ritual to be repeated every time I ate at Tawiil's establishment. 'Seventy rials, but because you are my friends, only sixty.'

The next morning my unease with the image presented of our project's success increased. I was highly envious of Susan as she was led away to visit local women in their compounds and to meet the traditional midwives BSDA had helped train and encourage. In comparison, Simon, the male doctor I had come to work alongside, seemed lacking in contacts and had no one to introduce me to. He talked at length and was at pains to explain the complexities of the filing system and to further my initiation into the mysteries of our Eze-Vu system of divination. He explained how the dusty, clearly-unread, books in our office were catalogued. I came across a series of pregnancy booklets, thought to be in Arabic, sent out from the London office for use by local women. I noticed that they were in Urdu and could be thrown away for all the good they would do. What, I wondered, was the point of having such an office and keeping all our Eze-Vu records in English and hidden from our 'counterparts'? Why did we have so much health-related literature and so many health information posters in Arabic sitting unread in an office to which Yemenis had no access? The files contained official letters in Arabic unaccompanied by translation or indication of their contents. A few contained scrawled comments admitting no one had been able to decipher what they were about.

We were introduced to our project vehicles and told how they should be maintained. Our organization owned a 4WD Toyota, and we also had charge of a smaller more economical 4WD vehicle, a Daihatsu Rocky, donated by UNICEF for primary health care promotion. On two occasions UNICEF had tried to allocate vehicles to our project but were thwarted by officials of the provincial health office who had commandeered them and were now driving them round Nakhwa as their own private vehicles. Only by dint of much protest had we recently succeeded in getting our Rocky delivered to Ahad.

In the afternoon our colleagues showed us more of the town

and its surrounds from the comfort of our Toyota. We first went to pay electricity bills as officials cut off those who fail to pay within two days of receiving demands. I heard from my colleagues that the supply was erratic and power-cuts common. Throughout the second summer of the project's life there had been no electricity for three months. I doubted my ability to live without fans and refrigeration. I was upset enough by the fact that the electricity went off at two in the morning. There was little point going to sleep under a ceiling fan as one had to wake up in the middle of the night, drenched in sweat, and move outside to catch whatever breeze was available. In the electricity office several clerks and technicians were crouching on mattresses, piles of *qat* set in front of them. None, however, were authorized to receive payment for bills in the absence of the director.

We moved on to visit the just-completed telephone office and be introduced to another allegedly great friend of the project and a very useful person. When I got to know the telephonist, and before he was sacked for expropriating money from telephone users, I disagreed. I found him an inquisitive bigot whose reasons for touching me were far from innocent, a contrast to the general, and quite congenial, Yemeni male love of physical conviviality.

We drove through the complex of government buildings and came down to the offices of the local development association where, it transpired, we had very few contacts. Hopes were expressed that I, with my Arabic, would remedy this and would also establish contacts with officials of the very impressive newly-built youth club. But why was this burden being put on me? We had already spent three years in Ahad. Should we not know these elected community leaders?

We drove out of town to the north passing the turnoff to the airport. We were warned that the military would not be pleased were we to go too close. We passed the town's only bank, the state-owned Agricultural Credit Bank providing loans, mostly to better-off farmers, for the purchase of tractors or drilling of tube wells. We came to another of the many military checkpoints littering the highways of Yemen. This one appeared to be more important than most as there seemed to be representatives of different branches of the army posted to watch each other. Scores of lorries and Toyota saloons with piles of goods precariously stacked above them were waiting to be checked and assessed for customs duties. Most had already been checked 50 km. to the north, while others had undoubtedly been driven across the Saudi border in the dead of night. Groups of men watching a search would suddenly dissolve as the driver and most important soldier strode off into the scrub for a hurried exchange of bank notes. A civilian from the local development association was collecting, not without protests from drivers, a 50 pence levy on each vehicle that passed through the checkpoint.

All this government vigilance could not hide the fact that just up the road smuggled petrol was being sold. So cheap is this petrol, brought into Yemen at night by trains of donkeys each carrying two 20 litre plastic jerrycans, that it is not profitable to build petrol stations in the North Tihama. We pulled up alongside a barrel on which a jerrycan was perched, tooting our horn to rouse the owner dozing under some thatch. He passed a hosepipe between the petrol tank and the jerrycan and, by blowing into the opening of the jerrycan, commenced the flow. Oblivious to the fumes swirling round him and the dangers posed by his cigarette, he wanted to know if we were Koreans or Bulgarians, apparently the only varieties of non-Arabs of whom he had knowledge. He was relieved to learn that the British, unlike the road-builders he had met, do not eat dogs.

After 2 km. we left the fine highway and paused to deflate our tyres and engage four-wheel drive. Our course lay down a wadi and there were many possible tracks, with varying degrees of corrugation, to follow. There are no permanent streams in Yemen and this valley like others is cultivable only alongside the shifting banks of the sporadically filled water-course. I hung on grimly in the back of the Toyota, uncomfortably seated at right angles to the direction of travel, ducking my head in anticipation of bumps. We joined a larger wadi some 300 metres wide and running between fields of sorghum. Groups of women and children were making their way down to the wadi where the only permanent wells are to be found. I was surprised that only a few wells are surrounded by relatively inexpensive concrete rings. Most lack protection from debris carried along at great momentum when flash floods come down from the neighbouring hills.

We came across two bulldozers engaged in building a levee right across the wadi. I had already seen how in Yemen the introduction of new technology – whether pumps, plastic piping or earthmovers – has greatly complicated questions of water usage and traditional systems of distribution and led to endless disputes. I had seen how foreign initiated water projects, implemented without social factors being investigated, had very often been sabotaged. Here it appeared that those able to hire bulldozers for the length of time needed to build an embankment of this size would, if their investment paid off and the wall held up, stop all floodwaters from irrigating fields downstream. A few minutes later we had to detour out of the wadi to avoid such an earthwork behind which were 100 metres of stagnant water, all that remained of a downpour a few weeks previously.

We passed a school, the first we had seen since leaving Ahad. I heard how the North Yemeni president, always referred to in official egalitarian-speak as 'the brother the president', had been driving along this wadi and had impulsively stopped to talk to the citizens, as is his wont. He had been appalled to find there was no school, had ordered one to be built on that very spot, and had pulled out a wad of the large denomination notes he always carries to show his concern for the people. No matter that there were no villages immediately adjacent and that a more convenient site could have been chosen. It was still a much needed and valued amenity. I later got to know youths who spent four hours on foot every day to come down to this school.

Further up the wadi, and closer to the mountains, surface water was flowing freely along the valley bed. Local drivers were using this opportunity to wash their cars, racing through at such a speed as to raise a bow-wave over their bonnets. Those standing up in the back of pickups were ducking to avoid a drenching, but still managed to wave a greeting.

We passed through Suq as Sebt, a small weekly market with a dozen permanent shops. Nearby was the site of one of the primary health care units supposed to have been completed two years previously. The contractor, a relative of the provincial health director, had declared the building finished and received payment. Yet there were no window frames. The flimsy wooden door had fallen off its hinges after being ravaged by termites. There was no sign of the electric generator, pump and roof water tank which UNICEF had provided to this and 200 similar buildings in North Yemen. Some boys who had been dozing inside the building made us welcome.

Our visit had attracted attention and men made their way across from nearby huts. Were we the promised doctors about to start work in their hospital? I began the explanatory spiel I was to repeat a thousand times. We had come to Yemen to help the training of Yemenis, to work with local people to find bright young men and women who could be trained for a year and then be in a position to treat most, but not all, cases of illness in their communities. The building we stood outside was not a hospital and would never have sophisticated equipment and facilities. However, God willing, there would one day soon be a skilled local person prescribing a limited number of useful drugs. Men listened politely, but were obviously sceptical. They had been told, they said, that a foreign doctor was coming to their community. When would he come? Would he have 'powerful medicine' and 'good injections'?

On our way back to Ahad I thought no more of this hint of the frustrations to come. Instead I marvelled at the beauty of the sunset and the proliferation of birds drinking in the wadi. We arrived home to find a group of people knocking on the door of the doctors' compound. They had come from the nearby pharmacy and had decided it would be better, or perhaps merely cheaper, to be injected by my colleagues rather than by the pharmacist. A plastic bag of drugs was handed to Elizabeth. Instead of quietly explaining why the various tonics, drips, antibiotics, vitamin and hormone cocktails were dangerous, worthless or grossly over-priced she immediately berated them and sent the bewildered visitors packing. Another educational opportunity had been wasted. But why, I reproached myself later, did I expect anything better? Elizabeth, like her colleagues, had received no proper training in Arabic. Though she had worked very hard at the language she had acquired the restricted technical vocabulary to diagnose and prescribe rather than the more complex language needed to persuade and change practices.

The next day, just as I was beginning to despair of setting foot inside a local house before returning to Sana'a, Simon took me on a social visit to Ali Ahmad, the bright young hospital administrator. We announced ourselves at the gate of his compound, allowing his wife, sister-in-law and other women to scuttle for cover. His mother shouted that we were to enter and a door opened to reveal a small boy who directed us through the compound and past a half dozen tethered sheep. The main hut into which we were taken was no disappointment. Tihami beds of various heights were arranged around the walls and, being important visitors, we were bidden to take the highest. Ali Ahmad's friends, interrupted in their *qat* chewing, competed with each other to offer us their places. The walls were decorated in traditional manner with a curious mixture of the utilitarian and the ornamental. Prestige objects such as Teflon frying pans, French drinking glasses, unopened bottles of colognes purporting to be also made in France, a pair of new sunglasses and a variety of Chinese enamel dishes, still bearing their labels of purchase, were nailed to the mud walls. Alongside were plastic flowers and portraits of singers and film stars from India and Egypt. Gamal Abdul Nasser was set alongside Ibrahim al Hamdi, the populist president of North Yemen assassinated in 1978, probably on Saudi orders, for fear he would re-unite Yemen. Highly heretical were the syncretic Indian posters similar to those I had previously seen in highland houses: Mary holding Jesus with Shiva looking on in the background; Burak, the horse which bore Mohammad heavenward, adorned with the head of an Indian film goddess. As in many other huts I was to see, the most common image of the collage was of the man of the house. He was shown as a shy boy, a bewildered teenage soldier and finally a confident self-important bureaucrat.

Despite our obligatory protests, we were each given a bottle of refrigerated mineral water. They cost 50 pence each, a not inconsiderable sum for a man earning a typical civil servant's salary of about £100 a month. A pleasant hour was spent chatting. Ali Ahmad was extremely knowledgeable about

Yemeni dialects and interested in analysing for me the difficulties of understanding the people of his town. I found him a congenial man and could not understand why the female doctor and the midwife both thought him an arrogant misogynist.

5

A JUNKET OF DISCOVERY

After Susan had completed her travesty of an Arabic course in
Sana'a one further experience was deemed necessary for our
job preparation. Since our organization had arrived in Yemen
it had been a tradition for new volunteers to be sent on an
'orientation tour' to visit other health projects. I had heard
scepticism about the educational value of such visits, particularly for those newly arrived in the country and sent to
discuss health issues with Yemenis who knew no English.
Still, the opportunity to be able to drive round Yemen and be
deferred to as a foreign 'expert' was not to be sneezed at.

On a fine morning a week before Christmas we left Sana'a
to visit our first project, a mother and child health clinic in the
southern city of Ibb set up with funding from the Norwegian
Save the Children Fund. We left the Sana'a plain and after an
hour came to the equally large plain of Dhamar, scene of an
earthquake in 1982 which had killed two thousand and left tens
of thousands homeless. After a few hours, we came to the pass
of Sumara, at 9,000 feet, more than a geographical boundary
between the arid north and the more fertile southern provinces
of Ibb and Ta'iz. For the north of the pass has traditionally
been the homeland of tribesmen belonging to the Zaydis, a
sect of Shi'i Islam now extinct elsewhere in the Muslim
world. All the Imams who ruled Yemen for twelve hundred
years were Zaydis. Zaydis are often dismissed by the half of
the Yemeni population not sharing their beliefs as unprogressive, bigoted, uneducated and quarrelsome. Inhabitants of the
southern mountains, like the Tihamis, belong to the Shafi'i
sect of mainstream Sunni Islam and were the earliest leaders of
the republican movement which triumphed in 1962. Because

of the proximity of Ibb and Ta'iz provinces to the former British enclave of Aden many Shafi'i exiles fled there for work and for education. Some have seen the world: travelled as seamen, been traders in Ethiopia, opened groceries in Cardiff, New York, Saigon or Marseilles, made cars in Detroit or picked fruit in California. The education system in Yemen is so recent that almost all the professional people and skilled technicians in Yemen still come from these southern Shafi'i regions and Aden. The atmosphere immediately felt more relaxed. After the suspicious soldiers who had scrutinized our papers and car at the checkpoints outside Sana'a, it was good to be waved through by more genial, relaxed men, some of whom spoke a little English.

In Ibb the deputy director met us and took us to a flat rented by the Ministry of Health. The next morning we arrived, as instructed, at the health centre at eight o'clock. I was amazed to find that the entire staff of a government institution had reported to work on time. We were treated like dignitaries and taken straight to the office of the director. The hospital was spotless, the staff professional looking in their western dress and white coats. I was instantly embarrassed by my error in coming dressed in a Yemeni *futa* (sarong). In other areas where the staff were, for the most part, similarly dressed, I was frequently commended for doing so. Here, however, I felt gauche, trying to be a Yemeni amongst Yemenis trying hard to show their European sophistication.

A very impressive service was being offered. The building had been well-designed with a specific flow of patients in mind. After paying a nominal fee, parents with their young children were led into a waiting room. They were then locked in and obliged to listen to a ten-minute health talk before having their children examined or treated. Some, especially the few fathers in the group, objected to this coercion and tried to leave but were firmly, albeit politely, prevented from doing so by the staff. A series of subjects were dealt with according to a roster.

The first topic that day was infant feeding. The introduction of widespread bottle-feeding in the 1970s in a country where less than 10 per cent of households have running water or modern cooking facilities, undoubtedly increased an already horrendous rate of infant mortality. Yemeni parents are, for the most part, convinced of the superiority and ease of milk powders. This is understandable because, until very recently, they have seen television advertisements making such claims. Protests by international organizations and a code of advertising practice forced on manufacturers eventually led North Yemen to stop screening quite such blatant anti-breastmilk propaganda. However, doctors and pharmacists still hand out free samples. Bonny Caucasian babies are featured on the tins of the two dozen or so brands of milk powder sold in Yemen. Bottle-feeding is inextricably connected with modernism in the popular imagination. So engrained is the habit of feeding babies with bottles that there are, I was to find, as many words for feeding bottle in colloquial Yemeni Arabic as the Eskimos have for varieties of snow.

The approach used to re-educate mothers was novel. The male nurse addressing the group started by asking what was the best way to feed a baby. The audience seemed startled at being spoken to in pithy colloquial language rather than talked at in high-falutin classical Arabic. Eventually, one mother spoke up. Of course, bottle-feeding was best. The nurse feigned much amazement and asked to see the bottle her baby was clutching. He sniffed it suspiciously and made as if to retch. He asked if she would herself want to drink such a foul liquid? He passed the bottle round the group. Surely only idiots would give such putrid stuff to their children? He asked the hapless mother where she had got the bottle. Did she not realize someone had taken advantage of her and exploited her ignorance? The audience were lapping it up, and beginning to laugh at the woman, even those who were themselves offering bottles to their babies. The technique seemed cruel, but eventually even the victim joined in the general merriment. For all their fierce pride, Yemenis have an admirable, often enchanting, ability to laugh at themselves.

A patriotic appeal was launched, appealing to the Yemeni fondness for *baladi* (local) foods. 'Citizens! Brothers and sisters! We do not need these foreign products. Artificial milk costs money our country needs for its development. We know what is best for our Yemeni children. Our grandmothers did not use this artificial milk but knew how breastmilk protects us from disease. They did not wean us on biscuits but on natural food, porridge made from the grains Allah has blessed us with. We are not stupid. Throw away your bottles.'

A new group was invited in and the old one moved into an adjoining room. Their children were weighed and weights recorded on the yellow road to health cards used throughout the developing world to record infants' progress. Efforts were made to explain to those attending for the first time the concept, difficult for the completely uneducated, of how an x and y axis can have any relation to their child's progress through the first years of life. Those whose cards indicated they had not completed a programme of vaccination were sent on to the vaccinators. Those underweight for their age were led to a kitchen where various weaning foods, mostly traditional recipes involving a mixture of the grains grown in highland Yemen, were being cooked.

A separate room was given over to rehydration. Diarrhoea and fever-inducing illnesses are so often fatal in Yemen, as elsewhere in the developing world, because of severe dehydration caused by the unfortunate belief that the ill should not drink. When presented with liquids the child may initially refuse but, after a while, will begin to take spoon-fed liquids and rapidly gain weight. Use of sachets of oral rehydration solution (ORS), provided by UNICEF, was being demonstrated and a few days' supply handed out. Parents were told how to mix it with clean water of a certain quantity. If using the bottled water freely available almost everywhere in the country, they were told to first pour off a quarter of the water so as not to make the solution too weak. The patience shown by the instructors was most impressive.

While Susan stayed with the midwives I spoke to those responsible for supervising the work of the far-flung rural health workers who depended on the hospital. I was told that communities had been mobilized to support their health worker. Citizens contributed funds, through the network of local development associations, for the construction and upkeep of health units. Almost all the health workers were receiving government salaries, had been given motorbikes donated by UNICEF for primary health care workers and were receiving money for petrol and maintenance. Kits of twenty-eight basic drugs, also supplied by UNICEF, had been transported to units.

It had been an instructive and full morning. We thanked the director for his kindness. He was modest about the achievements of the clinic and would not accept my comment that it was unlikely that parents taking their children to a similar institution in Britain would have such a stimulating and profitable time.

Little did we know it, but we had seen the model health project in the country, run by well-connected men able, at least for the time being, to tap influence in Sana'a and abroad. Everything which followed was to be a disappointing contrast to the Ibb project. In an optimistic mood we drove on to the southern capital of Ta'iz, forty years ago a large village, half of whose population were Jewish, but today the second largest city of North Yemen. We asked directions to the hotel we had been advised to stay in. We found it to be one of the poshest in the city and felt guilty about spending BSDA's money on such luxury. Our scruples lessened, however, when we saw the extraordinary panorama it offered of Ta'iz and Jabal Sabr, the mountain which looms over it.

We went down into the city to visit the market. Shafi'is from the south are renowned for their business acumen and dominate commerce throughout the country. Ta'iz has the further distinction of having female entrepreneurs who descend to the market each day from the scattered hamlets on the slopes of Jabal Sabr. They were selling qat, various kinds of bread and poppy seed heads (from which an infusion is made and used to pacify children). These unveiled women were flamboyantly occupying space, looking men in the face, proudly displaying their gold and fine costumes, their demeanour an extraordinary contrast to that of all other Yemeni women.

Nearby were tourist shops selling what remains of the intricate silver jewellery once made by Jews. In relation to most goods, the sentiment that baladi (native) is best survives in uneasy opposition to the contrary schema of status automatically according superiority to khaaraji (foreign) goods. In the case of silver jewellery, however, Yemeni women have come down decisively in favour of the kind of graceless poorly-worked gold ornaments beloved in the oil states. We entered a shop and fell into conversation with an old man. He said he had agents going round the countryside buying silver jewellery from elderly women, that tourists and European traders came to buy it, and that sadly there would soon be none left.

I asked about the Jews who left *en masse* in 1950. 'What Jews?', he replied, a twinkle in his eye. 'The ones who went to Palestine', I replied. 'Oh, they were not Jews. They were Muslims, God-fearing people who kept their word. Look around you today. Now Yemen is full of Jews.' He had used *yahudi* (Jew) in the pejorative sense now used by young Yemenis when talking of any amoral person, trickster or cowboy businessman. Yet his respect for Judaism, typical of men of his generation, was apparent. He talked of individual Jewish silversmiths he had known as friends, how they had chewed *qat* together and how their skills had never been picked up by Muslims after the Jews had been so cruelly tricked by Zionist emissaries who convinced them Palestine was a fabulous land where gold lay around for the taking.

I related a tale which I found always went down well. When working as a teacher in the occupied West Bank, Palestinian friends had introduced me to a young Yemeni Jew desperate to return to the Sana'a from which he had been removed in childhood. His fading memories were of the bounty of the Sana'a plain, the glories of the local grapes, the majesty of fruit trees in blossom and the grandeur of the multi-storey houses. I dared not disillusion him by talk of traffic jams, graceless concrete suburbs and the photo-chemical haze now shrouding the city. The Yemeni was already depressed enough. The Israelis would not let him leave to go to an Arab state. His only hope of going home was if he could somehow get enough money to first go to Europe. His meagre wages as a domestic, working alongside Palestinians in a tourist hotel, left him scant possibility of doing so.

One contemporary 'Jew', eager to practise his English, accosted me. I allowed myself to be taken on a tour of the old town, realizing too late the man was drunk. He made no effort to hide the fact. Islam, he insisted, does not prohibit alcohol. 'I have just had a drink but as long as I don't pray in this state no one will object.' To prove his point he led me into the city's main mosque. Shafi'is are very tolerant people in comparison with Zaydis and permit non-Muslims to enter their mosques, but this was testing their forbearance too much. Sure enough, my guide's condition was soon noticed. Old men, disturbed in their reading of the Koran, came over to berate him for the disgrace he had brought on Islam, especially in front of a *nasraani* (Christian). He argued back. I slunk away, leaving them to their theological dispute.

The next morning we presented ourselves at the Swedish Hospital, a mother and child clinic set up by Swedish Save the Children. Our reception was less enthusiastic than in Ibb. The Yemeni director gave us a quick briefing about the institution, laying great stress on his personal friendships with powerful people in Sana'a and how these would enable him to preserve the jobs of the ninety-seven staff and overcome any problems of drug supply or funding once the Swedes withdrew support. He passed us on to the only Swedes still left in the clinic, a couple who had arrived in Yemen only the previous week. They knew no Arabic and suspected the picture of complete success presented to them by the clinic director. They wished to learn from us of health problems in Yemen.

We wandered together round the large building, noting the confusion of patients unsure of the procedures to be followed. In the nutrition room the food being demonstrated contained none of the rich ingredients we had seen in the central market of this fertile area. Instead women were being shown by a man how to make scrambled eggs. The only posters on display had come from India, were written in Hindi and English, and showed pictures of vegetables unknown to Yemenis. We visited a classroom being used by what appeared to be the ladies auxiliary. Immaculately attired, obviously affluent, women were taking turns to record sections of a five-minute health slot broadcast once a week by the local radio station. In a country where the rate of rural female illiteracy is almost 100 per cent, and familiarity with classical Arabic minimal even amongst those women fortunate enough to have had a few years at school, I wondered what was the point of health messages broadcast in such fine classical language.

More impressive was the ante-natal section where we were warmly welcomed by a clearly experienced team. We discussed one of the major problems faced by midwives in

Yemen – the demand of mothers to be routinely given oxytocin injections at the beginning of labour. In the West such medication is given only after prolonged labour because of the dangers it can pose to the mother's health and her future ability to bear children. In Yemen, though theoretically only available with a doctor's prescription, it is freely administered by quack pharmacy owners. Young women have, in many areas, come to believe it is not possible to give birth without an injection. The Ta'izi midwives had produced an imaginative solution to the problem. They gave placebo injections and noticed how women, psychologically dependent on the drug, had more quickly completed labour as a result. They had decided not to disabuse the women by telling them of the ruse lest they not return for future deliveries.

Early next morning we descended from the mountains to the Tihama and arrived at the junction of the new highway leading to our next stop, Mocha. We slowed down, in search of some breakfast. Two groups of men leaped onto the bonnet and started disputing with each other. 'We saw the *nasraanis* first! They're ours!' I pulled up. I knew what the commotion was about but mischievously feigned ignorance. Could they direct me to a restaurant? Their faces fell. Did I not want whisky? Foreigners never stopped at the crossroads except to buy whisky. Why was I being difficult?

Mocha is today renowned in Arabia not for coffee but for whisky. One of the largest industries in Djibouti, a few hour's away by small boat on the other side of the Red Sea, is the illicit re-export of alcohol to Yemen and Saudi Arabia. It is relatively easy to land undetected along the sparsely populated Tihama coast.

We breakfasted on liver and went on to Mocha. As we neared the coast, humidity increased and a howling sandstorm blew up. Soldiers at the checkpoint outside the town had left their posts to get out of the wind. We drove on past the many abandoned mosques of what was once a grand and prosperous city. I got out to ask the way to the hospital and could barely stand up against the force of the gale and the pelting sand. It was a relief to find shelter in the hospital.

Waves and spray were dashing against the walls of the building. Given that the Red Sea is getting wider and that

Mocha is known to have declined as a port in recent centuries because it has silted up, why was this relatively new building, partly funded by the French aid organization which had just precipitously departed, not built further away from the sea? We searched for the man, reputedly a friend of BSDA, who was said to have been briefed of our arrival. He had gone to Sana'a and, so we later learned, had not been informed of our planned visit by our office. There was no one about at nine in the morning but we eventually met his sister, also a worker in the hospital, who shyly made us welcome until the director arrived.

His attitude was immediately antagonistic. How dare we arrive unannounced and without relevant papers from the ministry? His pique seemed justified. I felt let down by my organization. I imagined the chilly reception a Yemeni would get on turning up unexpectedly at a British hospital and asking for a tour of inspection. I grovelled as well as my Arabic would permit and the director was eventually slightly mollified. He passed us on to one of the two supervisors of the rural health care workers under the authority of the Mocha hospital.

He began by showing us around the hospital. We met a very dispirited vaccinator poring over his school textbooks. He vaccinated only about half a dozen children each day. He had been working for the hospital for eighteen months but his salary had never arrived from Sana'a. Most people, he lamented, were too poor to afford to bring their children into town to be vaccinated. In some outlying districts less than 1 per cent of children had received the three injections conferring immunity against the six major killers of children. I was told that the French had promised to provide a car and refrigeration equipment to allow a programme of rural vaccination to begin but nothing had happened. Could our organization help out? I explained that we were nobodies without power to decide such things. We had just come to see and to learn. He shrugged resignedly. No doubt he had seen many foreigners passing through, giving the same answer.

I felt guilt at being a development tourist, hearing of, but doing nothing about, real problems I was not the first to learn of. I was reminded of similar feelings three years previously when my German employers had sent me to investigate problems of water supply. After a long hot drive I had randomly selected a village on the fringes of the Tihama. I had assumed women drawing water from a well in such an isolated place could not have seen many foreigners. I got out and as I walked towards them a flirtatious young woman stepped forward. 'Another *nasraani* has arrived! What do you think, girls? Is this one Russian, Chinese, American, German, Korean? Perhaps he is a jinni. Will he first ask us when this well was dug, how deep it is, or when it runs dry? He will want to know the name of this district and who our sheikh is and then will get into his car and drive away and forget us.' She mimicked the expert gravely taking down information in his notebook. The audience were in stitches. I had to join in, regardless of lost dignity.

The tour of the hospital continued. We were shown a small room and told it was used as a health education centre and a rehydration room where children suffering from diarrhoea could be given oral rehydration solution until they were fit enough to be taken home. This was the only room in the hospital which lacked a ceiling fan, presumably reflecting low official priority given to its functions.

The supervisor was due to pay a visit to a health worker about 20 km. away and invited us along. As we picked our way through the dust storm, our thirty-five year old companion related his melancholy history. Though a native of the area he had been educated in Aden where his father had trading interests. After the 1962 revolution in the north his father had returned home, leaving his son to complete his secondary education in Aden. This he had done shortly before the British withdrawal in 1967. He had set out for home on a dhow which foundered near Bab al Mandab. Though everyone reached shore all their belongings were lost. These included the supervisor's matriculation certificate, a highly prized possession even today when there are many schools, but in the early 1970s a passport to any job in the new state. Heartbroken that his studies had been in vain, the supervisor had spent years trying to get official recognition of his educational achievements. Because of the chaos caused by the take-over of Aden by the National Liberation Front, the civil war in the north between royalists and republicans and the later mistrust between capitalist north and Marxist south, he had been unsuccessful. Eventually he had resigned himself to starting again from scratch. After he had once more completed primary education he was able to qualify for training as a nurse. He now combined his job as a primary health care supervisor with studying in secondary school. God willing, he would enter university, even if it was twenty years after he should have gone.

His fortitude was impressive as was the obvious conviction he brought to his work. The main enemy of primary health care, he said, is not the ignorance of the people but the privilege of doctors. To establish a real system of people-oriented health care meant a war on two fronts – against doctors and against the multinational drug companies. The World Health Organization slogan 'Health For All by 2000' was, in the case of his country, quite unrealistic. The Ministry of Health was staffed by apathetic mediocrities. He joked that they may try to hide their failures by handing out a packet of aspirins to every household in Yemen on New Year's Eve in the year 2000. The 'war' to build a real system of community health would not be won in his lifetime, but, have no fear, it would be won. Women were vital to its success, 'the petrol of primary health care'. He wished there were official encourage-ment to train a woman to work alongside a man in every health unit. The role of foreigners in building a relevant health system was minimal. They could provide funding but otherwise Yemenis could do it all for themselves. He had read how Nicaragua, against all the odds and with little help, had trained thousands of barefoot doctors since its revolution.

Thus he remained optimistic despite the many difficulties of his work. Half the health workers had no buildings to work from, some had not received the UNICEF motorbikes promised them and were not able to get out and visit homes in their scattered districts as they were supposed to. Basic drugs supplied by UNICEF had begun to run out and the ministry in Sana'a had sent no new supplies. Those with motorbikes received no money for fuel and maintenance and some had broken-down machines they could not afford to repair. Some workers had been unpaid for a year. Only one woman had received any recompense for her work and even then she was officially employed as a 'cleaner' and her hard-won qualifications not recognized.

We came to an unprepossessing collection of villages set against one of the few hills which reduce the monotony of the Tihama plain. Fields of stunted sorghum were half-covered by sand. We had no time to chat to the health worker in his one-room unit as he was already late for his weekly appointment with the school children. We all went off to the school and were taken to see the most senior class, sixth form primary students. There were no girls. As in other Yemeni schools, students were of all ages. Adult men previously deprived of any opportunity to study feel no shame about studying with boys a third their ages and there were a number amongst those who rose to greet us.

Almost all schoolteachers in North Yemen are Egyptian Muslims of a fundamentalist bent, recruited and paid for by the Saudi government, and this school was no exception. Such teachers, an embarrassment and a threat to their own government, earn at least a dozen times the meagre salaries paid them in Egypt. Again a paradox of development in Yemen came home to me. A government which wishes to be seen as a redeemer sweeping away 'backwardness' and illiteracy and creating self-sufficiency is forced to depend on foreigners who, though Arabs and Muslims, are often filled with contempt for Yemenis and their culture. Egyptian teachers were always trying to befriend me so they could vent their spleen to another foreigner. A common joke amongst them was that, God willing, in a hundred years the Egyptians might be able to bring Yemenis up to the educational level of donkeys.

The Egyptian whose lesson we interrupted seemed as surprised as his students to find a European man and woman walking into his classroom. The pupils were put through their paces to show what they had previously learnt. They all knew what carbohydrates and proteins were. Their teacher beamed. Would I like to ask the class a question? Taken aback, I asked if they knew where vitamin C might be obtained. A sea of arms arose. The Egyptian chose a pupil who rattled off an extensive list of fruits and vegetables. No doubt all could be found in

Cairo, but most of them were either completely unknown in Yemen or else unavailable in the drab village we were in.

With apologies to the teacher, the supervisor interrupted the class. He acquainted the students with the ideas of the Brazilian pedagogue Paulo Freire. 'We are here to learn from you. Theoretical knowledge has no value if we cannot relate it to our lives. Can you all think carefully and tell us what foods, available in this village at this particular season of the year, might have vitamin C?' The class had to think, but gradually answers were elicited. He then discussed sources of protein. As we all know, he said, at this time of year we cannot afford to eat the little fish which is caught because it is sent to urban markets. What substitutes can we find? Students offered their views, instead of parading their rote-learnt knowledge. The Egyptian teacher was apoplectic at this revolutionary challenge to his authority and seemed glad to see us leave.

We returned to Mocha and were taken to lunch in a local restaurant by the supervisor and his colleagues. We were joined by a female Eritrean nurse – unthinkable behaviour for Yemeni women who never eat in public. It was Thursday, the beginning of the weekend, and the supervisor was glad to be offered a lift to his home village. We went on down the coast to seek a place to camp for the night. Often our view of the sea was blocked by the mangroves which make it impossible to swim for most of the length of the North Yemeni coastline. We came across a break in the mangroves and found a small village with date palms. We changed and walked out to sea for several hundred yards before the water became deep enough for swimming. Further out, waves were breaking over the coral reef which hinders navigation along most of the coast. Flocks of flamingos retreated before us. Pelicans lumbered into the air.

On our return to the shore we found a wizened man busy watering some date palms. He came over and showed us to a thatched hut where we could stay the night. Despite his obvious poverty he refused our offers of money to rent his modest shelter. We walked along the beach chatting. I learned how during the windy winter months the fishermen could not set out to sea and times were hard. At this time of year they could only catch fish in the flimsy traps driven into the sand just off the beach. The earth was so saline that nothing but date palms could grow. He explained how trees were propagated and tended. No one in the village owned any of the trees and they had to hand over half the produce to absentee highland landowners.

Tihamis are accustomed to hardship. They have had no defences against those who for countless centuries have come from the sea or down from the mountains to rob them of their livestock and their produce. In very many communities it is absentee highland Yemenis or resident representatives of mountain families who control access to water and land. Relatively few Tihamis benefited from the employment opportunities in nearby Saudi Arabia in the 1970s and early 1980s. Because theirs is a hand-to-mouth existence, many could not afford the cost of transport and settlement expenses before beginning to remit money to their families. It is hardly surprising that Tihamis are more wary of strangers than their more forthcoming highland compatriots. This kindly man was fortunately an exception. He did not invite us into his home, I suspect out of shame at the undoubtedly shabby nature of his surrounds. He did fetch us a bucket of water for drinking during the night, but as it was only marginally less salty than seawater we could not bring ourselves to use it. We slyly used the bottled water we had brought with us.

The beach was littered with beer cans and whisky bottles. My companion pointed to them sadly. I apologized for the insensitivity of my fellow Europeans who so casually disposed of their left-overs. No, he said, it was not just the fault of the *khubaraa*, the foreign 'experts' who come down to the coast for the weekend; young Yemenis from the cities were just as much to blame. He himself had never tasted alcohol and at his age would go to his grave happy not to have done so. No, he did not condemn those who did. It was for Allah to judge. What did distress him was not their drinking but their thoughtlessness in not hiding the evidence of their habits. Never had I heard a better exposition of the essential tolerance of Arab society, the stress Islam puts not on prohibition of activities it deems sinful, but on their social concealment.

Returning to the highway the next morning, we were again accosted by booze sellers and this time allowed ourselves to be led off the highway into a secluded wadi. Susan was understandably nervous about being in an isolated place with armed men. Because I had been in Yemen before, I was worried not at the prospect of being robbed, for theft is extremely rare in rural Yemen, but at the fear of the whisky being diluted. Did I want yellow or white whisky? I did not want gin so ordered the former. The men took my money and disappeared into the hills on a motorbike. Within minutes they were back with an obviously unopened carton of Johnny Walker.

Having bought whisky, I was determined not to have to give it up at the first checkpoint. We pulled off the road to re-pack the booze and discard the carton and found that thousands of others must have had the same idea as the place was littered with used cartons and beer cans. We resumed our journey. Knowing how impressed Yemenis are by foreigners who appreciate qat, rather than instantly condemn it, I stopped to buy some and hurriedly began stuffing my cheek with leaves. My preparations were not in vain. At the first checkpoint I was immediately asked 'How much whisky have you got on board?'. I had barely begun my prepared lines approving of Islamic prohibitions on alcohol when one of the soldiers noticed my qat bulge. Another noticed my futa (sarong). Diligence gave way to delight and all thoughts of search vanished. So I liked Yemen, did I? I must return some time and chew with them. I am sure they knew of our alcohol but, like most Yemenis (and unlike Saudis), were eager to turn a blind eye to the habits of visitors to their country. They wished us a pleasant journey.

We went on and came to the ancient city of Zabid, once one of the major Shafi'i centres of religious study and a rival to the Al Azhar University in Cairo. We were directed to the hospital built fifteen years previously by Swedes. We had heard that the Swedes had withdrawn their personnel and support five years previously. An air of demoralization hung over the hospital. Dust was everywhere and litter lay in the corridors. Susan was invited into a delivery room to witness her first birth in Yemen and returned within minutes, obviously shaken by what she had seen. We were then led to the director's office and found him in a despondent mood.

The dozen outlying health workers supervised from the hospital had run out of drugs supplied by UNICEF. The ministry showed no interest in helping them and some had disappeared from official records. Nobody had any influence in Sana'a which might improve the situation. Most of the health workers had become drug sellers, had opened pharmacies and were administering medication they had once fought against. He could not blame them. How else were they to get by?

As elsewhere in rural Yemen a smart private pharmacy outside the hospital gates provided a contrast with the drab government building. Dozens of needles had been carelessly thrown away and were lying on the ground. More than once I heard stories of Yemeni children playing 'doctors and nurses' with such needles and of tetanus deaths which had resulted.

We went on to our next stop, Jabal Kahima, site of the project which I had been proudly shown on my first visit to the organization's London headquarters. We turned off the Russian built highway and passed by the hot springs where in his final years Ahmad, the last Imam, sought relief from injuries resulting from repeated attempts on his life. I was glad to climb away from the monstrous heat. I gritted my teeth as Susan had her first practice driving round the hairpin bends of Yemeni mountain tracks. I had met many Yemenis who had lost friends and relatives when their cars had toppled over ledges. Wrecks glinted in the sunshine hundreds of metres below us.

Myriad tiny hamlets lay above us, most accessible only by steep paths which are a challenge to man, woman and donkey. Here, as everywhere in highland Yemen, defence had been the prime consideration when siting houses with the result that water supplies are often hours away. We passed many groups of women patiently trudging up and down with plastic buckets and jerrycans perched on their heads. On seeing us they instinctively flipped down the panel to complete the veiling of their faces. Again I marvelled at the industry of the generations of Yemenis who had made settlement possible by constructing terraces out of such slopes.

At 7,000 feet we found ourselves in mist but climbed higher and burst through the enveloping gloom. We entered a pleasant sunlit town surrounded by lush fields of sorghum, wheat and barley. We were now too high for coffee or *qat*. We were directed to the old Ottoman fort, greeted the soldiers at the entrance and went on to the seven-roomed house solely occupied by Helen, the project co-ordinator.

I awoke early next morning and stumbled outside to see the day. The clarity of the air on a superb cold morning was incredible. Far below me I could see the wadi which led up to the town of Rahbaan, hidden from view, where our other project in the area was based. The whole Tihama lay below me, the coastline 40 km. away as clear as crystal. Beyond was the black mass of Hanish Island in the middle of the Red Sea lying 100 km. distant. The coast of Eritrea, 160 km. away, was clearly visible. I stood bewitched. How had I been stupid enough to volunteer to work in a hot horrid place like Ahad when I might have been about to work here amid such beauty?

But what was our work? Helen did not appear to have much. We were taken on a quick trot round the hospital where we met our Sudanese colleague, BSDA's only non-European employee. Having lived in Kahima for five years (though only employed by us for a year) he was well-connected and clearly liked. Helen, however, seemed to know hardly anybody in the town. We chatted for hours and walked aimlessly round the town before shutting the doors and pouring whiskies. We began a succession of Monopoly games, kidding ourselves we were practising Arabic because we were using an Arabic board.

I later found that Helen had been recruited because BSDA had thought that as an anthropologist she would learn the language quickly and wish to get to know the people. She had arrived to find herself alongside a highly respected Sudanese nurse and shortly afterwards a well-qualified Palestinian woman was recruited. Clearly Helen could not compete with native speakers for acceptance when she had been given inadequate training in the language. Her colleagues both had medical qualifications and Helen did not. How was she to present herself? To boost her standing, she let it be known that she was a doctor, but this only added to her problems. Locals know nothing of postgraduate qualifications and were naturally doubtful of someone calling herself a 'doctor', yet not even able to give an injection.

In the months to come I realized how Helen's problems paralleled Graham's. Her employer had not determined her authority *vis à vis* her colleagues. She claimed that when recruited she had been promised a car of her own and became embroiled in conflicts with colleagues who insisted she had no right to exclusive use of a vehicle. In her anger she retaliated – and gave more ammunition to her critics – by making a point of flying, at BSDA's expense, from Hodeidah to Sana'a rather than travelling by bus or shared taxi as all other volunteers did. More and more, she feared going out into the countryside. She hardly ever visited the Rahbaan project, on the other side of the Kahima massif, which she was also supposed to co-ordinate. Because of mounting ill-will she did not always heed her colleagues' hints that she should dress in a manner likely to win local approval. Unlike all the other women employed by the organization she did not routinely cover her hair as custom dictates nor wear trousers under dresses and, as a result, was sometimes taken for a man. Only after a year in the job, and as a result of nagging from colleagues, did she visit any of the health posts scattered round the mountain. Her Arabic did not get better. It was not surprising that as time went by, she retreated into the privacy of her house in Sana'a and adopted a façade of vigorous labour which further alienated her colleagues. To maintain her self-esteem she made much of her scanty knowledge of rural Yemen whilst dining out amongst the expatriate sets of Sana'a. Her high profile social life and first-name intimacy with several western ambassadors infuriated her colleagues toiling away in the countryside. Her predicament was tragic and insoluble.

I heard that other personal crises were also brewing atop this idyllic mountain. Our sister agency AFJAD, who had funded our Kahima project for many years, had recently sent one of their own employees to the area. Lucy, a water engineer, had been up the mountain for six months but had not managed to start work on any projects. Her morale had slumped due to her inadequate Arabic and AFJAD's failure to investigate the intrigues and conflicts over traditional water rights which made the ambitious tasks presented her impossible. She had fallen out with Helen and had moved out of her house. AFJAD were paying several thousand pounds to renovate a house in a nearby village for her sole use.

Problems also surrounded the appointment of a new member of our own organization. Julie, a linguist, had been recruited to carry out research on the prospects of reducing the rate of female illiteracy. Yemeni counterparts were not informed of her imminent arrival. Colleagues did not advise her how to present herself. Neither was she given language instruction, for BSDA naïvely imagined that as an Arabic graduate Julie would immediately understand the dialect. On arrival she found that her mere presence immediately gave rise to the belief that BSDA was about to provide teachers, materials and classrooms for local women. There is little overt opposition to such education even from the most benighted fundamentalists. It is considered most unprogressive to not want to educate women. Julie's attempts to explain that she had come simply to investigate if the citizens wanted a literacy programme puzzled people. Of course they did, when would classes start?

The director of health in Kahima, a member of a powerful sheikhly family, had been particularly annoyed at what he took to be the perfidy of foreigners. He telephoned Sana'a and found that Julie had no official clearance to be in the area. She had entered the country on a tourist visa which had expired. Her job had not been approved by the Central Planning Organization, the Interior Ministry, the Health Ministry or the security authorities. These formalities are essential for any development worker in North Yemen. Julie only found she was in breach of Yemeni regulations when the security authorities began taking an understandable interest in someone wandering round their country without papers and without a residence permit. She was banned from returning to Kahima. The programme co-ordinator and Helen competed to pass the buck. No one ever apologized to Julie or shouldered responsibility for the financial loss involved in paying a salary to someone who was never able to do the job for which she was recruited. For months Julie was in imminent danger of being taken to the airport and expelled from the country. Months of trudging round offices in Sana'a did not change official minds. She left Yemen in an understandably bitter mood.

On the way down the mountain Helen told us some of the

hidden history of our organization, the embarrassments purged from the bulging filing cabinets. For half the project's life there had been no road and volunteers had reached the town only after walking for twelve hours and climbing 7,000 feet. One of the early workers recruited in Britain had, so she alleged, not had this properly explained to her. She had arrived, hot and bothered, at the base of the mountain, taken one look upwards and insisted on returning to Britain at once. Later the isolation led to such tensions between two couples that they had swapped spouses. AFJAD, without consulting project workers, sent a male film team who outraged local sensibilities by dressing in shorts (regarded as underwear by Yemenis) and filming local women. Two midwives, who had lived together in a London flat and quarrelled, specifically requested, when both applied to the agency, that they not be posted to the same country. However, due to the recruiting crises which regularly bedevilled BSDA they had been sent, by themselves, to start an ill-fated offshoot of the project in a small market town halfway down the mountain. Work was hampered by the rigid social divisions which prevent tribal women from entering the *akhdaam* section of the community and vice versa. The midwives could not agree which part of the community to concentrate on, stopped speaking to each other, and the project was eventually abandoned.

An Australian doctor with no veterinary experience decided that what the area really needed was some virile goats – despite the fact that goats are not encouraged in highland communities because of the damage they can do to terraces. There are large herds in the Tihama where they range widely over the arid scrub but they are not valued in the mountains. If a goat gets onto a mature *qat* terrace thousands of pounds of damage can be done in no time at all. Nevertheless, the goat scheme was pushed forward. Two chunky files were filled with correspondence, assessment of the viability of the idea and extracts from various journals devoted to goat husbandry. Eventually seven super-large goats were recruited in Kenya and shipped from Mombasa to Hodeidah where they were met by a goat-herder employed by BSDA. The goats' orientation programme was a traumatic one. Three died before reaching the base of the mountain. Two more did not survive the climb and the remaining two expired from altitude sickness in the expensive lodgings built for them. In the end £15,000 pounds had been wasted.

The fiasco ranked amongst the crassest tales of misdevelopment in Yemen I had come across. Almost as bad as the advice given me by my former German boss, holder of a doctorate in development economics, yet unable to read contour lines on a map, a man who believed YMCAs could be found in Yemeni provincial towns. Blinded by his experience in the completely different environment of Sudan, he told me to try to persuade Yemenis to come down from their well-watered hills and resettle round wells in the arid wadis. He sent me to report on water projects implemented by the American Save the Children Fund. The Americans had built half a dozen covered water cisterns each with taps only 6 inches above the ground – far too low for the tall plastic jerrycans and buckets used by Yemeni women for carrying water. Recipients of this aid had to make holes in the water tanks through which to insert hose pipes and suck out water. Great pools of stagnant water, ideal for mosquitoes and for snails which host bilharzia schistosomes, were created by these projects. I noted this in a report to my German employers and urged them to build outlet taps a half metre above the ground. My warning was unheeded, my report remained unread. The Germans made exactly the same mistake.

Tales of American incompetence were legion. Perhaps apocryphal, perhaps black propaganda spread by rival agencies, was a report that the US Agency for International Development (USAID) had landed pigs to breed in Yemen before realizing Yemen was 100 per cent Muslim. Another tale was that USAID had brought a new strain of donkey to Yemen to replace allegedly inferior local beasts. To Yemenis the new donkeys looked so bizarre that they assumed they were pigs and would have nothing to do with them. I heard of a Peace Corps volunteer who walked round a rural town with a pet Dachshund which Yemenis were convinced was a pig. Definitely true was the tale of how solar panels and a computer with which to monitor their correct degree of inclination had been brought from America and set up to provide power to refrigerate soft drinks consumed by the high officials of the Central Planning Organization.

I was ready to believe anything of Americans after we had visited the next development enterprise on our list, a USAID-funded health project in Hodeidah. The American aid industry is largely privatized. Multinationals not widely known for their experience in health care have successfully tendered for USAID primary health training projects in politically sensitive countries such as North Yemen. For this, financially the biggest health project in Yemen, the contract for the first three years had not gone, as expected, to Westinghouse but to a smaller company.

The first impression on leaving the sweltering streets of Yemen's main port was the lavish surroundings of the project's suite of offices. So cold was the air-conditioning that I began shivering. Three expatriates, only one of whom spoke Arabic, were at their desks reading *Le Monde, Newsweek* and the *Wall Street Journal*. They made us welcome and began explaining the organizational details of the project in terms of befuddling acronyms. We learned they had difficulty in spending the $10 million annual budget and their annual underspend exceeded BSDA's total budget. We were shown the telex and facsimile machines keeping the project in touch with Boston and Washington. Pages and pages of instructions arrived each day. A directive had just come down from the American Embassy in Sana'a ordering them to cease using drugs, ordered by UNICEF, which were of Eastern European origin. We asked how they were overcoming problems of drug supply and non-arrival of salary that were threatening other health projects we had visited. We realized there were no problems because the Americans paid for everything. If salaries did not come they did not, as we did, make a nuisance of themselves in the ministry to find out why, but paid out their own money. Less than a third of their health workers were receiving government salaries. Though the American aid was due to end in a year, they did not seem concerned what might happen afterwards.

The rationale for the project seemed political, to win affection for the donors, rather than to establish a viable health system for the Tihama. State salaries of all Yemeni counter-parts were augmented by the Americans, with the highest-ranking Ministry of Health employees receiving the most. The extent of this topping-up was a closely guarded secret though I

later heard how a rival company in Egypt boosted the salaries
of departmental heads in the Egyptian Health Ministry by a
factor of forty-three. We were told there were frequent
opportunities for overseas study tours. Senior Yemeni personnel were sent to the United States for three months at a time
for 'language' and 'management' courses. All the males
involved in the project, and the few females whose fathers
gave approval, had been to Cyprus for a refresher course
during the holy month of Ramadan. We asked the benefit of
sending even the lowest-ranking health workers to study
abroad in such a different culture and were told that in Cyprus
there were no 'distractions' of the kind which would impede
their study in Yemen. I later heard of the acute disorientation
experienced by some of those taken from a Yemeni village
straight to a decadent tourist resort complete with nudist
beaches and easily available alcohol. Another trip was being
planned to see USAID-funded health projects in Bangkok and
Manila. The Americans joked as to who was going to have the
pleasant job of accompanying 'the boys' and 'seeing they
behave themselves'.

Such largesse undoubtedly wins hearts and minds. Other
nations compete to send Yemenis round the world. I came to
realize that all the Yemenis we worked with had heard of the
exciting travel possibilities provided by the western aid
community. Corridors of Sana'a ministries are filled with
rumours of forthcoming trips, of talk, both boastful and
envious, of sponsored visits to the bars and brothels of Addis
Ababa, Cairo and London, of those who have converted a
study tour or a hospital stay into a round-the-world trip. Why,
we were all asked, did BSDA not do the same? Why couldn't
our 'counterparts' go to England to study English or be sent
round the Arab world? I was to spend hours and hours trying
to explain why we saw little benefit, or cost effectiveness, in
doing so.

The Americans seemed infatuated with their computers.
They stressed the value of collation, inputting and analysis of
data and talked, misty-eyed, of creating a nation-wide
computerized data base on indicators of rural health. I
wondered how the ministry could digest and analyse information in such form when it had no computer-literate personnel.

I learned that the Hodeidah project ran computer courses for all health workers and possessed five computers. Now that the health workers had dispersed to their far-flung communities the machines, kept in a permanently air-conditioned room, were unused by Yemenis and records not updated. Protecting hardware from heat seemed unnecessary for the machines were permanently turned off and only occasionally used by the bored expatriates to teach themselves word-processing. I was intrigued at this consequence of the developmentalist credo that the computer brings progress and banishes inefficiency wherever it goes.

We were taken to lunch and introduced to a woman employed by the largest Dutch project in Yemen. A private company had been given the contract to introduce a rubbish disposal system for Hodeidah. Metal skips had been imported and distributed all over the city. A fleet of Dutch rubbish trucks had been given to the Hodeidah municipality. Already, after only a few months, a third of them were out of order. The hydraulic lifts to hoist the skips and empty them into the trucks had become clogged with sand. The Dutch employed several non-Arabic speaking 'specialists', each with a luxury apartment in the beach suburb reserved for foreigners and leading compradore merchants. The Dutch were spending no money on teaching Yemeni mechanics how to maintain the vehicles. I later saw a video they produced in the hope of encouraging awareness of sanitation problems amongst inhabitants of the shanty towns ringing Hodeidah. The commentary was entirely in classical Arabic and thus incomprehensible to its target audience. The video had been so skilfully shot that scenes of rotting rubbish, decaying animal carcasses and flying plastic bags had an eerie surrealist beauty and conveyed little of the filth and squalor of the city.

The next morning we left humid Hodeidah and headed out along the pot-holed highway with its rutted, half-melted carriageway. We passed an impressive Chinese-built weigh-bridge and lorry inspection station where few of the over-loaded lorries beginning the slow haul up to Sana'a were bothering to stop. We were startled to see an immense structure looming out of the haze. I was to learn it is one of the six largest flour mills in the world. Yemeni production of wheat would keep the mill busy for only one week a year yet such is the desire for white bread, that the plant runs at full capacity.

We passed through the town of Bajil, once a sleepy Turkish garrison now a thriving entrepôt where imported goods are off-loaded from containers onto four-wheel drive Toyotas, the only vehicles capable of carrying them up the nearby mountains. We turned off onto an almost completed highway which provides an alternate, but longer, route to the central plateau. The road is well built with none of the hairpin bends and awesome drops which make driving on the old Chinese highway so perilous. I was surprised to see it lacked bridges and we had to descend the wadis and gullies dissecting the plain across which we were driving. I later learned that the North Yemeni government, keen to prevent saboteurs threatening the artery, had instructed the Korean road-builders to build fords not bridges, even though this meant the road would be blocked after rainstorms. We waved at industrious Koreans completing the final touches to the highway before Saudi royals flew in to declare it open. We were halted at a checkpoint outside the Koreans' main construction camp. As our papers were examined a new shift of soldier-workers crossed the company parade-ground and saluted their corporate flag.

We arrived at Dowran, our destination, the site of the final project on our list. The old town of Dowran was completely destroyed by the earthquake of December 1982. Six hundred people, half the population, died when the earthquake struck at noon on a Friday. They had little chance as the heavy stone buildings found everywhere in the mountains fell about them. The death toll was so high because men were gathered in the mosques and women were indoors preparing the most important meal of the week. I was in Yemen at the time, 100 km. from the epicentre. The quake came as an enormous shock as Yemen had not been known to lie on notable fault lines. People in my area regarded the destruction as Allah's judgement on the sins of their Zaydi sectarian rivals. They must, I was told, have been sleeping with their sisters, or drinking huge amounts of whisky for Allah to have sent such fearful punishment. Some suggested that Bilkis, the Queen of

Sheba, had been so disgusted at the immorality of the nation she had helped create, that she had literally turned in her grave thus triggering the waves of destruction.

Dowran had been sited, for reasons of defence, on a mountain overlooking a wide plain. The surviving population were grouped down on the plain alongside the hospital, one of the very few buildings in the area to have withstood the quake. We went into the hospital and were directed to the mother and child room. A Dutch nurse, whose enthusiasm was sadly not matched by her ability in spoken Arabic, was battling to talk about the nutritional value of pulses. A group of men, all of them smoking, were occupying the available seats, while local women, most clutching young children, squatted, as inconspicuously as possible, on the floor.

We were warmly welcomed and told that this crowd had come in to pass the time while waiting for the vaccinator to be fetched out of his classroom and come to the hospital. We left Arabia behind and adjourned to a well-appointed European apartment. Over cups of Dutch coffee we learned how the nurse and a midwife colleague had been sent to the hospital to advise and to train local men and women. But, as was often the case, the presence of qualified foreigners had served as an excuse for the ministry to reduce the number of medical workers they would have to recruit. The Dutch were thus kept busy in a curative capacity and had not been able to arrange any training courses for local women.

We discussed problems of contraception. The Dutch had made surprising progress. Over one hundred local women had intra-uterine devices fitted with the full blessing of their husbands, an extraordinary achievement in the context of rural Yemen. Two women had been unofficially trained in how to insert them. The ministry had not been told for fear they might object.

Official policy on contraception is tentative and often inconsistent. Given pride of place in the modest office of the Yemeni Family Planning Association in Sana'a is a pro-natalist message from the president stating that the future of Yemen lies in the expansion of its youth. Large amounts of donated contraceptives are held in store in Sana'a and allowed to expire by officials opposed to their use or fearful of those who might be. Contraception is rarely available in any government health facility, especially in the countryside and in the less progressive Zaydi provinces where religious objections carry more weight. Yet there is a great demand for contraception from Yemeni women desperate for a rest between pregnancies. Wherever I went I was approached by veiled strangers pleading for contraceptive pills. Men, who in large groups would invariably condemn all forms of contraception as *haraam* (unlawful), also often took me aside to ask for advice. In some areas the pill is sold by pharmacists themselves unsure of how it should be used. Many women believe it is only required on days when they have intercourse. Several women told me they had tried it but found it very dangerous. Because the pill is wrongly used many Yemenis now associate it with severe bleeding and other complications.

From puberty to menopause the lives of rural Yemeni women are dominated by constant child-bearing. I have met middle-aged women who have been pregnant so often they have never had a period. The IUD and Depo-Provera injections are suitable forms of contraception in a society where already poor female health is worsened by inability to space births and the near complete absence of reliable contraceptive advice. Both forms of contraception have the further benefit of only requiring the husband to give permission once. Depo-Provera, because of side effects, may not be the contraceptive of choice in the West, but in contexts such as rural Yemen has some advantages. It is a lesser evil than death from anaemia, a common fate for Yemeni women of child-bearing age. Yet, due to an international campaign in the late 1970s, it is illegal in Yemen, as in most countries. In the name of feminism, western women may have worsened the plight of millions of their sisters. Depo-Provera is very popular in Yemen and widely available, yet because it has been banned is administered solely by untrained people whose only considerations are profit.

After lunch a ghoulish fascination drew us up to the ruined town. As we walked away from the temporary settlement of corrugated iron shacks, the old town looming above us seemed intact. Only as we drew nearer did the scale of devastation become more apparent. Though houses in villages only 500 metres away had stood up, every building in old Dowran had been rendered uninhabitable. The town was deserted except for some girls herding sheep who curiously came to join us. We clambered over the mess of fallen stones and found pages from the Koran still lying about the destroyed central mosque.

After the earthquake North Yemen was inundated with assistance quite disproportionate to the degree of damage. Within months tents, blankets and antibiotics had reached the marketplace. I myself had bought a fold-up camp bed at a ridiculously cheap price. The oil states, and particularly Saudi Arabia, followed up with reconstruction projects. Along all the highways were signs applauding the activities of His Highness King Fahd and the Higher Supreme Committee for Reconstruction. Below us the results could be seen. Built right alongside a new highway running down the middle of the plain were row after ordered row of tiny single-storey bungalows. Throughout the area of devastation I saw similar estates being put up by Turkish, Korean and Indian contractors.

We went down to watch the last of hundreds of these boxes being completed. The Bengali labourers spoke neither Arabic nor English so no information could be gathered. But it was obvious how socially insensitive such aid was. Yemenis have large families, married sons often stay in the parental home, and it is common to find fifteen people living in the three or four-storey stone houses found throughout the mountains. A large *diwaan* forms a communal space used by groups of men when chewing *qat* and where large groups of kinsmen and neighbours gather in the evening. These two-bedroom monstrosities contained no such room. They were built cheek by jowl, allowing neither horizontal nor vertical expansion. If Yemenis were to move into such houses they would have to reorganize themselves into nuclear families and start practising birth control.

We met an inhabitant of the town of corrugated iron buildings which had sprung up in the three years since the earthquake. They clearly lacked the beauty of traditional architecture but reflected the priorities of Yemenis – space to allow separation of men and women, to stable animals and to expand. I was told that the president was facing a dilemma. He could not offend the Saudis by telling them that their houses were not required, but neither could he coerce the citizens into moving in against their expressed wishes.

AFJAD, our sister British agency, ran a modest and more sensitive project in the area of devastation. Recognizing that Yemenis take enormous pride in their architecture – the humblest Yemeni knows that his people built the first multi-storey houses in the world – the agency focused on making traditional houses stronger, not on redesigning them. They employed an architect who ran short courses for local builders. He demonstrated how if windows were placed further away from corners of rooms, and a course of cement built around each room atop the layers of shaped stones, buildings would probably hold up if Yemen is ever unfortunate enough to have another major earthquake. The architect developed excellent relations with local builders. Many showed talent as budding actors and starred in and directed a series of videos paid for by AFJAD. The builders also wrote the dialogue which was colloquial and comic. Unlike the great majority of informa-tional videos produced by 'experts' in Yemen, these were in great demand as popular entertainment, especially during *qat* afternoons when public opinion in Yemen is moulded.

We returned to Sana'a, glad of a rest after our journey. We went to eat in the restaurant nearest our transit house. It was Christmas Eve and the proprietor, a highly westernized emigré from Saigon, was even more depressed than usual. I had first eaten in his restaurant in 1978. Then he had been a bright and confident young man, clad in high-heeled boots, baseball cap and Levis. His mini-skirted daughters were even more inappropriately dressed in this very traditional city. He had cheerily told me, in his American accented English, that for him Sana'a was only a point of call. He had no affinity with Yemenis and did not wish to bring up his daughters in Yemen. He had only used his father's Yemeni nationality to get out of Vietnam. Any day now he would receive his green card and settle in the States. Now many Christmases had come and gone and he was still waiting. He had lost his English. His faded New York Jets sweatshirt looked as forlorn as his prematurely middle-aged face.

Over supper we chatted with a group of newly arrived,

fresh-faced Peace Corps volunteers. One confided that she was terrified of all the weaponry she had seen. I tried to reassure her. I explained that the homicide rate in Yemeni is very low. The carrying of arms is essential to self-image, a kind of male fashion accessory very rarely discharged in anger. It is highly shameful for a Yemeni to use his pistol or Kalashnikov without first trying to avert danger with his fists, his club or his dagger. I stressed the importance Yemenis put on welcoming and protecting foreigners. The last person to be shot in Yemen would be a foreigner and I had never heard of a case. The young American, however, could not be disabused. 'Our Peace Corps trainers have told us that Yemenis are especially likely to use their weapons on us.'

We left the Americans to their prejudices as we had to take part in the festivities of our compatriots and negotiate our social position in the British community. As newcomers our ambiguity afforded us some mobility. The separate festivities of the Embassy, British Council, Overseas Development Administration, Cable and Wireless, assorted engineers and businessmen and the many finely-differentiated castes of English language teachers echoed both the hierarchy of the raj and contemporary Britain. Out of charity we had been invited to several parties but nowhere were we made to feel welcome. No Yemenis were to be seen. The British were organized in cliques, strangers in a hostile land, full of complaints about Yemen, Yemenis and other foreigners. The ever affable ambassador, an Arabist keenly interested in the problems of development, dashed from party to party in an effort to gloss over such divisions.

Few Yemenis have any inkling of Christmas for there is no Christian minority in Yemen nor much knowledge about the beliefs of other religions. Considering this, the soldiers at the checkpoints monitoring the nightly curfew in Sana'a were amenably congenial as drunken *nasraanis* wove their way home in the early hours of Christmas morning.

6

WHAT TO FACILITATE?

It was New Year, time to go to Ahad to stay and to begin work in earnest. First of all, accommodation had to be found. I had been assured that this was a responsibility of Graham, the project co-ordinator but arrived to find he knew hardly anyone in town and there was nowhere for me to live. I fretted at the prospect of having to spend too long sharing Graham's one-roomed compound and was guiltily grateful when he soon returned to Sana'a. Fortunately, Irene, the outgoing midwife – the member of the project with the widest contacts in the town – came to my rescue. One of the town's richest merchants sent word he had a flat to rent.

I went in search of the flamboyant Sheikh Ahmad. At first glance it was clear he was not a local. I found that he came from Aden and like many entrepreneurial Yemenis had left with the British. I was warmly invited into his crowded hardware store. *Kanadas* were produced from his freezer and he told me how honoured he was to have an Englishman to talk to again. His English had become rusty: 'special price', 'you my friend', 'no charge for looking' and other shop boy's phrases no doubt much inflicted on P & O transit passengers in search of duty-free goods. 'I swear to God', he proclaimed in voluble Arabic, 'the years of the British in Aden were like Paradise.' Life was ordered, the administration efficient, the beer cheap and, so he whispered, the brothels supervised and hygienic. What a shame it had all gone! Why had the British not fought harder against the anarchists who had ruined the good life? He could never forgive Harold Wilson.

I had heard this many times before from nostalgic, fiercely anti-communist exiles. To staunch the flow of reminiscence I asked why everyone called him a sheikh. 'I help people with problems', he replied. 'I never asked to become a sheikh. The people made me one.' I heard how he had begun as just another pedlar squatting in the dust of the weekly *suq* and had worked himself up. Clearly he was very well connected, a man worth knowing. His warehouses lay directly under the nose of the government and yet, after I had moved in, I would be woken in the dead of night to see trucks with no number-plates arrive. A gang of porters would materialize from nowhere and contraband bags of cement, sacks of wheat and lengths of timber would quickly disappear into his buildings.

Enough time had been spent chatting. The subject of my visit could now be broached. Sheikh Ahmad oozed bene-volence. His unctuous flattery, uncommon among real north-ern Yemenis, was well over the top. His prayers, he said, had been answered. He would be delighted, truly honoured, to have an Englishman as a friend, neighbour and tenant. The flat was greatly in demand. The government prefect had himself just been round to plead to be able to rent it. But Yemenis were dishonest, the English renowned for their probity. How, but by moral example, could they have built an empire on which the sun never set? He had been offered 1,500 rials a month (£150) for the flat. Because the English were his friends I could have it for only 1,000. Would I care to have a look?

Though the place was in a mess I was immediately attracted. The building made no concessions to Tihami taste and was a two-storey concrete block construction with a large, flat, enclosed roof from which I could look out over the town, the marketplace and the nearby government buildings. I had dreaded having to move into one of the typically featureless compounds with rectangular rooms. The kitchen was blackened with soot from the traditional wood-burning ovens and lacked any kind of ventilation, but then I did not plan to spend much time cooking in such heat. I imagined living mainly on the first floor, hopefully catching the breeze and being away from scorpions and insects. I could prepare a highland-style reception room-cum-bedroom and imagine that I was living in the mountains.

To assure me that I would be well protected Sheikh Ahmad pushed aside a cupboard to reveal a Kalashnikov. He lived right next door and I would only have to shout in the event of trouble. But no one would be foolish enough to rob Sheikh Ahmad. He flung open his safe to show me a wadge of large denomination Saudi banknotes. He paused in mid flow, having noticed something he had failed to put away – a can of Stud Delay Spray For Men – a 'medicine' much employed by Yemeni hypochondriacs afraid for their virility.

The rent seemed reasonable, especially considering there were amenities I had not dreamed of enjoying – a shower and, in one room, an air-conditioner. I reported back to my colleagues and there was much headshaking. The shower was acceptable, though it would mean that I would have to have more water delivered by truck than was used by Simon and Elizabeth, the two doctors, who lacked this amenity. But the air-conditioner, low-powered though it was, was an unjustifiable luxury. If I wished to use it I would have to do so at my own expense. The rent, £100 a month, was more than the two doctors paid between them and could only be justified if Graham also moved in with me. Irene, who had fought hard for her own privacy and comfort, and who was living on her own in even more relatively expensive accommodation, seemed unsure. She said nothing, not wishing to have more disagreements with her colleagues during her last weeks in Ahad. As a result I paid 20 per cent of my salary for the extra electricity in order to be able to sleep at night and function more efficiently in the horrendous climate which had taken its toll on all my predecessors in Ahad.

I was keen to move in and to begin putting my new house in order. I poured my energies into preparing my nest, an escape from having to think what I was supposed to do. The amount of money I spent on paint met with disapproval but I persisted. To justify the expense, it was decided that my room, once furnished and painted, would make a good meeting place when we held discussions with our Yemeni counterparts. I was warned not to overdo the labour in the heat as the midwife we had briefly met in Sana'a before her departure had fainted while painting her room. I woke early and it was with reluctance that I abandoned my housepainting at eight each morning to walk across town, past the shabby *akhdaam* huts and through the dusty lanes of the tribal quarters, to begin 'work'. Simon, having seen Elizabeth off to the hospital, would be ready waiting for me in our office. I itched to know what we were supposed to do. For the first few days we did little but chat, go shopping in the *suq*, prepare lunch for the women of the project who were actually working, have desultory drives round the immediate countryside and, again and again, pore over the files.

Further discrepancies in the image which had been presented to me became apparent. We had now been in Ahad for three and a half years and yet we and the provincial health office did not agree upon the geographical boundaries of the area we were supposed to be working in. BSDA variously referred to our project as the Ahad health project and the Ahad rural health project, reflecting our own uncertainty about who were the beneficiaries of our presence. Had I been recruited to help the five or six thousand people of the town, the two hundred thousand of Ahad and surrounding districts, or the half million or more living in the north Tihama? I learned how three years previously BSDA had signed a document offering to support primary health care training in both the Tihama and mountain districts of Nakhwa, one of Yemen's largest provinces, as well as to train nurses, technicians and administrators for the Ahad hospital. Subsequently we had insisted that we could only work in Ahad and two neighbouring districts, yet the provincial health office kept reminding us of our original commitment to train health workers from eight districts with a combined population of one million.

I had already seen how in Yemen the arrival of foreigners in isolated places gives rise to overblown expectations but had thought that BSDA, after a decade in the country, would have had the savvy to deflate such hopes. How could we have promised so much with so few resources? A high-level quadripartite committee including the provincial governor and other luminaries had been set up in 1982 but had never met. A twelve-month course for training male primary health care workers should have started in 1982 but was still as far away as ever. No candidates had been selected and it was unclear who would choose them. It had been agreed that five small health centres would be built before the end of 1982 but, three years later, still not one had been.

Simon was determined to look on the bright side. He explained the procedure by which the team evaluated our work. I learned how after many hours of 'brain-storming' and 'Eze-Vu' sessions fourteen project objectives had been identified. These linked visionary plans – 'improving the position of women', 'making health education widely available', 'encouraging community involvement', 'participating in national and international health campaigns' and 'aiding the political development of project workers' – with mundane objectives described as 'project evaluation' and 'project management'. On a semantic level, it was hard to see these as objectives. I wondered if there could be a project which does not seek to manage, if not always evaluate, itself.

Each project worker was required to draft six-monthly reports citing individual progress in furthering the fourteen objectives. After discussion in the project, and democratically-determined revisions, these reports would go on to Sana'a and to London. To improve the layout of reports Graham designed a word-processing template. In order to save time typing out the impressive list of aspirations – or to avoid thinking too much about them? – he added the project objectives to this template file.

The London desk person and the Sana'a-based programme co-ordinator would formally reply to our reports. When feedback had been received, and other reports compared, it would be possible to accurately evaluate our success. I was told this process culminated in periodic revisions to the touchstone of BSDA's faith, a tatty folder containing the grandiosely-entitled 'Yemen country analysis'. I already knew that in fact this holy book had not been changed since being written three years previously, but Simon insisted an up-date was imminent. It all sounded very impressive, if a touch self-congratulatory.

One of the objectives dealt with 'health link persons' (HLPs). I had been told in London of innumerable such uneducated, but good-hearted people, identified by project members as sympathetic to our aims and whose interest I was to further. A three-hour meeting had assessed the various 'degree of fit' such people had with the objectives of our project, our national programme and our organization. 'Eze-Vu' decreed this form of quantification. The overall result was

8.2 over 10, apparently a great and encouraging indication of success. It quickly became clear that these 'health link persons' were another fiction fed back to London; there were none for Simon to introduce me to in our aimless drives round the environs of Ahad.

The idea was floated that HLPs be given basic drugs from the Ahad health centre to dispense in their communities. This was seriously discussed despite the fact that the drug supply to the hospital was itself grossly inadequate. No thought was given by the expatriates to the ministry's predictable, and undoubtedly justifiable, objection to untrained personnel handing out a valuable resource.

It was clear that Simon had been forced by events to keep a very low profile in the town. Lack of interest in primary health care had meant he had achieved little. He had acquired reasonable Arabic considering he had started from scratch a year before, but was not widely known in the community. Indeed, I was startled a few weeks later to be asked if I was the husband of the saintly female doctor who treated children for free. Simon avoided showing his face at the hospital too often lest it be thought his job was also to provide a curative service. He had tried and tried to explain to the old *mudiir* that his job was to encourage primary health care but had got nowhere. Though itching to work, he was perceived by Yemenis as indolent because he had the courage to avoid confirming expectations that doctors could only cure. Clearly the socialization of young doctors in British society had not prepared Simon for the degree of unwanted enforced leisure he had to cope with in Yemen.

My other colleagues conformed to local expectations by adopting Arabic names and I soon became known as Abdullah. Graham, who had a much higher profile than Simon, was, in contrast, addressed and referred to by all the hospital employees as 'Mister Graham'. His job seemed more and more absurd, especially when I saw the job description which he, without his colleagues' approval, had immediately amended on his arrival in project. He was forever using the word-processor to tinker with his 'JD'.

He described his main task as 'strengthening the Ahad health centre', a goal he advanced by stamping all receipts before they were sent on up to the provincial health office. Why we should be involved in such financial management, when we provided no funding for the work of the Ahad hospital, was puzzling. He lobbied in Sana'a in the interests of the Ahad health centre but no colleague stopped to ask why he had taken on a job which by rights should have belonged to a Yemeni. Clearly escapist were such tasks as monitoring droughts, use of agricultural chemicals, the price of grains in local markets and changes in land ownership. How, with his minimal Arabic, could he possibly do this? Oddest of all was his oft-repeated insistence that primary health care had nothing to do with him. Because he perceived his job as hospital based he had never visited any of the rural areas where we had hopes of training men and women and seeing health posts built.

Graham imitated his predecessor and composed lengthy reports to the ministry, the provincial health office and the Central Planning Organization which were translated into correctly flowery Arabic and typed at great expense. Renewal of the modest, and blandly cosmetic, project agreement also took up months of Graham's time and involved countless drafts, and repeated translations before the ministry was finally satisfied. In every communication to the health office and the ministry Graham listed all the employees of the hospital as if somehow he, or we, were their employer. Prompt submission of these meaningless reports made Graham popular in Sana'a and in Nakhwa, the provincial capital. He was proud of the fact that important bureaucrats had flattered him that no other foreign organization presented such fine reports. Graham's six-monthly evaluations, like the welter of statistics demanded of Yemeni health workers, were duly filed away unread. Thus was the god of bureaucracy propitiated.

Success was also proclaimed in reports to our funders. Graham wrote to the Overseas Development Administration that 'the primary goal of strengthening the Ahad health centre has been achieved'. His predecessor had written to London that 'through control over who the ministry supplies as personnel we will ensure that unethical health workers are removed from the staff'. Graham continued this delusion and was forever talking of 'Yemenization'. He used the computer to draw up

staff projections of the health centre into the late 1990s. He
continued to do this though it was abundantly clear that the
provincial health director preferred employing tractable foreigners such as Egyptians and Somalis to training up his own
countrymen. With his ubiquitous briefcase and the mystery
which surrounded his ever more frequent absences and
meetings with big men in Sana'a, Graham increasingly
reminded me of a colonial district officer. In trying to become
indispensable he alienated his colleagues but succeeded in
making the old director of the health centre totally dependent.
Whenever I ran into him he would greet me with an anxious
enquiry: 'Where is Mr Graham? When is he coming back?'

Our files had much to say about the old man. In early 1982,
when BSDA first thought of working in Ahad, the programme co-ordinator in Sana'a had described him as 'well-
liked in the town and in the clinic' – a bold conclusion given
his admission in the same document that 'little contact has been
made directly with the Ahad community'. A month later, with
the decision to begin work having already been made
following this inadequate 'baseline survey', he again wrote to
London. He noted that 'casual conversations in the market at
Ahad have left us with the idea that the present service is not
respected'. One of the first BSDA volunteers, a doctor from
Tigre, was savagely contemptuous of the way we had started
working in Ahad. In a report, not shown to new volunteers in
London, he compared our original project agreement with a
'colonial treaty forced on subject chiefs'. He wrote of his
amazement that the *mudiir* saw nothing untoward in selling
drugs openly stacked on top of his desk in the office where all
patients were required to register. The Tigrean, who resigned
from BSDA in frustration at our failure to stand up to the
mudiir and the provincial health boss, described the hospital as
'a business centre, not a health centre'.

I learned that in the intervening years the old drug dealer had
started humouring us by storing only a basic cache in the
drawer of his desk. A young boy employed as a runner fetched
other medicines from the old man's pharmacy. Graham, for
want of anything more constructive to do during his brief
visits to Ahad, spent much time sitting round in the *mudiir*'s
office. I began to wonder what kind of message this apparent

conviviality with a corrupt official was giving of BSDA and its aims?

My impression of our neo-colonialism was reinforced on reading the files and finding that the former co-ordinator, an Australian dentist, had been engaged in some very curious activities. His enthusiasms and displacement activities had been catholic. He imported, and cleared through customs with much difficulty and expense, a cine camera and a slide projector, now broken and collecting dust, with which to entertain the natives. This he had previously done in the wilds of New Guinea but in Ahad slides of falciparum malaria or accounts of the life cycle of the bilharzia schistosome could not compete with the pleasures brought into peoples' lives by the televisions and videos found in almost every household. Though he could not read and write Arabic, and spoke only haltingly, he collected school textbooks to assess the potential for presenting preventive health messages to local school students. He wrote all around the world investigating the possibilities of introducing solar power, improved seeds, fruit trees, more benign – albeit expensive – pesticides, better irrigation techniques, new kinds of vegetables and more appropriate building materials. A flood of obscure journals and newsletters – all in English – still arrived with every post and were dutifully filed away unread. He also convened meetings of his colleagues to Eze-Vu the possibility of training local people to construct latrines. This despite the fact all households in the town already had well-dug pits. In contrast to mountain Yemen, there is little health threat from human waste.

The former co-ordinator had even thought of introducing the infamous Australian dunny seat, a wooden contraption quite unsuited to Arabs accustomed from earliest childhood to squatting. He built a prototype which lay rotting in the compound. I later cannibalized it to make a table. He also took an interest in the activities of the youth club, which he patronizingly referred to in the many memos he had written as the boys' club. He tried, without success, to arouse interest in quiz evenings and a competition to design T-shirts. Even more optimistic, given the strict sexual segregation of the society, were his plans to involve himself in promoting women's income-generating activities, handicrafts and collective market gardening.

The files also helped explain why Simon and I had so little to do. Apart from the fact that the catchment area from which trainee health workers would be selected and the procedure for selecting them had not been agreed with our Yemeni counterparts, there was nobody to teach them. There seemed no point in raising the hopes of local men if there was no one to teach them. Teaching had to be the task of a qualified Yemeni, not ourselves, even supposing our Arabic was up to the task of organizing a year's course. But who was qualified to teach? After much chopping and changing of policy, the ministry had decreed that the trainer supervisor had to be a three-year-trained nurse who had also completed a six-week training course in Sana'a. For BSDA, as for other development organizations, this was an unwelcome change of policy. We knew that experienced village health workers, familiar with rural health needs but uncontaminated by the lure of high technology medicine found in hospitals, made more sympathetic supervisors. Also, in the case of the north Tihama, demanding high qualifications further complicated problems because there were no trained medical personnel from the area.

For years BSDA had been discussing with Yemeni officials the problem of finding a suitably qualified trainer. The lack of urgency with which the provincial health office approached the problem had confirmed the impression that we were being fobbed off with insincere protestations of support. Did they see the nonsense we talked about preventative, community-based, health care as the price to be paid for the main benefit they gained from our presence, the provision of a free female doctor and a midwife?

Two years previously a nurse, Tihama-born though not from our area, had been ordered by the ministry to come to Ahad to begin teaching a course. However, he had been seduced by the Americans in Hodeidah who were topping up his salary by 300 per cent. He had been sent on several overseas trips and now had no desire to come to Ahad to work for the mean British. The Americans now had a proprietary attitude towards the man, even though they had acquired seven such trainer supervisors and could have managed without him.

In effect, USAID largesse had set up a primary health care

project which far from encouraging trained health workers to leave the city and work in the countryside had done the opposite – a complete contradiction of one of the bases of primary health care. Trained nurses from one of the most backward areas of North Yemen had been drawn into the city of Hodeidah despite the fact there was an oversupply of nurses in both hospitals in the city. Those in the pay of the foreigners were manifestly underemployed and hung round enjoying the cool comfortable offices of the American project.

We decided to try once more to resolve the situation and to go to Hodeidah to talk to the Americans and to the provincial health director. Also in Hodeidah were two local men from our project area whom we had financed to go on a nine-month primary health course organized by the Americans. Their period of study was about to come to an end and we wished to learn of their progress. Two other men, both from the town of Ahad but not supported by us, were about to finish a three-year period of nursing training at the main hospital in Hodeidah. We wondered if they would be amenable to the idea of returning to their home town, or whether they too would join the Americans' payroll.

On arrival in Hodeidah we were introduced to the trainer supervisor who had been supposed to come to Ahad. He obligingly signed a piece of paper confirming his unwillingness to do so. The Americans assured us that the health director, whose equally lavish suite of offices lay above theirs, was a genial and co-operative man. He had just returned from another three-month trip to the States. Though his English had improved, we were advised to speak to him in Arabic. The Americans refused to accompany us upstairs, not wishing to enter into the problems of another health project. On the way up I prepared the Arabic necessary to explain that the citizens of our project area would benefit if the two soon-to-graduate nurses were allowed to work in their home town.

The director was brusque, grudging us his time, clearly not willing to bother with representatives of an organization so poor it could not recruit its own Yemenis. He barely listened as I outlined our problems. He told us there was nothing he could do. The two Ahadi nurses would have to stay in Hodeidah as they were bonded to work for the next three

years in the hospital where they had trained. I repeated that
this would mean the Ahad hospital had not a single Yemeni
nurse while Hodeidah had too many, but he was unimpressed
and shrugged his shoulders. We took our leave.

Back downstairs, we asked the Americans to give us some
idea of what they had been teaching our two men. Despite the
ranks of filing cabinets and secretaries, the syllabus they were
using could not be found. But would we like to sit in on a
refresher class being run for previously graduated primary
health care workers? We took up the offer and were taken to a
cool pleasant room where five trainer supervisors, including
the man who should have come to Ahad, were teaching three
health workers how to fill in weight and height details of
children on the road to health cards already described. Such a
gross waste of personnel and resources in a developing country
made us angry and frustrated.

Not for the last time we sought consolation in shopping, a
useful therapy after meeting with unhelpful bureaucrats.
Hodeidah, the only city in the Yemeni Tihama and North
Yemen's main port, had already become for me, after only a
short time in Ahad, a consumerist paradise. We filled the car
with cushions and mattresses I would need to set up my room.
We bought fruits and vegetables not available in Ahad. We
purchased a cheap Chinese bicycle, far too small for my non-
Yemeni frame. I could not resist buying a cologne called
Sexylia, supposedly French-made, which promised to be the
'partner of my happyness' and enable me to 'attract women
much more than the usual'. We visited the supermarkets,
stocking up on foods which might be about to be included on
the import restriction list. We saw the counterfeit import
substitutes, packaged so as to be virtually indistinguishable
from the originals – Clinics tissues, Blanty bars, Kin Kan
chocolate wafers, Marz bars, Silvikrit, Silcovertin and Heat
and Shelter shampoo and, best of all, Blank ink.

To save foreign exchange, and to encourage Yemeni farmers
and manufacturers, the government had embarked on a series
of import-substitution initiatives. Nescafé had just been
banned. I welcomed the move but, being an instant coffee
addict and not liking the fermented taste of Yemeni beans, I
guiltily needed my fix. After a whispered conversation with a

supermarket owner I was led to a back room and surreptitiously offered smuggled jars. Our supplies secured, we started back to Ahad in a dust-storm. We peered through the gloom, hoping not to hit a camel and add to the festering carcasses lining the approaches to Hodeidah.

The next morning I tried out our new bicycle. The project had paid half its cost on the understanding that Graham and I would use it to get around town. Two years before a visiting black American anthropologist, researching amongst the ostracized *akhdaam* community in Ahad, had advised us to stop exhibiting our wealth by driving through the *akhdaam* quarter. We now did so more than ever before as Graham and I lived only a few hundred yards from their ramshackle huts. I had thought that Graham should try to use our cars less but had not said anything. I had not been without fault myself as my determination to always walk across town lapsed in the enervating heat. Admittedly we had not been driving through the *akhdaam* section with the reckless abandon characteristic of rich *qabiili* drivers, especially young men from the family of the traditional sheikh, who know from experience that if they are unfortunate enough to kill an *akhdaam* child the compensation to their parents will be minimal. Nevertheless, it seemed a good idea to finally take up the suggestion that we project a more humble image.

I mounted the bicycle but had only gone 200 yards before trouble arose. No adults ride bicycles in Yemen and they are considered as toys for children. A throng of *akhdaam* children impeded my progress. Unlike the children of tribesmen few attend school. They were endearing kids but the necessity of declining offers to shake outstretched hands and refusing requests to let them ride with me brought me to a standstill. Eventually I broke free but they continued to run after me. Several adults stopped and stared in amazement. One stood, arms akimbo, in my path, obliging me to stop. He was not being unfriendly but simply wanted to chat and know what on earth I was doing riding a bicycle. I explained with whatever patience I could muster in the heat. I persisted for several weeks in trying to ride across town but eventually had to give up. Constant ridicule from the youths of the town eventually put paid to this abortive public relations effort.

Many days passed as Simon and I wondered what to do to expedite matters. I finished my decorating and occupied myself rewiring my rooms and putting mosquito mesh over every opening. I acquired a cat as a companion and defender against the swarms of locusts which arrived following the end of the drought in Ethiopia. Unfortunately he only ate the fleshy parts leaving me to sweep up the legs. He also gorged himself on a plague of moths which descended after the locusts had passed on. The cat's arrival led to the departure of the tiny gecko who had patrolled the area round my mattress, dutifully snapping up insects. I acquired a television, hoping to practise my classical Arabic by watching the wildly inaccurate pseudo-historical soap operas depicting the early days of Islam.

I started getting up later and later, wishing my indolence were not so obvious to the world. I would engage the real world by listening to the news from the BBC World Service and leave my relatively cool room at a quarter past nine. Right outside my door I would find a group of labourers, employed by Sheikh Ahmad, who had been toiling making bricks since shortly after dawn. The size of Sheikh Ahmad's work force fluctuated according to demand for bricks. Trade peaked at certain times of the year, particularly before the fasting month of Ramadan, when migrants returned home with cash to add rooms to their houses. The only permanent brick maker, whose age could have been anything between forty and eighty, stopped me one morning to ask about his youngest son's health. In vain did I tell him I was not a doctor and suggest that he take the boy across town to the hospital. He did not, he said, have enough money to go to hospital. He earned only 50 rials (£5) for a ten-hour day toiling, unprotected, in the blistering heat. He was *miskiin* – poor and deserving. Could I not give him some 'powerful medicine'? He knew we had some for he had seen me unloading boxes of drugs. I felt wretched as I finally managed to get away. I salved my conscience by regularly overpaying for the car-borne water whose delivery he negotiated.

We had just installed an electronic bell when a man rang and asked to see our *mudiir*. I replied that we did not have a director and that the co-ordinator, one amongst equals, was in Sana'a. Naturally this puzzled him, but eventually he told me why he had come. He was a builder and had heard that more work was needed on the hospital extension. Could he have the contract? I told him it was none of our business, that it would be better to approach the hospital management. He was unconvinced. 'The hospital is your hospital. It is not Yemeni', he insisted. In horror, I wondered how many others had this impression of us, and how this had come about.

My inactivity was getting me down, especially as I could not talk about it with my male colleagues who maintained the fiction of being fully employed. I wondered why the team had recruited me to work alongside Simon, considering that he seemed to find time lying heavy on his hands and still had almost a year of his contract to go. I wished I was a woman and a midwife and could go and share Susan's exciting new life amongst the friendly females of the town. I was beginning to long for a respite from my earnest colleagues and the pressure of having to appear contentedly busy.

I was glad when a friend arrived unexpectedly in Ahad. In Sana'a I had suggested that she drop in while visiting the Tihama and that we might go to visit the coast. However, she had turned up in mid-week, not on Friday, the one day of the week we were officially at rest. She was keen to try the locally available Nafaq *qat*, famed throughout Yemen for its potency. It was afternoon so legitimate, in Yemeni terms, to do so, but I felt my colleagues' disapproval as we sat and chewed. Before sunset we went to join a crowd of several thousand who had come to watch the local football team playing a Sana'a club. Such matches between highlanders and Tihamis are often one-sided. Our boys had been trounced on their last outing in Sana'a, having got straight off their mini-bus and soon run out of energy in the rarefied air. The crowd expected revenge as the equally unacclimatized mountain men would not be able to deal with the heat. We climbed a ladder to the flat roof of the hospital to command a better view. The spectators were extraordinarily well-behaved, accepting unfavourable judgements from the referee with good grace. The local team, all short men, had roped in a tall Somali and a Sudanese from the expatriate community of teachers, doctors and nurses in Ahad. Some of the Ahad players displayed considerable individual skills but did not gell as a team. Did this, I wondered, reflect the general breakdown of the cohesion of traditional society? Ahad won the match.

Another football club, the *Wahda* (Unity) Club from Sana'a, were responsible for one of the crassest of the errors made by BSDA in trying to take the political pulse of the Yemen Arab Republic. One morning in the early 1980s Sana'anis awoke to find graffiti artists had written *wahda* in large letters all over the city. The programme co-ordinator wrote excitedly to London of this clear manifestation of a popular desire to unite North and South Yemen. A colleague, who spoke better Arabic and had more contacts outside the expatriate ghetto, had to point out that apolitical football fans had been responsible.

That night my friend was kindly put up by Irene the midwife, it being out of the question for me to offend local sensibilities by offering her accommodation. But what to do the next day? I agonized for hours and finally plucked up courage to ask if I might go away with the more economical Daihatsu after 'work' in the morning. There was obvious disapproval from the doctors. I had the feeling I was being chided not to make a habit of such dereliction of duty and left town with my tail between my legs.

Perhaps they were merely expressing their sub-conscious envy or doubts about the devotion to duty they forced upon themselves. Elizabeth, a martyr to her work, had not been away from the town for months. Her colleagues had all urged her to take more frequent breaks outside the town, if only for a day. On one disastrous occasion she, Simon and Irene had embarked on an expedition to the sea in the heavy Toyota, powerful but less well-suited for the sand than the Daihatsu. They had become embedded in the middle of nowhere. Simon trudged off into the wastes and eventually re-emerged from the enveloping dust haze with an avaricious tractor owner who, after protracted negotiations, agreed to pull them free. The whole dehydrated party was by then so furious with each other they turned back, did not repeat the experiment and now regarded the approaches to the Red Sea with undeserved awe.

There are no graded roads across the Tihama, merely a myriad of changing tracks covered over by the wind. The only way to find our way to the coast, some 30 km. distant, was by leaving the mountains behind us. However, soon after leaving a dust haze came down, reducing visibility to a kilometre. The mountains and the sun disappeared and we began to suspect that we were driving in circles. We pressed on through the heat, pausing at a few scattered villages to ask people the way. Most hamlets were no more than a couple of huts inhabited by women, children and a few goats and cows. In the absence of their men some women seemed frightened of us and ran away into their huts. The few elderly men I did manage to speak to had no idea which tracks we should take to the sea. It gradually dawned on me that they had no reason to go across the sand dunes and the bleak salt flats which lie parallel to the coast. Their lives are entirely oriented to the inhabited fertile parts of the Tihama.

Eventually we began to smell the sea and came to a fishing village at the edge of a salt pan. We fell into conversation with a group of men and were offered tremendously saline water. To be polite we forced ourselves to drink a little. Some men on motorbikes, used for carrying fish to markets along the highway, accompanied us across the salt flat. We stopped next to a mound commanding a view of the mangroves and the surf breaking over the reef. It turned out to be the grave of a saint, to whom no one could put a name, who offered protection to fishermen. For his pains the saint had been left some dates.

We said goodbye to the living and the dead and began driving north along the salt flat. The beauty of the bleak landscape in the fading light was awesome. Not a sign of habitation was to be seen. So engrossed was I, that I did not notice that the ground over which we were travelling was becoming softer. Soon we were completely embedded in the clinging black mud which lies just under the glistening surface of salt. We had no choice but to camp for the night. After dark, we saw the lights of two or three cars cautiously picking their way along the coast but were too far away to summon help. The cars were probably smugglers running goods down the coast from Saudi Arabia.

The next morning we noticed amounts of driftwood lying along the shore. An hour spent digging, collecting timber and laying a track of driftwood in front of our car was ultimately rewarded. We had prudently moved away from the sea to the landward side of the salt flat when we came across a military patrol and were flagged down. I was apprehensive as we had no authority to be where we were. Yemenis are justifiably nervous about foreigners along their isolated coastline, lest they be spying on behalf of Israel. A bad mistake between related Arabic words did nothing to allay these fears. Instead of saying that we had come to the coast to 'observe birds', I said our purpose was to 'observe aeroplanes'. The soldiers looked shocked but I quickly corrected myself. Fortunately, like the great majority of Yemeni military men, they were amiably disposed, joked at my error and wished us a pleasant journey.

Ahead of us a mountain seemed to loom out of the salt flats. For half an hour we were sure it was just another mirage and then realized we were approaching the town of Luhayyah. Luhayyah, like Mocha, was once a major port but has also fallen on hard times because of deposition of silt. No longer a bustling entrepôt, Luhayyah still has an ethnically hetero-genous population, Yemeni blood mixed with that of the Levant, Ethiopia, Somalia and India. A few women scuttled past clad in the *sharshaf*, the climatically inappropriate all-enveloping black covering fast becoming the mark of female members of the bourgeoisie throughout Yemen. Other, unveiled, women and crowds of delightful children were far from shy in coming up to greet us. We stopped to watch fishing boats being made and learned it is a skill greatly in decline due to the introduction of fibre-glass. We watched as fish were gutted and put into clay ovens to be smoked. Such fish is one of the cheapest sources of protein for the people of the Tihama. We popped into a house where a former Lascar proudly displayed a fading shipping company testimonial. He had rounded the Horn and was 'a man of sober habits'.

Luhayyah is noted for its bizarre architecture, multi-storey houses of coral blocks constructed by merchants with large families who have now moved away. Palatial homes have been abandoned to bats and the swift ravages of time in this perpetually humid and windy climate. These houses we hoped to see, but on our arrival in the town centre were immediately nabbed by a man who introduced himself as the town's tourist director. Could he see our permission to visit the town? I had no pass and had not tried to get one as I knew that the tourist office in Sana'a routinely refused authorization to visit anywhere in the north Tihama, even including Ahad, our place of work. I thought to fob him off with one of the many official permits I had by now accumulated. I groped into the envelope containing my growing wadge of papers.

He was not impressed and ordered us to leave the town and not to return. I did come back many times in the course of the next eighteen months, always trying to avoid the tourist official charged with discouraging tourism. I adopted progressively more cunning tactics of guerrilla tourism: driving into the town across the dunes and ducking into deserted houses to avoid detection. To no avail. My adversary was the most vigilant public official I ever encountered in Yemen. Within minutes of my arrival he would pop up from nowhere and berate me for disobeying his previous instructions. I would invent one fanciful explanation after another, claiming to have been authorized by various important men and generally making a nuisance of myself. As time went by the official seemed to enjoy the game of hide-and-seek and verbal jousting as much as I did. He never carried out his dire threats to denounce me as a spy and have me expelled from Yemen.

After my return to Ahad 'work' continued in the same desultory manner as before. After a week or so Simon suggested that we go to Rahbaan, BSDA's third project which I had not yet visited. We drove beyond Hodeidah, left the highway and lost our way in the sandy wastes lying below Jabal Kahima. After countless false trails, meeting few others from whom to ask directions, we scraped our way along the rutted track which leads to Rahbaan. We found the town to be in a bowl surrounded by mountains towering above it on three sides. One by one the scattered highland hamlets lit up as private generators chugged into life. A local joke had it that newly arrived Egyptian teachers, not realizing there are tens of thousands of people living on the slopes, are convinced they are looking at the galaxies unfolding before them.

Our hosts, a married couple nearing the end of their period of service, explained the history of the project. It had been set up less than two years previously as an offshoot of the Kahima project. Kahima, although only 20 km. away, takes two days to reach on foot and a day by car. Co-ordination between the two sets of expatriates had been poor. After a series of bitter disagreements between the three people based in Rahbaan and Helen, their co-ordinator, the project had split off and was now separately funded and administered.

A training course for men had recently been completed and one by one the male barefoot doctors were beginning to start work. We were up early the next morning to attend the opening of a primary health care unit. We helped load a donkey hired for the occasion to carry up the UNICEF drugs and equipment. A daunting three-hour ascent of over 2,000 metres lay in front of us. The slopes we had to tackle are far too steep for car tracks and the mountainside has not been scarred by debris moved by bulldozers as is often the case in the mountains of Yemen. The going was relatively easy as we found a magnificent staircase spiralling into the sky. Basalt in the region breaks up into metre-sized hexagonal blocks and in the days before the revolution labour was mobilized to lay the blocks to build these improbable stair highways.

As we trudged exhausted up the final few hundred stairs we glanced upwards and saw all the local schoolboys being marshalled to greet us. As we came nearer they burst into the national anthem and one boy with a megaphone stepped forward to stiffly recite a formal poem of welcome. Women shyly watched from the safety of rooftops as we trooped through their village to the recently completed one-roomed health post. Banners were draped everywhere and men with Kalashnikovs fired volleys of welcome into the air. Speeches began and were unexceptional in their praise of the president and the glories of the revolution. Nothing was said of the nature of primary health care. In a pause between speeches I heard men in the crowd saying how the building was only a temporary structure pending the construction of a hospital and that the health worker, a local man, would soon be replaced by a foreign doctor.

Such beliefs were vigorously repulsed by the next speaker, the local director of health. A greater contrast to the old man we had to contend with in Ahad could not be imagined. Mujahid, the Rahbaan director, is a determined man in his forties who not only does not have his own pharmacy outside the gate of his hospital, but is resolutely opposed to private medicine in all forms. An acknowledged leader of the progressive camp in his district, he had recently been re-elected to the local development association. He bravely dispensed with all the conventions of Yemeni public speaking. He did not begin his speech with the obligatory pious phrase 'in the name of God', nor did he once mention the president or end by citing the divinity. But he did give a good account of the principles of primary health care and exhorted the local community to support their health worker.

From heady socialism we returned to feudalism, as we were led away to a massive fortress belonging to the local sheikh. Pride of place in his five-storey house was his top-floor *diwaan*, furnished with fine carpets and brassware and enjoying a superb view. As we waited for food to be brought, an unfortunate incident happened. The middle-aged sheikh, like many men of his generation, is a hypochondriac convinced that he needs regular injections of assorted tonics. He had just come back from Sana'a with ampoules of calcium, vitamin B and testosterone. To our horror, he called on the health worker to inject him. The poor man was put on the spot. Acceding to the order would mean contradicting all that he had learnt. He looked at us for sympathy, but did as bidden. My colleagues later tried to persuade the sheikh that the substances he had been injected with were at best worthless and expensive, and possibly harmful. But the public damage had been done. It put a blight on an otherwise enjoyable and encouraging day.

The descent to Rahbaan was exhilarating. I ran and skipped all the way down the staircase, descending in half an hour and destroying my thigh muscles for days afterwards. I paused only once to be offered reviving cups of *gishr*, an infusion made from the husks of coffee to which ginger is added. Yemenis sell beans for export and utilize the husks usually discarded by coffee producers.

That evening we were introduced to Abdul Hamiid, a local tailor devotedly wedded to the notions of primary health care. His gratitude to my colleagues verged on the embarrassing. If only, he immediately told me, we had started work in Rahbaan earlier, he would not have lost four children. Such is his enthusiasm for the oral rehydration solution he is convinced would have saved them, that he embarked on a tediously long explanation of its use. I had been warned that Abdul Hamiid could be a preventative health bore with an endless capacity for telling us things we had taught him. More entertaining was his account of a recent unsuccessful visit to Sana'a in search of a government salary. On first hearing the details were sparse. When I heard the story a year later, with the subtle embellishments added in the course of many *qat* afternoons, a major contemporary epic of human resilience had been forged.

Abdul Hamiid had never visited the capital and imagined that the British would be as well known in Sana'a as in his own small community. To his surprise, no one was able to direct him to our office. The Europeans he stopped in the streets of Sana'a did not speak Arabic. He spent days walking the length of the growing city looking for BSDA. He was about to give up and return home when he thought of going to the British Embassy. He had met the ambassador months before when he had visited Rahbaan. But when he asked the guards outside the ambassadorial residence for admission they fell about with derisive laughter. How could a country bumpkin, and an unprepossessing cripple to boot, know so mighty a personage? They shooed the madman away and cuffed him when he persisted in hanging around. Day after day he returned, submitting to all kinds of humiliation. Eventually the soldiers grew tired of him and they reached a compact. The ambassador would be called. If he did not immediately recognize him, Abdul Hamiid would give the soldiers everything he had and allow himself to be imprisoned for as long as they liked. The valiant little man was vindicated, as indeed he is in all such sagas of the humble Yemeni citizen fighting for his rights. The ambassador had embraced Abdul Hamiid as a long-lost brother and invited him in for tea. An hour later the soldiers turned pale with shock as the ambassadorial chauffeur was detailed to bring Abdul Hamiid to our house.

The next day we dragged our tired bodies up the other magnificent staircase leading into the mountains. On the way I got to know the health director and he told me his life story.

Mujahid had hardly any formal education and passed his formative years as a young shop assistant in Aden. This experience, he said, opened his eyes to the nature of imperialism and started his voracious reading. He saw building a network of primary health care in his region as an integral step towards a restructuring of society giving people more charge of their lives. For his pains, he has been briefly imprisoned several times by the suspicious security authorities. Yet he has allies in the community and by maintaining good relations with various government prefects sent to the area has succeeded in restricting the number of pharmacies to one. Regrettably, he has to spend at least a third of his time in Sana'a fighting for funds for the health services in his region. He has gone greatly into debt because state support had been so niggardly. He does not wish to hand any ammunition to the Muslim Brothers who are competing with his group for influence in the district. He goes through the motions of praying and attending the mosque, for it would be social and political death not to do so. On occasion he has even delivered the sermon after Friday prayers.

After a few hours' walk we arrived at Mujahid's house. In honour of his guests he turned on the generator which remains unused during his long absences from home. Aspirant leaders in rural Yemen have to conspicuously display their material possessions – I have seen refrigerators and washing machines, still wrapped in their packaging materials, displayed outside big men's houses – but Mujahid cannot afford to use much electricity. Usually his wife and family have to make do with paraffin lamps and a black and white television powered by a car battery.

We spent the evening in Mujahid's house, watching colour television and chatting to the neighbours and friends who arrived. As always the programmes which excited the greatest interest were the advertisements endorsing foreign products or the substitutes made in Yemen. Almost all actors in these ads were Europeans. No Yemenis were shown and the few Arabs who appeared – to promote soft drinks, washing powders and biscuits – were pale-skinned Lebanese masquerading as Europeans. Caucasians came on to extol the virtues of Yamany milk – UHT milk now available throughout Yemen. Yemenis take pride in the achievements of this company and are deluded into thinking the milk comes from cows grazed in Yemen. In fact it is reconstituted milk salvaged from the EEC milk lake. A 'doctor', complete with white coat and stethoscope, sang a ditty that Yamany milk is 'natural' and 'healthy'.

Immediately afterwards similarly clad figures, this time real doctors, presented the weekly health programme. We were shown a wardful of men in traction after car accidents. Doctors denounced traditional bone setters, warned the citizens against 'superstition' in all forms and advised them to come to hospitals to have broken bones set. This provoked others in the audience. Though there are growing doubts about the efficacy of traditional medical practices bone-setters are still held in high repute. Several viewers came to their defence. They mocked as we saw uncomfortable-looking patients being interviewed and obligingly endorsing the propaganda by reporting how satisfied they were with the hospital. My host lamented that the Ministry of Health concentrates resources in the cities where less than 10 per cent of the population live. He was upset that all aspects of folk medicine are routinely denigrated.

Great problems surrounded the Rahbaan project. The budget from the ministry had just been further reduced, many health workers received no salaries and supplies of drugs for some units were already running low. The Muslim Brothers, wishing to have nothing to do with foreigners and minimal contact with the state so they could be seen as the sole provider of amenities, had not allowed health workers to begin work in some districts. But at least there was a committed director struggling to do his best, albeit in unpropitious circumstances. We returned to Ahad, wishing we had a similar counterpart sharing our aims.

On arrival we found two young boys from the mountains impatiently awaiting our return. They had been sent to Ahad by the provincial health office and told that a training course, run and financed by the British, was about to begin. In our absence Ali Ahmad, the young hospital administrator, had repeatedly told the youths there were no plans to begin a course, but they had insisted on staying to meet us. We found that they came from a mountain area of the province, some ten hours drive away. Even when we did begin training it was quite unrealistic for such distant health posts to be effectively supervised from Ahad. We felt sorry for these innocent victims of a propaganda ruse designed to lower our credibility. We spent hours explaining the national primary health care plan, the limited and temporary input of foreigners and our problems in finding a suitable instructor. The youths were bitterly disappointed at this frustration of their hopes to become 'doctors'. We gave them Arabic copies of the excellent health manual 'Where There Is No Doctor' and eventually persuaded them to go home.

We discussed our problems with the Yemen field director of AFJAD, our funding agency, on one of her periodic visits to our project. We agreed that there was only one way to approach the impasse which had prevented training for so many years – we would have to make a nuisance of ourselves in the provincial health office. Graham, the project co-ordinator, had returned from Sana'a in order to stamp receipts before taking them up to Nakhwa to be endorsed before he took them on to the ministry. Simon and I decided to accompany him as far as Nakhwa.

We planned to tackle another serious problem – the lack of oral rehydration solution. For three years we had been trying to interest the Ahad hospital director in persuading parents of dehydrated children to use ORS. Yet, though the use of such sachets had increased, none had ever been delivered through the Ministry of Health. Sachets supplied by UNICEF were to be found in great numbers in ministry store-rooms in Sana'a. Since the start of our project we had badgered cartons of ORS out of the ministry and transported them to Ahad. Doing so had given the impression that it was a medicine popular with foreigners but not approved by Yemeni medical workers who, for commercial reasons, instead prescribe intravenous drips. We hoped that if we goaded the provincial office into writing letters of authorization a permanent system for ORS supply could be set up.

We also wished to discuss a matter which Nuriya, the local woman working as a registrar and advice giver alongside Elizabeth, had asked us to raise. She had recently been ordered by officials in the Nakhwa office to register the name, address,

sex and age of every single recipient of ORS. In no other
province was this necessary and we had learnt that such
statistics were soon lost amidst the chaos of the Nakhwa office
and not passed on to the ministry. Nuriya had her work cut
out trying to impose order on the crowd of patients and to
teach about vaccination, weaning and other subjects. She had
to spend hours of her own time at home catching up with this
and other nonsensical paperwork.

The evening before our trip Graham sat at one end of the
cool and comfortable room I had built around me. He was
flanked by Ali Ahmad on one side and the hospital's deputy
director on the other. For two hours they took receipts from
one file, handed them to Graham for stamping, and put them
away in another file. Graham seemed quite unaware of what
most of the receipts were for and did not welcome help in
interpreting. The AFJAD representative sat transfixed at
Graham's absorption in a ritual of verification which, sadly,
seemed essential to his flagging self-esteem. She had worked
for BSDA and had known the Ahad project and its workers
since its foundation. She later confided that every BSDA
employee sent to Ahad had exhibited equally disturbed
displacement behaviour. She told me I was the first person sent
to Ahad who had made any effort to create a congenial living
space. My predecessors had 'camped' and made much of the
hardships they had needlessly worsened.

Nakhwa is only 100 km. from Sana'a, yet because of its
spectacular terrain is an isolated town with a reputation for
backwardness. The province has always been a bastion of the
Zaydi sect of Islam and of powerful sheikhs who rallied
support for Imams in time of trouble. Under the Imamate
republicans were tortured and imprisoned in the dungeons of
the spectacular fort dominating the town. When civil war
broke out following Imam Ahmad's death in September 1962
the new republican administration in Sana'a needed Egyptian
air and ground support to capture and hold Nakhwa town
against the opposition of surrounding royalist tribesmen.
When conflicts with the state arise tribesmen still block the
approaches to the town and force soldiers manning checkpoints to retreat along the road to Sana'a.

I first visited Nakhwa in 1981, just as the sealed road linking it with the capital had been opened. The journey from Sana'a had been cut from five days to three hours. Tribesmen travelling with me in a taxi were as amazed as I was at the formidable achievement of the Chinese engineers who had built the highway. We stopped to take photographs at the memorial to the Chinese and Yemenis who had died building the road. Several had fallen to their deaths dangling by ropes off sheer cliffs into which they were drilling holes for explosives. A tale was told me which illustrated the restricted horizons of the Nakhwa tribesmen. Some time previously Pierre Trudeau, while still Canadian Premier, had flown in by helicopter. *Kanada* denotes in Yemen either carbonated drinks or sacks of imported wheat. A large crowd of tribesmen had gathered in expectation they would receive free gifts of soft drinks and grain.

Prior to my first visit I had been given a letter of introduction to three young men employed by the Peace Corps. As is so often the case in the developing world, the arrival of the road coincided with the arrival of foreign experts. The Americans had brought with them a load of traffic signs donated by USAID and the first traffic light. I found my hosts sitting in a fine office projecting traffic needs into the next century, drawing up plans for roundabouts, ring roads and contra-flow systems for a town where there was only a handful of cars and which had a population of a few thousand. None of the Americans spoke Arabic. Each had a new model American 4WD car and a house. They made me welcome and we passed what they said was a typical evening. Southern Comfort and hashish flowed freely. Such vices should be indulged in Yemen only behind securely closed doors. The generous Americans kept an imprudently open house and many Yemeni visitors came and went through the unlocked front door in the course of the long evening. I was not surprised to hear that the Peace Corps had been expelled from the province a few months later.

On my return to Nakhwa no crowds awaited us but people still stared in surprise at the sight of *nasraanis*. We made our way into the temporary offices of the health department and were bidden to wait, as the director, the only Yemeni doctor in the province, was in the nearby hospital. I had heard that Dr Thaalib came from a powerful royalist family, had received a scholarship to Bulgaria, become a surgeon and was often absent from Yemen on UN and US-funded trips. Fifteen others awaited him, settled into the plush leather sofas ranged round the walls. The usual questions followed – was I married, did I like Yemen, which was better Yemen or my country, did I chew *qat*, why had I not converted to Islam? In the silence which followed my inadequate reply to the last question I practised Arabic by trying to make sense of the large framed map of health facilities in the province which hung over the director's desk.

The director returned and was gushingly affable. In a room full of lean, arms-bearing, skirt-wearing warriors the portly, balding, suit-clad doctor seemed incongruous. He expressed his great surprise at finding a third man had joined the Ahad project. We tried to talk about the problem of not having a trainer of health workers, but got nowhere. The problem was quite out of his control, he was just a loyal servant of the ministry and our inquiries should be taken to Sana'a. We were interrupted by fresh arrivals in his office. They wanted a medical consultation. A charade repeated for our benefit every time I met Dr Thaalib was enacted before us. 'How dare you come to me on private business at this hour! I am doing government work! Come back and see me this afternoon!' Only once was I to catch him spoiling his performance by winking.

We changed tack and asked if we might have some supplies of oral rehydration solution. Of course, supplies were in the storeroom, but did we have an official letter requesting this from the Ahad health centre? We produced one but fault was immediately found with the way it had been written. Could we write another letter ourselves? So in place of Ali Ahmad's impressively signed and stamped letter in Arabic, we wrote a letter of request in English. Dr Thaalib stamped it and scrawled an explanatory note before sending me off to the hospital. When I got there and eventually found the correct official I was most surprised to be offered ampoules of DPT (diphtheria, whooping cough and tetanus) vaccine. I declined and returned to the health office. After I had finally caught Dr Thaalib's attention it became clear that the director, who had been abroad on countless primary health care seminars conducted in English, did not know the meaning of 'oral rehydration solution'. He was not at all abashed, but surprised that we should imagine he should have such supplies. We should go to Sana'a. When we mentioned that Nuriya had no time to provide copious details about a medicine his office did not deliver, he referred us to his deputy who was insistent that Nuriya had to do her duty. Her job responsibilities were a Yemeni matter, no concern of foreigners. If she did not provide this vital information she would be dismissed, and another woman found.

Dr Thaalib was most concerned that the security authorities should be informed without delay of my having taken up residence in Nakhwa province. Could I provide his office with six photocopies of my passport, residence permit and various letters of authority from the security headquarters, Ministry of Health and the Central Planning Organization in Sana'a, have them verified and then go to the governor's office? This took the remainder of the morning and it was already time for the noon prayer, the end of the working day for important men, when I toiled up the hill to the governor's office. A friendly soldier guarding the building told me the governor was absent but that the deputy governor and the provincial security director were present.

I made my way nervously into a room full of important men. My obligatory salutation of 'Peace be upon you' produced no response. I was upset as this had not happened to me for ages. I was reminded of how zealous Zaydis often refuse to acknowledge the greetings of non-Muslims. I squatted near the doorway like other supplicants, my papers clutched in my outstretched hand. The big men seated at the far end of the *diwaan* had noticed my arrival and began discussing me, assuming that like other foreigners I did not understand Arabic. The comments of the security chief were unflattering: 'What does this *nasraani* want? What's he got to offer us? Why doesn't he go and 'develop' his own country? I'm fed up with these experts without expertise.' The whole room laughed appreciatively. I waited five minutes, gradually gravitating towards the powerful end of the long narrow room as fellow supplicants were dealt with. In silence, I passed up my papers to be stamped and then left. I appreciated the reasons for resentment against the hordes of foreign *khubaraa*, but was nevertheless chilled by the sarcasm and degree of hostility displayed.

The first of many unsuccessful visits to the health office had produced only one result – the receipts from the Ahad hospital had been accepted. But what did this have to do with our work of setting up a preventative-oriented, non hospital-based, community-financed health system? We cheered ourselves up with the prospect of having a good Yemeni lunch. We clambered up a hill to Bayt al Baydani, a private house owned by a southerner who has kin in Ahad. He and his family earn their living feeding and housing travellers, a shamefully polluting occupation in the eyes of *qabiili*. We were ushered into a small room where an unveiled serving girl was flirting with her tribal customers, giving as good as she got in a flow of badinage and innuendo I could barely follow. Large trays were brought in and we all squatted. As always when a multi-course meal is served in Yemen the first course was sweet – in this case an excellent *bint as sahn* (literally 'daughter of the plate'), pastry dripping with honey. The girl insisted the honey was *baladi* (indigenous). But as *baladi* honey is very expensive – the standard measure, a Johnny Walker bottle full, costs £50 – it was an improbable claim. The main course was a whip of fenugreek on a base of meat stock into which freshly-baked bread is dipped. This is the staple of highland Yemeni food and I had been disappointed to find it is not widely eaten in the Tihama. Finally chunks of meat were torn apart, the assembled men all being very attentive that we should receive more than our fair shares. I was enjoying myself, being back among gregarious highland men whose dialect was more accessible than that of the Tihamis. I was delighted to find long-forgotten words coming back to me. Glasses of cardamon-flavoured tea were passed round as water pipes were set up. It was with reluctance that I heeded the wishes of my colleagues and refused pressing invitations to chew *qat*. We returned down the bumpy road to the heat and dust of Ahad.

Another problem presented itself. To complement male training we had been trying for three years to begin a twelve-month course to train local women in basic midwifery and primary health. It was envisaged that these local birth attendants would, unlike traditional birth attendants only trained for a few weeks, receive a state salary on completion of their year-long course. It had been hoped that we could train one woman from each of ten or more rural areas scattered throughout the three government districts which we believed were our catchment area. Problems had arisen because officials in Sana'a insisted that all LBA candidates entering such a course had to have completed primary school education. However, with the exception of girls who study in the town of Ahad, none go to school in any of the three districts and thus no women from rural areas could be trained. Such a catch-22, if enforced, would mean that disparities in numbers of trained health workers between various sections of the country would become even more marked. Because of the backwardness of our area we had tried to have this ruling interpreted flexibly by the ministry, but without success. Indeed, it was taken as an indicator of how much the country had progressed that it was now said to be possible to insist that all health workers were properly educated. Why, it was hinted, should BSDA seek to stand in the way of progress?

More pragmatic was the only important woman official in the ministry, who said we might be able to get away with selecting women who had one or two years of primary education. We had searched for such women in rural districts only to find that even if there were any, there was intense hostility to the notion of local women being allowed to go to the town of Ahad to study. In common with most government centres and market towns in Yemen, Ahad has an insalubrious reputation in the eyes of those living in its rural hinterland. The presence of strange men makes fathers fear for their daughter's virtue. We had thus been left with the prospect of training women from the town who after graduation would have neither the intention nor the possibility of working as barefoot doctors in the countryside as the national PHC plan insisted.

Despite these difficulties, the number of women putting themselves forward for training was greater than necessary. A dozen came from the town of Ahad, many spuriously claiming to have completed primary school. Three women from a community ten minutes away up the highway had also applied. From the start it was clear none would become the kind of rural health worker envisaged by UNICEF but would be employees of the hospital. In effect, we were adding to the process of centralization of health resources which we told our funders we were doing our best to avoid.

Who was to decide who should be selected and who was to pay for their training? Report after report to London had claimed that training of female health workers was a high priority of the local people and their representatives in the local development association. Yet soon after my arrival I had begun to hear rumours that the LDA had no intention of meeting half the cost of the course. To clarify the situation Simon and I decided to seek a meeting with LDA officials to discuss plans for both male and female training.

I had heard that the president of the association, the eldest son of the sheikh of the town, had been nominated for the post by his father, the previous incumbent. He was said to take little interest in the job and was often absent in Saudi Arabia on business or in search of medication for various, probably imaginary, ailments. The real power behind the association, whose office-holders are elected every four years by adult males, was Mohammad Ali, the secretary-general.

Finding Mohammad Ali was not easy as he wished to avoid us. He could not be found in the LDA office alongside the rusting Egyptian tank below the government buildings and the guard professed to have no idea where he was. Neither was he in his compound or, at least, his wife had been instructed to say so from behind the security of a barred door. Having been told he was often found reclining on a bed in the *suq* drinking tea, I wandered round the market and an obliging man pointed out the important official. Mohammad Ali pleaded urgent business and made an appintment for the following day.

Simon and I duly went to his office and waited half an hour. Through the guard we arranged another appointment. Mohammad Ali again failed to turn up. When he calculatedly insulted us for the third time I proposed that we would gain more respect by expressing our resentment. I eventually persuaded my nervous colleagues to allow me to write a letter. I expressed our regret that representatives of the citizens showed no willingness to discuss plans to improve health services. If Mohammad Ali was not in his office at nine the following morning then we would sadly have no choice but to inform the governor, the Minister of Health and the president of the co-operative association headquarters in Sana'a of his indifference. Lo and behold, Mohammad Ali was waiting for us and immediately dispatched his *akhdaam* retainer to fetch tea and bottled water. Mohammad Ali chastised me for my unnecessary note but a twinkle in his eye seemed to indicate acknowledgement that we had more spunk than he had reckoned. He heard our description of the national primary health plan and our hopes for training men and women in Ahad, but was non-committal. He was more concerned to know when BSDA would start training radiographers and laboratory technicians. It was agreed he would come the next day to meet the female candidates.

The fifteen women who assembled in our office were understandably nervous. To spare them embarrassment I and the other men stood outside under the sweltering sun while waiting for Mohammad Ali to arrive. This he eventually did an hour late. Without a word of apology he launched into a diatribe against the women. 'What is this I hear about you girls wanting to take the citizens' money. Shame on you! We do not need to train more people as, thanks be to God, we have a hospital and fine pharmacies in this town. If you want to study it is for your own benefit and you have to make sacrifices. If you loved your country you wouldn't be so greedy.' His rate of delivery was so rapid that my colleagues did not understand the gist of his comments. I tried to voice protests that we were only asking the LDA to meet obligations clearly laid out in their own government's primary health care plan, but to no avail. 'I am a busy man. Hands up those patriotic girls prepared to study without our support.' One by one, under the pressure of Mohammad Ali's intense gaze, the women shyly raised their hands. Ali Ahmad, the capable young hospital employee, was ordered to take down their names and to act as witness that they had agreed to drop their claims. The secretary-general departed, looking satisfied.

He left behind consternation. The browbeaten women sat silently as the men filed out. Encouraged by the presence of my female colleagues they gradually recovered confidence.

They voiced their dissatisfaction at not being paid. Some said they would not be able to study with the money we would provide and would have to return to dressmaking, one of the few ways for 'decent' women in the town to earn money. Meanwhile I had become locked in conflict with Ali Ahmad who said that he had been a witness to the agreement of the women not to seek a training allowance and that the matter was closed.

Another thorny problem divided us. Two of those who had come forward for selection are most unusual Yemeni women. They live together in their own house, next to the police station, and neutrally placed between the tribal and non-tribal sections of town. By their physique they are obviously highland Yemenis. One drives a car and both smoke cigarettes in public. Such violations of traditional norms of female modesty unsurprisingly lead them to be branded as prostitutes. They may well be, but they are also working midwives with an established clientele in the town. Midwifery has always been a low-status occupation and the roles of prostitute and midwife are not mutually exclusive. Both women had completed a brief traditional birth attendant course a year earlier and were literate. They seemed ideal candidates for further training and had been recommended by a previous project midwife. Ali Ahmad, no doubt fearing such strong women, was adamant they could not be allowed on the course. The women were equally insistent and drove up the mountains to enlist the help of their kinsmen. The dispute dragged on for some time but in the end I was unable to dissuade my colleagues from the view that it would be 'interventionist' to fight for these women. They were not permitted to study.

We were more united in opposition to food aid provided by the World Food Programme (WFP). Elizabeth and Nuriya and Amina, the two Yemeni women who assisted her, had been ordered to arrange the distribution of white flour, cooking oil and tinned fish long past their expiry date. A lorry load of such food had arrived unannounced from Nakhwa. Such food was neither needed nor suitable. The Tihama is not Tigre. Although it is subject to drought, there is no comparable over-population and degradation of the land. The Tihamis are not only perfectly capable of growing enough grain for their own subsistence but in most years produce sorghum for sale in the mountain areas of Yemen and in Saudi Arabia. Furthermore, because of their relative isolation and lack of access to cash, people of the Tihama have not yet been seduced into the belief that white wheat flour is preferable to their own unhusked grains. The arrival of hundreds of sacks of white flour from the developed world was sending a clear message that such food was superior to local foods.

The food aid issue had agitated BSDA since the inception of the project. At first we had assumed that our mere presence would cause the problem to go away. The Sana'a co-ordinator had assured the desk person in London that 'WFP aid will be stopped because of our involvement in the Ahad health centre.' The vanity of our presumption that we could lead by our moral influence had been clearly revealed. Countless letters, all in English, had been written to various officials in Sana'a and Nakhwa arguing why such aid was nutritionally retrograde and a disincentive to Yemeni agriculture. Again and again officials had professed to share our concerns but done nothing. Dr Thaalib had been most adept at diverting our anger. As the man credited with dispensing the World Food Programme largesse he earned the gratitude of the vulnerable Tihamis whose diet was 'improved' by such gifts.

We held yet another interminably long team meeting to discuss what to do about this and our other problems. I argued we had never tried to explain to the hospital staff why we were campaigning against such aid. We could not expect to win over the hospital officials simply by losing our tempers and stubbornly refusing to co-operate. A meeting with our colleagues in my house to discuss the issue was convened. Nuriya, and the two boldest of the nine women chosen to begin the course, attended the meeting, creating a precedent. They huddled at the end of my room chewing melon seeds with my female colleagues while the men reclined at more leisure chewing *qat*.

We had gone through the issues involved and I had prepared my arguments in Arabic. The young vaccinators, Uthman and Lutf, took the point and were interested to know of the political pressures in Western Europe and North America leading to over-production of food. The old *mudiir* however

was insistent that donated food was needed by the poor and
that it was government policy to hand it out through the
hospital system. We should discuss how to distribute food to
the needy, not how to stop it. His disingenuous concern for
those less well off unleashed a flood of bitter comments and
accusations that particular individuals were profiting from
selling the food or distributing it to friends and relatives. I was
later to be shown such WFP sacks and hear complaints that
people had gone all the way to Ahad to buy 'quality western
food' at a cheap price, only to find the sacks seething with
weevils. We were all surprised, and rather pleased, when one
of the women shed her reserve and started accusing the deputy
director of the hospital of giving food to his kinsmen and
friends. He, in turn, threw allegations at another woman. A
slanging match ensued. The meeting broke up with nothing
resolved. More food aid continued to arrive.

Comic relief from our difficulties was provided by the visit
of the British Minister for Overseas Development. We had
little choice but to receive him as the Overseas Development
Administration (ODA) had just agreed to begin funding 50 per
cent of our project. After the visit of the AFJAD representative
our sister agency had announced that they wished to halve
their suppport for the Ahad, but not our other two better-
regarded projects. I approved of the decision but dared not say
so to my colleagues who all loyally shared our corporate
distrust of our sister non-governmental agency. Both the
London desk person and the Sana'a co-ordinator seemed
pleased to be receiving British government support as an ODA
grant, once given, is renewed without the on-site investigation
insisted on by AFJAD. BSDA hoped that ODA would assume
the full burden of supporting the Ahad project so that our rival
agency would no longer be able to 'interfere' in our affairs. In
other countries where our agency sends volunteers almost the
entire funding is provided by ODA.

We agonized over what to feed our esteemed guest. Should
we dig into our special food reserves, brought at some effort
from western supermarkets in Sana'a and Hodeidah? In the
end we decided it would further the minister's education to
offer him only foods which could be bought locally. At mid
morning, with the temperature over 40° (104°F), the minister

and his wife, accompanied by the ambassador, half the Embassy and two car-loads of Yemeni soldiers and officials, arrived. The minister had flown that morning from Sana'a down to Hodeidah and had come straight on in an air-conditioned vehicle so the heat and confusion of the Ahad hospital came as a shock to his system. As he was shown round he appeared, unlike his wife, to be taking in very little. I hung round at the back of the entourage and answered the questions of confused locals wishing to know his relationship to *al Hadiidiiya* (the woman of iron) and the Queen. The minister was a bit taken aback when Elizabeth, deluged by the usual number of scrimmaging parents and children, barely glanced up to acknowledge his intrusive presence. The ministerial party crowded into our office, jostling for a position under the fan.

While awaiting lunch the minister got up to have a look round and I took him up to the flat roof to gain an overall view of the town. I was pointing out places of interest when I noticed he was instead staring at my Campaign for Nuclear Disarmament T-shirt. He interrupted in mid-sentence: 'Is there a large CND cell here? Are you inciting the local ladies to protest at the nearest American base?' he drawled, smirking at his wit. Ignoring him, I tried to talk about the problems of health workers needing hard-wearing motorbikes capable of getting round the scattered hamlets of the vast sandy plain which lay before us. 'You mean to say there is not an adequate provision of rural bus services?' was his only comment. The man had just come from Sudan and had, presumably, been to far more developing countries than most people could name. His comment suggested he had never been off a sealed road or got out of his air-conditioned car. As he sped off to his next brief appointment en route to Sana'a, I wondered what I was doing in Yemen when there was such ignorance about the developing world to be tackled at home in Britain. Two ODA officials stayed behind for half an hour, seemingly eager to shed formality and speak frankly. Their boss, they confided, knew little of development problems in the countries he visited. It would be up to them to write the 'what-I-did-on-my-holidays compo' for the minister to read to a bored House of Commons.

Local faith in the 'good word' of the British was illustrated by reaction to the bloodshed in Aden in January 1986. As Marxist factions fought for two weeks for control of the city, half the men of Ahad seemed to be walking round with transistors trying to catch the news from the BBC Arabic Service. Throughout Yemen there is the most extraordinary devotion to listening to London. A one-day strike of the BBC External Services in protest at government censorship was noted by a great number of men who told me this was clinching proof that the BBC 'speaks the truth'. On isolated mountaintops, where almost everyone is non-literate and no papers and magazines ever arrive, I have come across men who are, thanks to the BBC, extraordinarily well-informed about world events, even if rather ignorant of Britain itself. Again and again I was asked how it was that women ruled my country. How could there be social order if wives could be obtained without payment to their fathers? Some would-be-sociologists extrapolated further: was everything back-to-front where I came from, a mirror image of their own patriarchal society?

I had got into the habit of getting a daily digest of world news from a neighbour in Ahad who missed not a minute of the BBC Arabic service. From this self-taught man I had learnt much Arabic, including the complex technical vocabulary of the arms race with which he was conversant. I was thus filled with sadness when one day, his radio as always glued to his ear, he stopped me in the *suq*. 'I thought the British loved the Arabs. Why have you done this? Why have you killed children?' I had to ask what we had done and was stunned to hear Britain had supported the bombing of Libya. For days I was reproached wherever I went. Reprisals against Britain seemed inevitable. The death in Beirut of Leigh Douglas, a British teacher whom I had got to know during his time in Yemen, added to my anxiety and anger. The leader of my country had, in effect, sacrificed him on the altar of Anglo-American friendship.

The problem of the women's training dragged on. We now had candidates but no teacher. We went up to Nafaq, the mountain from which local *qat* supplies come, to meet Maryam, an experienced Sudanese midwifery trainer whose work there was just finishing. Her substantial salary – twenty-five times that she had received while working for the Sudanese government – was paid for by the World Health Organization but it was the Yemeni authorities who decided where she should work. We offered to provide her with accommodation if she would come to Ahad. She said she would be happy to do so but had to go wherever the Nakhwa office sent her. A week later she arrived at the Ahad hospital with the deputy director of health for the province. He insisted they were only stopping off en route to Nakhwa where her services were required.

As the project Arabic speaker I was propelled into a confrontational role. I argued the case that Maryam should stay in Ahad where trainees, a training room and accommodation were all prepared. The official from Nakhwa was contemptuous. From that moment onwards there was enmity between us. 'These people', he told Maryam in a loud voice, 'are backward, Bedouin savages who know nothing of civilization. You can't teach them anything. Look how dirty they are! Don't believe the promises of these Christians. Come back with me to Nakhwa where you can be of use.' The fact that a crowd of patients and the curious had gathered to witness this confrontation seemed not to disturb him in the slightest. Amongst mountain Yemenis such aspersions would meet with instant unsheathing of daggers or brandishing of firearms. The poor Tihamis, long inured to such put-downs, merely shuffled round, staring at their flip-flops.

A week later, after we had made complaints in Sana'a, Dr Thaalib, the provincial health director, was forced to come down from Nakhwa to placate the foreigners. A meeting was convened in the office of the *mudiir an naahia*, the government prefect. The usual pack of petitioners was kept at bay by a cordon of soldiers while we discussed how to begin a course. Dr Thaalib shook his head sadly. There were no funds available. In any case there was, he told the *mudiir an naahia*, not much to learn about midwifery. Babies lived or died according to the will of Allah.

The elusive secretary-general of the development association, though summoned by the prefect, had not come to the meeting. A soldier was dispatched to Mohammad Ali's house but returned to report that he had not been allowed access and that hidden women had told him that his quarry was too sick to be disturbed. 'I don't believe him' was the prefect's very public comment. 'Go and get him. If you don't come back with him within ten minutes you will both find yourself in chains.' The threat worked. Within minutes a hale and hearty Mohammad Ali swept into the room. He breezily repeated all he had previously said. It was quite out of the question for the funds of the LDA to be used for such a low priority purpose.

An impasse ensued. The meeting seemed about to break up. BSDA's programme co-ordinator had come down from Sana'a and asked to have a word in private with Dr Thaalib. His message was threatening: 'We came here to encourage training of Yemenis. If you do not support this course we are taking away our female doctor and midwife immediately.' They returned to the room, a wry smile on the face of the health director. Elizabeth was later furious that her services had been brandished as a bargaining counter, but the move was undoubtedly necessary if we were to start training women. I was delighted we were adopting more aggressive tactics and was sorry to hear that the programme co-ordinator was shortly to be replaced.

Dr Thaalib's reputation would have suffered if he had been judged responsible for the loss of a sympathetic doctor who did not charge patients. He changed tack completely and for five minutes spoke passionately on how important it was to train female health workers, cadres who could serve the national interest. It seemed that during his many trips abroad he had, after all, picked up the jargon and philosophy of primary health care. If I had not known better, he would have sounded convincing.

Mohammad Ali's case collapsed once his ally switched sides. A document was drawn up pledging that the development association would pay 500 rials (£50) a month to each of the nine women selected and we would also pay 500. The LDA was also to pay for the driver who would bring the three non-Ahadi women into town each day. We all shook hands, a display of *bonhomie* in accordance with the emphasis Yemeni culture puts on resolution of conflicts.

To celebrate our triumph Susan and I went to visit our

nearest expatriate neighbours, three German health workers based outside the town of Arbat, some 50 km. from Ahad. Arbat is a traditional market and administrative centre in the middle of the Tihama, on the banks of one of the four major wadi systems pouring water down from the mountains to the arid Tihama plain. Today it is at the heart of a massive $50 million irrigation scheme, aiming to dam the rainwaters which race down the wadi and divert it into irrigation channels. The justification for this, as for similar large-scale projects in the other wadi systems, is debatable. Yemenis have always been proficient at catching spate run off. Water is precious and rules and conventions for its use have grown over many centuries. Even during major storms, water was only occasionally allowed to run across the Tihama into the sea. A likely effect of damming and storing water will be to concentrate land ownership in the hands of the well-connected. Elsewhere land used to grow sorghum, a hardy plant adapted to the harsh environment and producing a nutritious grain, has been given over to less wholesome fruits profligate in their water demands. Damming water will increase the rate of evaporation. The maze of irrigation channels will quickly be coated with silt and provide an ideal environment for the snail required for the life-cycle of the bilharzia schistosome. The Tihama Development Authority, the autonomous government body which oversees these huge foreign-funded schemes, has done nothing about this health risk.

Headquarters of the Arbat project and home to Yemeni administrators, a handful of British engineers and the German health workers, is a camp ringed by a high fence. It is guarded by a security force recruited by the Tihama Development Authority. We stopped at the well-guarded entry gate, were immediately refused entry and told to go away. I said we had been invited. The Germans, I was told, could not receive visitors without permission from Sana'a. I stood my ground, obstinacy turning to anger. When the armed guards refused to send someone to inform the Germans of our arrival I suddenly started towards their house. The guards were taken aback. One ran after me and planted a hand firmly on my chest, the other resting nervously on his pistol. Out of earshot of his colleagues he pleaded with me. 'Please don't make a fuss. I shall lose my job and be put in prison.' I turned back and the man agreed to go and inform our hosts. Eventually two German women were fetched and told they could receive us provided we were out by nightfall.

The Germans, a midwife and a laboratory technician, took us to their home – a large Western style villa of a kind found in construction camps throughout the developing world. The only way to live in such unsuitably designed buildings in the Tihama climate is to have permanent air-conditioning. Other inhabitants of the camp had this facility but the German women had been denied it in a dispute over payment for electricity. The midwife was supposed to be training local midwives and assisting in the case of difficult deliveries. But as the guards routinely turned back all visitors, and no local woman had the courage to do what we had just done, she only worked from eight to one in the hospital outside the camp. The rest of the day was hers and it was an empty life devoid of the social contact with Yemenis she would have liked. She had asked to be allowed to rent a house in the town but permission had been refused.

We were dripping sweat in their airless house and were invited to go for a swim. Unfortunately the swimming pool lay outside the compound. The Germans checked the guards were not watching and we all ran across to the perimeter fence and clambered over a section half covered with drifting sand. Inevitably, I was reminded of escapes from Nazi concentration camps but thought it tactless to say so. Across the road was a work .camp run by a Finnish company supplying drilling equipment. When we arrived we were asked if we would first like to have a sauna. I had checked the temperature before leaving Ahad and it was 45° (113°F). The humidity, now we were closer to the coast, must have been approaching 100 per cent. Why had the Finns built themselves a sauna when Allah already had? We went in and found a thermometer reading 48°. Susan and I had never been in a sauna before and were unsure of the etiquette. I looked round to find the German women had removed all their clothes. Was this not scandalous behaviour in Yemen? Could I really do the same? I took my lead from the embarrassed Susan. We both remained British in this incongruously placed sauna.

A new problem awaited us on our return to Ahad: Ali Ahmad had not received his government salary. He had telephoned the health office in Nakhwa and been told that his file had disappeared. He had not been sacked, simply ceased to be the recipient of a salary. To a Yemeni civil servant the loss of one's file is tantamount to official death. After working for the ministry for five years Ali Ahmad had become a non-person. Could we do something to help him?

His effective dismissal was a veiled attack on BSDA for Ali Ahmad had been associated with our project since its inception. He was the only official of the hospital who showed any indication of understanding the principles and philosophy of primary health care. BSDA paid him a modest stipend of 300 rials (£30) a month which boosted his official earnings by a quarter. We were not prepared to pay his entire salary and something had to be done to restore his rights. We decided to go to Sana'a to tackle this and other matters. We passed through Nakhwa and popped into the health office to discuss the problem. Everyone we spoke to feigned astonishment at the loss of the file and enacted a charade of searching through their filing cabinets.

His capricious return to official favour was indicative of the nature of power in the ministry. My male colleagues and I spent several days in Sana'a trying in vain to gain an audience with the deputy minister whose approval would be needed to restore Ali Ahmad to the payroll. We sought advice from Sarah, a colleague associated with our project in Rahbaan. By virtue of her gender, charm and excellent Arabic she had, on occasion, access to corridors of power denied to the rest of us. Once she had even managed to reach the ultimate seat of authority – the afternoon *qat* chew in the deputy's house.

Sarah agreed to take Ali Ahmad to the ministry and see what she could do. She caught the guardian of the deputy minister's door in a good mood and the great man himself was equally well-disposed. He took a shine to Ali Ahmad and immediately wrote an order making him 'administrative assistant' to the Ahad health centre. Our colleague returned to Ahad in triumph, imagining that he had become deputy director of the hospital, the *de facto* position he had held for the previous few years. He later found there was no such position as 'administrative assistant' in the official hierarchy and that his position remained precariously ambiguous.

A further minor success resulted from this trip to the capital. After several days the ministry was prompted to write a directive stating that the two male nurses from Ahad, who had by now completed their training as nurses in Hodeidah, were to return to their home town to commence work. The letter also mentioned the hope that they might obtain the further qualification required to become trainer supervisors of primary health care workers. We had in the meantime spoken to the two nurses who indicated their keenness to work at home and become trainers. Copies of this order were addressed to the directors of health in Nakhwa and Hodeidah province and I was entrusted with their delivery. However, when I presented it in Nakhwa on my way back to Ahad the letter excited little interest. Dr Thaalib shuffled it away under the pile of letters on his desk and said the matter was in his hands. He would resolve the situation with his friend and 'brother', his counterpart in Hodeidah province. I was chided for having bothered the busy officials in Sana'a. Such piddling matters could best be sorted out by himself. There was no need for correspondence. He shook his head sadly. Really, I should have more trust.

On our return to Ahad, Simon and I were approached by a minor official of the local development association. He required our signature and stamp of approval for the five-year development plan his association was sending to Sana'a for consideration. We asked what the lengthy hand-written document had to say about the development of health resources. The official was impatient and unwilling to provide details. Ali Ahmad, who had accompanied him, took us aside. He urged us to sign. What the document said was not important. Its existence, not its contents, were what counted. The LDA had to present such plans to Sana'a and it would be in everybody's interests if the hospital, the development association and BSDA were seen to share the same hopes. Much against our better judgement, we reluctantly signed and stamped.

Weeks went by without any news about the two nurses, Yahya and Yusuf. They returned to Ahad but could not work in the health centre as they were nominally attached to the Al Aulafi hospital in Hodeidah, 150 km. away. In any case, there were now too many doctors and nurses in the Ahad hospital as Dr Thaalib had renewed the contract of the Sudanese. For appearances' sake, the two Yemeni nurses showed their faces in the Al Aulafi once or twice a week, but had not been given any work to do.

Simon and I resolved to return to Hodeidah, this time with the two men. We had decided that we would forbid smoking in our Toyota and had obtained Arabic language anti-smoking stickers. However, when Yahya and Yusuf lit up our resolve lapsed, lest our behaviour be thought dictatorial. We put up with their chain-smoking all the way to Hodeidah. The rate of cigarette consumption amongst Yemeni males is horrendous and there are no public buildings, including hospitals, which are not perpetually shrouded in smoke. Rothmans, the largest British company in Yemen, have an excellent marketing network spearheaded by Arabic-speaking British executives driving round in flashy cars. I was later to meet some of the Rothmans expatriate personnel, late at night in a drunken party in Hodeidah. In a maudlin state the carcinogen makers praised me for the good work we were doing 'at the opposite end of the health equation' and then each individual proceeded, without prompting, to bring out rationalizations. I had seen how Rothmans operated when they had come to Ahad and my disgusted colleagues had refused to speak to the bustling young cigarette promoter based in Hodeidah. Without so much as a by-your-leave, his team had gone through the *suq* plastering Rothmans ads on every shop. Calendars and other promotional material were liberally distributed. Every road-sign the length of the highway from Hodeidah to the Saudi border is festooned with a Rothmans poster. On this highway, as on all others in Yemen, there are no municipal sign posts announcing towns. Instead we were welcomed and bidden farewell by Rothmans in every dusty little settlement we passed through.

As we crossed the sandy wastes on the approaches to Hodeidah I reflected on the subtlety of the cigarette advertisers and the much greater understanding they showed of contemporary Yemeni culture than anybody in the 'development community'. Yemenis are torn between admiration of things *baladi* (indigenous) and *khaaraji* (external). Unlike us, the cigarette makers successfully appealed to both poles of this status system. Rothmans, in all its advertising material claimed to be 'the best tobacco money can buy'. Such a slogan, in English and Arabic, was embossed on all the ashtrays, thermos flasks, calendars, car decals and umbrellas it distributed to Yemenis. A rival brand, Kamaran, is named after an island in the Red Sea which North Yemen seized from South Yemen after the withdrawal of its British garrison in 1967. Kamaran does not need to stake a claim to international standards for it is the patriotic smoke *par excellence*. I had seen many Yemenis going into stores, asking for the *baladi* cigarette and chiding Rothmans smokers. Kamaran's promotional material is unashamedly nationalistic. Unlike Rothmans, its calendars show no pictures of racing cars, western women or even of cigarettes but are filled with idealized nostalgic tableaux of an already vanishing Yemen: fishermen reaping the bounty of the sea, artisans contentedly at work, peasants ploughing fields and men sitting round chewing *qat* and puffing on a traditional water pipe. The rivalry is pure hype. Both brands are made in the same factory using tobacco and rolling papers imported by Rothmans.

Yahya and Yusuf had struck me as confident young men, proud of their achievements as the first from the area to have gained a prestigious nursing qualification. I thought we would have to say little on their behalf. Armed with the official letter of appointment surely they could explain themselves? We found our way to the office of the provincial health director and were made to wait in an anteroom. After some minutes the door opened, the director spotted us and beckoned us to come in. We sat down but found we had lost our counterparts. I looked round. Both had shyly remained in the anteroom, further evidence of Tihami diffidence in the presence of powerful highlanders. Again, the letter from the deputy minister cut no ice. The autonomy of powerful individuals makes a mockery of notional bureaucratic chains of command. The Hodeidah health chief told us that it was up to him to decide how to allocate staff in his province. He did not require assistance from foreigners. Out of sheer goodwill, he would send us one of the nurses. The other was required to work in

Salif, a bleak port an hour from Hodeidah. The men could decide among themselves who was to go where.

In vain did I point to the orders from Sana'a. He had made his offer. Did we accept or did we not? Completely unprepared for this eventuality, we nodded acceptance and withdrew. Our two colleagues when told the news were downcast. Neither wanted to go to Salif and both would rather have stayed in the city of Hodeidah. They discussed who would be allowed to return home. It turned out that Yusuf, although the older man, was the nephew of Yahya, and was therefore obliged to accept the inferior posting. In the end Yusuf remained in Salif for another two months before further intervention finally allowed him to come home. I exchanged sad farewells with the two men and drove despondently back to Ahad. How on earth, I kept asking myself, had I become embroiled in such an absurd situation?

7

GLIMMERS OF HOPE?

The training course for nine female health workers had begun but Simon and I had still made no progress with their male counterparts. I had only briefly met our two primary health care workers while they were passing through Ahad on the way back from their training in Hodeidah. Some weeks had since gone by and no one in authority had seemed concerned by the fact that neither had any prospect of starting work. We decided to invite them to come to Ahad for a few days at our expense to get to know them better.

Abdul Kariim, a resident of a village ninety minutes drive from Ahad, is in his late twenties. He is among the first from the district of Zahir, an area of some 80,000 people, to have obtained a primary school certificate. He is the father of six daughters and no live sons, a misfortune he bears with much grace. His family are relatively prosperous in that they have a small income from land. This had been an important factor in BSDA deciding to support him a year earlier. We had feared that the local development association would not match our 500 rial a month stipend and that he would have to depend on his family for expenses needed in Hodeidah. This had, indeed, been the case.

Salah, the other health worker, comes from a foothill district called Bani Salim, an hour out of Ahad. His is a desolate and bleak district completely lacking amenities such as the schools, electric generators, and shops now taken for granted in most of rural Yemen. Before beginning his course in Hodeidah he had no formal education apart from a few weeks at a Koranic school. Miraculously, through rote learning of part of the Koran, he acquired the rudiments of literacy. He had impressed my colleagues by his innate intelligence. Only by dint of arguing had we succeeded in gaining permission for Salah to enter the training course in Hodeidah. Had the course started a few months later he would have been barred from entering because of not having a primary school certificate. Like Abdul Kariim he had not received any money from his local development association during his course. Salah's family were in no position to support him and he had led a hand-to-mouth existence. We had been 'lending' him money in the ridiculous expectation he would one day be able to pay it back.

Before their course in Hodeidah neither man had visited a city. Salah, a shy nineteen-year-old, had been embarrassed by his lack of education in comparison to all the other trainees. He had persevered only because of help he had received from Abdul Kariim. Night after night he had gone over his notes as Salah had, in effect, acquired literacy and knowledge of health at the same time. Despite these enormous handicaps, he had, in the end, finished as the best student on his course. His morale had been greatly boosted, yet when I met him he still seemed an unimposing boy, unlikely to be taken seriously as a giver of advice.

I was glad to have Yemeni guests staying in my house. Salah's enthusiasm was infectious, a tonic after the frustrations I had experienced during the previous months. He was itching to start work but had neither drugs to dispense nor a building to work from. He had begun his medical career literally at home. His young nephew had recently had malaria and Salah had advised his parents to dose him for three days with a few rials' worth of chloroquine tablets which he gave them. His relatives had all disagreed with his advice and stated the well-nigh universal belief, fostered by unscrupulous pharmacists, that malaria can only be cured by injections. Believing he would be vindicated, Salah risked his credibility on a wager. They would all go down to the hospital in Ahad. If the Sudanese doctor working there did not endorse the view that malaria could be cured by tablets then he, Salah, would stop giving advice and acknowledge his ignorance. Off they went. To his shame, the doctor insisted that injections were the only cure and charged 100 rials for giving one on the spot. Salah was humiliated. Convinced he was right, his eyes were opened to the uneasy fit between the ideals of primary health care and the interests of doctors.

The procedure for supplying drugs and equipment to the two men was bizarre. BSDA had spent weeks nagging officials in the ministry to pass on the cartons donated by UNICEF and earmarked for the two units in which Abdul Kariim and Salah were to work. By harrying officials for signatures and stamps Graham eventually succeeded in acquiring the drugs and equipment, loaded the cartons into our Toyota and carried them to our house in Sana'a for safe-keeping. We hired a lorry to carry them down to Ahad where they were stored in our large house. When we opened the cartons of drugs we were distressed to find that many of the twenty-eight kinds of medicine were already close to their expiry dates. Eighteen months had passed while the drugs were being cleared through the port of Hodeidah, taken up to Sana'a and passed through the ministry. Some appeared to have suffered from being stored in the heat of the Tihama. As their effective shelf life was ending, and the Rahbaan project had run out, we surreptitiously slipped them some cartons of ampicillin.

When the director of the Ahad hospital heard what we had done he immediately assumed that he would take charge of the drugs. We had refused, both out of suspicion that the old man would sell them in his own pharmacy, and because he had said he was not interested in the establishment of 'little hospitals' outside the town. We had tried and tried to explain to him the nature of primary health care but to no avail. Our control of drugs provided by the United Nations to a sovereign state had first struck me as highly undesirable. The need to conceal from our Yemeni counterparts the extent of the drug supplies we were holding seemed unjustifiable. By now I had come to realize that with us lay the only hope that the drugs could be used by the intended beneficiaries – the rural poor without any access to pharmacies.

We showed Salah and Abdul Kariim samples of the drugs they were to use. They had only seen a few of them before and we wondered what the Americans had been teaching them. The list of drugs had been standard for many years yet the trainees had not been taught the scientific and trade names of the drugs nor the appropriate dosages. We had to start from scratch and help the men prepare charts containing such information. Salah immediately caught on though he was still embarrassed by his poor writing and constantly deferred to the older man. We also did some role-playing to improve the men's ability to sell themselves and the apparently fanciful notions they had learnt. I delighted in playing the kind of demanding patients I had seen in my time in Yemen: an obstreperous tribesman demanding a calcium injection for a cold, a young hypochondriac asking for a valium injection for his 'nerves', a mother complaining that her dehydrated son had not been given a drip, an obsequious man persistently calling the health workers 'Doctor' while asking for an X-ray, and a whining old man asking for a vitamin B12 and testosterone shot to restore his potency. Salah began shyly but warmed to the game. He countered my feigned ignorance with much patience and humour. Abdul Kariim, having been through the school system, had a much greater tendency to lecture and correct. I enjoyed our little course and the opportunities it provided to learn more about health problems and local conceptualization of illness patterns. I learned much colloquial language and started composing a glossary of local medical terms.

Salah was supposed to work in the unit I had earlier visited near Suq as Sebt, the weekly market up the wadi from Ahad. Salah knew nobody in the area which is three hours' walk, and an hour by four-wheel-drive vehicle, from his own district. He wanted to work at home. Dr Thaalib had insisted, however, that he should work in Suq as Sebt despite the fact he had no salary, no means of transport and no completed building to work in. Problems preventing Abdul Kariim starting work were similar. Fortunately he lived only five minutes away from his projected place of work and attended a school sited on a hill overlooking his health post. However, his building, identical to the one in Suq as Sebt, could also not be used, despite having been declared 'finished'. It lacked window frames or doors.

An opportunity to move forward presented itself. We were invited to attend a graduation ceremony for female health workers in Nafaq, the *qat* area two hours distant. The governor of Nakhwa province, the deputy minister of health and the World Health Organization representative were all going to attend and we thought to put our problems before them.

As we drove up the atrocious track to Nafaq Simon suddenly unburdened himself. 'I'm really worried about my wife. I don't know what to do.' I was pleased the subject was now out in the open. For months the rest of us had wondered what to do about the great stress Elizabeth was under. Her problems had been compounded the month before when a child had run in front of the Toyota she was driving. In avoiding him, she ran off the road, turned over several times and had incurred a head wound requiring several stitches. The badly damaged Toyota was never the same again. We had feared it would be disloyal to take the initiative and raise the issue of Elizabeth's stress or mention it to our superiors in Sana'a or London. A visitor from the British headquarters of AFJAD felt the problem had to be faced and mentioned Elizabeth's plight in an official report on his visit. Because of inter-agency tensions his intervention only served to bolster BSDA's refusal to acknowledge the symptoms of impending crisis. I told Simon I thought the important thing was for all of us to urge her to think about leaving Ahad early, not to feel guilty about doing so, but to see her exhaustion as the inevitable product of the incredible pressures she had been subjected to. After all, of those recruited by BSDA since the Ahad project started, half had failed to complete their two-year periods of service. Her problem was far from unique. Fortunately, within a few weeks the couple decided to leave Ahad. A month later Elizabeth, crippled with guilt, departed for some much deserved rest.

We arrived in Nafaq after the ceremony had started. Hundreds of curious tribesmen were crowded into the courtyard of the local school. The dignitaries, their military guards and the recipients of certificates were cramped behind tiny school desks lined up for the occasion. A provincial official was praising the president. We were recognized and ushered forward. Minor soldiers were unseated to make way for us. Bottles of mineral water and *kanada*, essential props for such formal occasions, were pressed on us.

The governor rose to much applause. He began a low-key

speech, in classical Arabic, which was filmed by the television crew present for the occasion. The crowd seemed to understand little but clapped politely on cue whenever the governor paused. A succession of other officials gave brief speeches, also in the classical language, followed by the World Health Organization representative who talked ramblingly in English. No one bothered to translate his platitudes. The crowd looked restless and seemed more interested in the soft drink vendors circulating amongst them. The women, all but one veiled, shyly came forward to receive their certificates. One recited a poem in favour of the revolution in a nervous, but suitably declamatory, manner.

The governor returned to the microphone. He switched from classical Arabic to the pithy vernacular. The television crew turned off their cameras for such populist behaviour is considered unbecoming. He was a man transformed. 'Citizens', he began grandiloquently, gesturing to the hills of qat terraces which surrounded us on all sides. 'There is a poison in our land. It saps our energies and is destroying our country. It is called qat. I look forward to the day when I come back to your beautiful town and every single bush is uprooted.' The crowd went wild with excitement, a curious spectacle considering that no other marketable crop is grown in Nafaq and most of the crowd probably derived their livelihoods from its cultivation or distribution. Never had I seen a more vigorous crusader against the leaf. I was even more impressed when the governor went on to give a pitch for female education and women's rights. He criticized Saudi Arabia for not recognizing the role of women. This ceremony, he said, was just the beginning. Soon there would be female doctors and engineers from the area.

To great applause, the governor suddenly strode off to his Range Rover. As accompanying Toyota pickups blared their sirens his motorcade whizzed away leaving a cloud of dust. Soldiers clung on, their guns drawn and pointed at the crowd. The other dignitaries struggled to reach their cars and join the motorcade. Traffic became greatly congested trying to get out of the school gates. There was much tooting of horns. Amidst the confusion I spoke to a passer-by about the speech. I was surprised how unenthused he seemed. Did the governor really hate *qat* so much, I asked. He smiled enigmatically and told me to wait for the afternoon.

We were forgotten in the press to catch up with the governor and made our way into the town, unsure what to do next. An officer suddenly remembered us and led us back to the official party. Lunch was just about to be served and 100 or so men were squatting expectantly around the plastic sheets laid on the ground. The governor saw us, barked at a few soldiers and places were made for us just in front of him. He asked how we were. Apropos of nothing, and in the midst of an Arabic sentence, a long-forgotten phrase from his English studies came back to him. 'The weather England bad, yes?' he beamed, looking pleased with himself. In Arabic he asked me what I thought of *al Hadiidiiya* (the Iron Lady). 'A jinni take her!' I replied, using a popular phrase. The entourage laughed appreciatively but the governor looked displeased at such lese-majesty. He turned to speak to his other guests and expressed surprise that there was much to learn about midwifery; he wondered why women had to spend so many months picking up an easy skill like delivering a child. With the arrival of food, silence fell upon the room. The governor was an attentive host and directed a sheep's head to be placed in front of us.

Amidst the commotion we had no chance to talk about the problems of our project and no one seemed interested to ask us. After lunch we managed to briefly detain Dr Thaalib and to speak about the problem of Salah having to work so far from his home. Would it be all right if the citizens of his area and the local development association raised money for a small unit to be built near his home village? Dr Thaalib was keen to get away from us to insinuate himself into a good position to catch the governor's ear and did not really listen. He clearly indicated his consent to our proposal, told us to speak to his deputy and rushed off. We did not see him again for another four months. Only later did we learn of his departure, accompanied by his friend the director of health in Hodeidah province, for another long visit to the United States financed by USAID.

We were led off to an enormous long thin room, some 50 metres by 5. Half a dozen dark-skinned *akhdaam* attendants were bustling round, setting cushions in place, lighting a score of water-pipes and arranging their sinuous hoses around the room. Men drifted in until there were some 250 in our room. We were not sure where to sit, receiving many conflicting instructions. Such a jostle for position is characteristic of the early stages of the *qat* afternoon as men compete both to gain more prestigious places and to show their generosity of spirit in abandoning them to others. Servants staggered in, laden down with such mounds of *qat* that they could barely see where they were going. One stumbled into a water pipe, spilling its coals over the fine carpet. The piles of *qat* were laid down at the far end of the room where the furnishings were most lavish. The governor entered and seated himself in front of the *qat*.

We were seated a third of the way down the room, within range of the group conversations at the big men's end of the room but out of earshot of the more intimate conclaves which develop as the *qat* afternoon takes its course. On the governor's instructions *qat* was distributed amongst those in the upper half of the room. The governor personally lobbed bunches of *qat* into the laps of the more favoured dignitaries. In the midst of a conversation I was startled by the arrival of a bunch of twigs. As custom dictated, I pressed the bunch to my forehead and asked Allah to reward the governor for his generosity. Some men lower down the room received bunches but most had to make do with the private supplies they had brought with them. The governor was amongst the most enthusiastic of those who started packing juicy leaves into their mouths. He soon developed a characteristic *qat* bulge. A man next to me, when asked to guess how much money had been spent buying *qat* for the occasion, estimated £5,000. We had been given a prodigious amount and though I stuffed it in with great gusto I was unable to get through even half the leaves given me. I later handed the remainder to grateful soldiers at checkpoints on the way back down to Ahad.

As we were the only foreigners in this vast gathering, people were interested in speaking to us. But with all the noise of mingled conversations it was hard to exchange more than a few words with those at some distance from us. Those seated nearby turned out to be soldiers who, like all military men, had changed into civilian gear of *futa* (sarong), brightly coloured western jacket and dagger for the afternoon chewing. I was rather hurt when one asked if Simon, three years my junior, was my son but remembered how difficult it is for Yemenis to place a clean-shaven Westerner. After a while I shifted place and entered into a theological conversation with a *haakim* (judge) and other Islamic scholars. After the bullying conversations I had endured from men in Nakhwa province who are so ignorant of the Koran that they do not know that Christians are also 'people of the Book' (monotheists) it was entertaining to be amongst men who were well-informed about Christianity and had studied the Bible. Conversation turned to Palestine, the arms race and the Iran–Iraq war, perennial subjects of interest in Yemen. An enjoyable afternoon was passed. Conversations lapsed as the light in the room faded. The 'hour of Solomon' had arrived. Men became lost in thought and gazed out at the swirling mists rising up to envelop the town. The silence was broken only by the gurgling of water pipes and the mutterings of the more pious men who broke out of their reveries to exclaim 'there is no God but God'. As the call to prayer rang out over the town and was picked up by other mosques men rose to their feet, mumbled 'Peace be upon you', and took their leave. We did the same.

The *qat* was having a pleasing effect. I raced down the mountain oblivious to the bumps. We had been shivering but within an hour were back in the foetid heat. *Qat* is dehydrating and I was soon pouring sweat even more than usual, disgusting myself by my body odour. In Ahad I had a brief wash before rushing off to a social function being held by the British engineers at the irrigation project in Arbat. When we took our place amongst the engineers, their wives, our German hosts and expatriate guests from Hodeidah I was struck by the suddenness of the cultural and climatic change. I dripped onto the carpet all evening, wondering, not for the first time, why I found it so easy to strike up conversations with strange Arabs, yet so hard with those of my own culture. Despite the alcohol I had drunk, I was still buzzing with restless energy from the *qat* as we made our way back to Ahad in the early hours of the morning. I could not sleep until the dawn.

We thought it best to act on the scope Dr Thaalib had, perhaps inadvertently, given us to get a unit opened for Salah. To avoid offending Ali Ahmad, the hospital's administrative assistant, I suggested that he come with me to Bani Salim which he had never visited. I had been warned by my colleagues that he would insist on driving and that I was to resist. Ali Ahmad had no licence and the terms of the insurance for our Daihatsu Rocky specified that any driver had to be licensed. Unfortunately, such reasons cut little ice with rural Yemenis who are not even aware that it is possible to insure a car. So, rather than appear high-handed, I allowed Ali Ahmad to take the wheel. Ours was a high profile departure. He revved the engine loudly so attention would be drawn to the sight of a local driving a *nasraani*'s car. We skidded out of town at high speed with me fearing for my life and for Rocky's springs. Once past the checkpoint, however, it became clear Ali Ahmad did know how to drive soberly and correctly and had only been showing off.

We stopped for cool drinks. On finishing his water, Ali Ahmad immediately threw the plastic bottle out of the car. Plastic and cardboard have arrived so recently that it has not occurred to people that their disposal could constitute a problem. Simon's efforts to persuade our counterparts to keep their rubbish with them and dispose of it later were regarded as eccentric. It was ironic, I thought, that BSDA had identified Ali Ahmad as someone keenly interested in problems of waste. In a report to our funders AFJAD, which I had read, he had been proposed as a candidate for training as a public health sanitarian.

We made a detour in the hope of explaining our plans to the treasurer of the local development association. He owns one of the largest shops in the small market village of Suq as Sebt. He was elsewhere but a son, running the shop despite his tender years, invited us in. A large crowd of men was hanging round as is common in the vicinity of a freezer-full of relatively cold drinks in such a hot climate. They plied us with questions, eager to know of plans to build hospitals and train local men. I tried to counter some of their misconceptions, but with little success. The men had heard the phrase *ri'ayya as sahhiia al awliiaa* (primary health care) on television and wanted to know what it meant. Ali Ahmad thought he was wasting his time with unimportant people and was keen to get on. He said it referred to 'first aid' and agreed with an assessment that it was a 'temporary' arrangement until more comprehensive health care could be provided by rural hospitals. We drove off, clutching extra bottles of water given us by the hospitable citizens. After a while I asked Ali Ahmad why he had not taken the opportunity to explain the nature of primary health care and to encourage the locals to get involved. 'They have no education here. They would not understand', was his infuriating reply.

We finally arrived in Bani Salim and sat down with Salah and other men to discuss whether local people might be interested in helping build a health post. First of all we had to identify men of standing in the community. This proved surprisingly difficult. When we asked various men who their sheikhs were there was much head-shaking and disagreement. Various individuals were named, then others said they were no longer sheikhs. We were advised to take our ideas to Nasar Mohammad, a powerful old man living nearby, the former president of the local development association for the entire government district. Others said there was no point. Nasar Mohammad was exhausted by all the squabbling in the community. In the recent elections he had been defeated by a younger man from the other side of the district, some two Toyota hours distant. He was now sulking in his house attending only to his own affairs.

The mood was pessimistic. The majority seemed to imagine it most unlikely that Salah could provide any benefit to their community. They preferred to wait for the doctor and hospital which had apparently been promised the community by the Nakhwa health office. One or two men seemed amenable to the idea of raising money so that Salah could commence work. Most, however, were dubious about the chances of the citizens agreeing about anything.

Not for the first time I heard people bitterly berating themselves for their factionalism and backwardness. For so long had they been put down as inadequate approximations to the ideal of co-operative tribesmen that they had come to internalize these negative images. The developmental monopoly claimed by the state had eroded these people's confidence in their ability to take matters into their own hands. Again and again I was told 'we are like animals here', 'we are uncivilized Bedouins', 'all we know how to do is to fight amongst ourselves', 'we are no better than cattle'. I learned that a year earlier, when Nasar Mohammad had been their LDA president, he had succeeded in getting the provincial education office to offer to pay 50 per cent of the cost of constructing a school. However, the citizens of the score of tiny hamlets who would have benefited fell out over the question of where to site the school. They squabbled so much that the opportunity passed them by. The bitterness thus produced was not forgotten. I was told the same would happen if men discussed building a health post. Enthusiasm would quickly give way to bitter division. Gratitude was expressed for my interest, but my time would be better spent elsewhere. The people of Bani Salim were only *karatiin* (cardboard boxes), incapable of realizing, or acting to further, their own interests.

Salah was disappointed but persevered in his efforts. He thought to shame the men from his immediate vicinity by offering to set up a few kilometres away. A few days later he and I went to speak to the headmen and sheikhs of this area but got nowhere. However, his actions had the desired effect and a number of men who had been initially reluctant came forward. A third meeting was convened, this time with Nasar Mohammad who, it was said, had thrown off his sloth. Thirty or more men crowded into his modest reception room and perched on the half dozen beds. From his circumstances it was clear that Nasar Mohammad was merely a first amongst equals, not the kind of powerful, educated land-owning sheikh characteristically found in the mountains. I found his dialect impenetrable and needed Salah's help to translate his words into more accessible Arabic.

In previous meetings I had exhausted all the arguments I could think of to encourage the local men. Fortunately, the government came to our rescue. The state had suddenly become much more determined to catch drivers of cars on which no import duty had been paid or which did not have number plates or registration discs. Some soldiers at checkpoints had even tried to earn some 'tea-money' by demanding that drivers produce driving licences. Few local men had ever seen a Yemeni licence and some had previously shown an interest in seeing mine. Prior to this clampdown, no cars in Salah's region had Yemeni number plates though a few have Saudi number plates which are taken on and off depending on circumstances. The blitz had led to hundreds of vehicles being impounded in Ahad while their desperate owners negotiated the terms of release with various government officials. Those with fairly new Toyotas were suddenly being forced to pay thousands of pounds. Would it not be easier and cheaper, I suggested, to have a local health facility, rather than face the risk of trying to drive into Ahad by back roads and being nabbed?

This practical consideration was listened to with interest. Nasar Mohammad agreed, as a purely temporary arrangement, to lend his efforts to raising money from the community to build Salah a one-roomed 'small hospital'. I had spoken to the British ambassador who had promised up to £2,500 for the scheme. This would have been enough to build a suitable unit but we had decided that the people had to be involved for Salah to have success. Thus I told the men that the British would provide 50 per cent and that the other 50 per cent had to come from them.

The men talked amongst themselves for ages, arguing about how much could be raised and where the building should be put. As discussion raged backwards and forwards I became completely lost. Salah attentively provided me with a running synopsis. He also whispered apologies for the seemingly rude behaviour of his friends and neighbours. 'This is the way things get decided round here', he explained. 'We are all backward and you need to be patient.' I had witnessed this egalitarian style of decision making among the 'real' tribes of Yemen and was impressed to see the Bani Salim tribesmen getting heatedly involved. I knew it took time and everyone with a view had to have it aired. Ali Ahmad, the rather self-important bureaucrat, was less patient and keen to get back down to Ahad before nightfall. It was eventually agreed that each household in fourteen hamlets would contribute money according to their means and that a man from each tiny village would be responsible for its collection.

Things now moved quickly. The next day I went with Salah

and some local men to inform their *mudiir an naahiya* of developments. The *markaz*, the government post, lies about one hour's drive distant at the top of a mountain. The prefect had only that week arrived in his job and was apologetic about the shabby state of his *diwaan*. He promised to clean up the desiccated *qat* leaves littering the building and said that he himself only chewed on special occasions. He explained that he was amongst a new batch of prefects, all young men in their early twenties, who had graduated from the army college. The president had sent them out from Sana'a in a sweeping nation-wide reform designed to remove the stain of corruption which had attached to their less well-educated predecessors. The new prefect was very congenial, listened with interest to our plans and expressed great support. Once an agreement was drawn up he would send soldiers to arrest any men who refused to pay their share.

A meeting to chew *qat* was convened in Ali Ahmad's house in Ahad and several Toyota loads of citizens descended for the occasion. A local building contractor had offered to build the unit and had come along. Again there were hours and hours of discussion, but eventually a document was drawn up. It was expected that before the meeting broke up the important men would sign it. However, just before the call for the sunset prayer Ali Ahmad announced that the document would need typing and everybody was to come back in a few days. There were rumblings of disappointment at this news. I cursed myself for having encouraged Ali Ahmad to investigate crates of UNICEF equipment which had been lying round the hospital unopened for the past two years. He had been delighted to find an Arabic typewriter, the first to be provided to the hospital and perhaps the only one in Ahad, and had immediately commandeered it and begun to teach himself typing. Typed documents are virtually unknown and it was quite unnecessary for our agreement to be typed. Ali Ahmad was simply aggrandizing himself. As tactfully as I could, I tried to suggest that we could all append our signatures (or, by implication, thumbprints in the case of the illiterate) to the hand-written document we had completed. Under pressure, Ali Ahmad eventually agreed. I lent authority to the piece of paper by solemnly wielding our project stamp.

The site for the unit was ideal. The building would be on the top of a hill and clearly visible for miles around. It was barren unused land on the interstices of territory belonging to several villages. A number of people could claim to have generously given up their claims in the common good. The contractor proved diligent and set to work at once. Within a week foundations and walls were in place.

A brief hiccup occurred. A local man, recently returned from Saudi Arabia and looking for a business venture to invest his savings in, persuaded his kinsmen to refuse to contribute to the cost of building. He went up to Nakhwa to try to get a licence to open a pharmacy in Bani Salim. Perhaps he did not offer sufficient inducement for he returned empty-handed. Salah informed the prefect who showed his mettle by sending soldiers to arrest those who had refused to pay. In Yemen having a soldier sent to your home is a time-honoured and highly effective procedure for coercing litigants into agreement. For not only do you have to recompense the soldier for the expense of getting to your area and escorting you back to the government *markaz*, but also you have to provide him with food and *qat* for as long as he chooses to stay. After a few days, the last resistance to paying crumbled and work resumed.

Thus exactly three weeks after the signing of the agreement the building was completed. A more telling contrast to the laborious procedure by which the official UNICEF-designed units had been 'built' by a corrupt absentee contractor over three years could not be imagined. It was hardly surprising that such a spectacle of citizens efficiently co-operating to develop their area was an obvious threat to some in high position. When Ali Ahmad rang the Nakhwa office to tell them the building was finished and to ask about arrangements for the official opening ceremony he found Dr Thaalib was in Los Angeles. His deputy professed astonishment. Dr Thaalib had not mentioned that an 'unofficial' unit was to be built in Bani Salim. The opening ceremony, if there was to be one, would have to have Dr Thaalib's approval and nothing could be done for several months.

The vigorous prefect thought otherwise and set a date for the opening. We realized that for the ceremony to be legitimate

a public show had to be put on. But who was to provide soft
drinks, meat and *qat* for the *mudiir an naahiya*, his entourage of
soldiers, office holders from the LDA and other important
men who might come for the occasion? We were worried lest
Salah go further into debt providing hospitality so took it upon
ourselves to pay for some meat and take up crates of *kanadas*.
Ali Ahmad persuaded the local director of schools to allow
fifty chairs to be borrowed for the day. To lend kudos and
official status to the health post I paid an Ahadi tailor to run up
a North Yemeni flag which I mounted over the building.

BSDA's recently arrived new programme co-ordinator came
down from Sana'a for the opening. Brian's appointment had
aroused controversy amongst my colleagues. The job was not
widely advertised and only two people had applied for the
post. As neither were ideal candidates some volunteers
requested the job be more widely re-advertised but London
had gone ahead with the appointment.

I was relieved that Simon, in his last days in the project,
would be able to be present rather than having to go home
with no achievements whatsoever to show for his dogged
efforts. Also present and enjoying the final days of her highly
frustrating stay in Yemen was Julie, the linguist-cum-literacy
promoter recruited for the Kahima project. I was glad of her
presence as we sat writing the speech I was to deliver on behalf
of BSDA at the opening ceremony. Together we sprinkled the
talk with references to the revolution, the president and the
sterling qualities of the Yemeni people.

We arrived in Bani Salim early and unloaded the school
chairs and the soft drinks together with the drugs cabinet we
had bought but which should have been provided by the
provincial health office. A ramshackle marquee made from a
dozen different coloured tarpaulins had been built overnight
and dwarfed the modest little health building. A troupe of
musicians with flutes and drums provided accompaniment for
men who started dancing while awaiting the ceremony.
Amidst much merriment I borrowed a dagger and began
waving it above my head in imitation of my fellow dancers.
Abdul Kariim had come to Bani Salim for the day and he and
Ali Ahmad helped a nervous Salah to go through his speech to
weed it of unclassical neologisms. Hundreds gathered, many

having to wait in the hot sun. The president of the local development association had said he was coming but did not turn up, presumably because he did not want to witness his rival, Nasar Mohammad the former president, basking in glory.

The prefect's entourage was spotted. Local people are too poor to be able to afford the bursts of rifle fire with which they should have honoured the visitors and instead threw fireworks into the air. For half an hour speeches were made. I overcame my nervousness and stood up to make my speech. My talk about the notions of primary health care and their relevance for a country with a dispersed population like Yemen seemed to be understood. At least I did not put the audience to sleep for they burst into applause at the appropriate moments whenever 'the glorious and eternal September revolution' was mentioned. I praised the citizenry for their co-operation and Salah for his achievements during his training course. I compared pharmacy owners to the disgraced Imams – hoarding knowledge and power and profiting from the ignorance of the people.

The prefect cut a ribbon held out for him by local men, applauded himself as is the Yemeni fashion and went in to inspect the health unit. He expressed disappointment at the paucity of the drugs and I was much occupied trying to persuade people of their value. The occasion was slightly spoilt by the prefect complaining of a headache and then protesting at the ineffectiveness of the modest aspirin which Salah immediately produced. A marvellous lunch was provided, food being carried by men from a great number of distant households. The prefect then showed signs of wanting to leave but his soldiers seemed reluctant. Nothing was said, but eventually a car came racing up to the unit. Nasar Mohammad had arranged for a Toyota to be sent down to Ahad to get *qat*. The prefect had to be persuaded to accept, saying he did not feel like chewing that day. He eventually took the offering, his soldiers looking relieved that their visit would not be in vain. They drove away and the party slowly broke up. We repacked the chairs, collected the empty bottles and made our way back down the perilous track to Ahad.

With the help of an important government ally encouraging

progress had been achieved. Unfortunately the new *mudiir an naahiya* stationed in Ahad was far less co-operative. Our first meeting set the tone for our relationship. It was the fasting month of Ramadan and I had readjusted my schedule like other inhabitants of the town. I had just come out of my house at midnight when a car driven by a very young man and with a number of youthful passengers drew alongside. My greeting was not returned and my papers were brusquely demanded. Swallowing my anger, I replied that his excellency, the brother the *mudiir an naahiya*, had already seen my papers and that my existence was officially known. As I spoke he merely shook his head and stared at me. A silence ensued. 'I', he said haughtily, 'am the *mudiir an naahiya*. I have not seen your papers. Report to me later!' So, at two in the morning and feeling like a chastened schoolboy summonsed to the head's study, I forced my way into his crowded *diwaan* to have my right to live in Ahad officially reconfirmed. The prefect did not appear interested in hearing my brief account of our plans. He told me he wished to be notified every time we planned to leave the town.

We decided not to accept this restriction on our movements and did not inform him. I managed to avoid the prefect for another three months until events compelled another encounter. With the onset of slightly cooler weather the numbers of mosquitoes had increased and with it the incidence of malaria. As most adults have acquired some degree of immunity in the course of growing up, it is children who are most at risk. Persuading young children to take bitter chloroquine tablets, even when crushed, is difficult. More suitable is flavoured chloroquine syrup but for months there had not been any in the hospital pharmacy. One day Susan came across a man who had just left one of the pharmacies with a bottle of syrup clearly marked as a gift of UNICEF. She learned that he had paid 50 rials (£5) for it. We had become fed up at the failure to improve the hospital's drug supply and thought we had clear evidence of corruption and might be able to achieve something. We decided I should go to see the prefect to inform him of the theft of UNICEF drugs and to present him with a similar bottle of chloroquine syrup so he would know what to look out for. He received me and thanked me for the information. Like a fool, I told Ali Ahmad what I had done. He was furious and also went to see the prefect. The upshot was that nothing happened for a week. By the time the prefect got round to sending a soldier to search the pharmacy the owner had ample time to remove the chloroquine and other medication purchased illegally.

The proud young prefect also soon began to offend one of our few allies in the hospital, Dr Tawfiq, a Somali sympathetic to the aims of primary health care. He told me how, whenever the prefect sent sick soldiers to him, they came with a note diagnosing their problems and proposing a prescription. Once a corpse was brought in to the hospital late at night. A man, suspecting his niece of an adulterous relationship had approached her hut, a pistol in his hand. He had called for her lover to come out but the intended victim stayed put and screamed for help. A neighbour who tried to placate the armed man was accidentally shot and died instantly. Despite his education, the *mudiir an naahiya* clearly believed in the kind of miraculous resurrection stories common among the peasantry. He rejected the death notice and told Dr Tawfiq to keep the man under observation until the morning. There being no facilities for storing cadavers in a hot climate, the Somali refused. The prefect threatened him with prison. He avoided this fate but a few weeks later was again brought by a soldier to the government buildings. A man had been denounced for drinking alcohol and soldiers had hauled him before the prefect. Medical corroboration of his intoxication was required. Dr Tawfiq could find no evidence the man had been drinking and suspected the accusation had something to do with a local feud. The prefect accused him of incompetence.

We had also received no help in getting the new hospital building in use. Amongst ourselves we had discussed ad nauseam what to do about the problem of the unfinished extension. Graham, our co-ordinator, justified spending three-quarters of his time in Sana'a by saying he was working on the problem. The rest of us were doubtful about whether he could achieve anything for in the eyes of officialdom the building was completed and in use. Some months previously word had come that the governor was to pass through Ahad to open the building. The provincial health office ordered all staff to transfer to the new building for the day to give the impression it was functioning efficiently. We had refused to take part in this charade, but all the other hospital workers, including those who, according to our plans, would never work in the new building, carried tables, filing cabinets and equipment over to the new building and carted them back after the official 'opening'. The ceremony was shown on the television news. For foreigners now to imply the building was not completed was to doubt the veracity of the news service and, by implication, the state itself.

Electricity had been connected for the occasion after which the building was locked up. A few shops and a house had gone up next to the new building and would no doubt become private pharmacies when the extension actually opened. In the meantime, electricity was being drained from the hospital to provide power for the family of one of the pharmacists who was living in the new buildings. After several fruitless complaints to the old *mudiir* Susan launched a campaign of attrition. Each day on her way to work she cut the flex in several places. Each night her adversary patched the cable together and in the end had more endurance and managed to retain his free supply of electricity.

I had been with Graham on one of his many visits to the Sana'a headquarters of the local development association to present letters about the problem of the new building. In the LDA headquarters none of the high officials spoke English and Graham dealt entirely through a genial English-speaking Sudanese whose position in the organization was unclear. Graham did not welcome help from myself or other Arabic-speaking colleagues in dealing with important officials. He constantly sent word back to us that positive developments were just around the corner. In the face of his isolation from the rest of the team he held on desperately to what he believed were areas of competence. It was only after bitter arguments that we agreed enough time had been wasted arguing about the new building. Nobody was going to pay to tile the building if we did not. I sought out a local contractor who agreed to tile the building for £2,000. Ali Ahmad drew up a contract and promised to oversee the work. Tiling took some time as the original contractor, to avoid having to lay tiles, had raised the floors so high that tiles could not be laid. This concrete had first to be removed.

Graham was further estranged from the team by a thoughtless jape. We forwarded to Sana'a for his consideration the fictitious minutes of a team meeting which never took place. We pretended to have 'Eze-Vued' the possibility of building a project swimming pool. I wrote up our deliberations in the solemn style of the copious memos clogging our files. We did not for a moment suppose that Graham would really believe a proposal that we approach the British government for funds to build a swimming pool and establish a programme for training local men in pool maintenance. Unfortunately he did not see the joke. He fulminated in the Sana'a office against his colleagues down in Ahad who had gone so soft they not only wanted air conditioning but also the luxury of a swimming pool.

Sadly, my relations with Graham went from bad to worse. Because of his depression he took little interest in his surroundings while in Ahad. He was not concerned to fight the dust which billowed into our house with every gust of wind. The already large cockroach community increased whenever washing-up was not done or rubbish bags not speedily removed. I managed to contain my irritation but clumsily expressed my resentment in a meeting when Graham told us that he was planning to take another holiday outside Yemen. He had only recently returned from Britain. From overheard comments I had realized that our local reputation was poor, that all of us, with the exception of Susan, were perceived as indolent. I suggested it might be good for our image if Graham did not specifically tell our Yemeni counterparts that he was going to the Seychelles but let them believe he was staying in Sana'a. He was deeply hurt and left the meeting. I later apologized for my clumsiness but was convinced I had a valid point. Our frequent and prolonged holidays provoked much envy. Nevertheless, for months afterwards I squirmed with recollected embarrassment at my cruelty. I remembered how Irene, reflecting in her final week on the bitterness engendered by personal tensions, said she had been reminded of *Lord of the Flies* while working for BSDA in Ahad. An individual had to be singled out and made to feel inadequate so the majority might stay sane in a hostile environment.

Graham had delivered countless letters of protest in Sana'a but BSDA had still not managed to persuade the Ahad LDA to pay their share of the stipends for the women trainees, now nine months into their course. I went into the classroom to explain the impasse to the women. I knocked and Maryam, the Sudanese teacher, called me in. My entry provoked a flurry of activity as every woman immediately veiled herself in embarrassment. This, despite the fact that Tihami women do not veil and I had already seen the faces of all but one of them, a woman of highland ancestry. When they were together, each woman had to outdo the others by her propriety.

The driver employed to bring three of the trainees into town from their village 10 km. away had also not been paid. For a while he kept on driving, unwilling to let the women down, but eventually became fed up with providing a free chauffeur service. We argued amongst ourselves whether we should offer transport. Would it be 'interventionist' or 'developmentally sound' to do so? If there was such lack of interest in training women should we not give up? Caroline, a newly arrived doctor who had applied to work for our agency in Latin America but had ended up in Ahad as successor to Elizabeth, had her first glimpse of the bitterness amongst her new colleagues. As a compromise, we decided to drive the women to and fro, but only for a few weeks. Under no circumstances would we 'back-stop' the Yemeni system and ourselves pay the driver. Eventually, as with so many of our irrevocable decisions overtaken by subsequent events, we forgot this resolution. We ended up not only paying the driver for the remainder of the course, but also paying for him to get his decrepit car back on the road.

I had by now despaired of making friends amongst the men of the town. While living in the mountains I had enjoyed a rich social life and could not understand why local men seemed so aloof. I wondered whether the fault lay with me and was relieved when Dr Tawfiq, the Somali who had been in Yemen for years and was generally more sympathetic towards Yemenis than the average foreign doctor, described the townsmen as 'cold, just like the English'. From the start of our project, reports had spoken of the greater friendliness of the women. I was thus glad pragmatism had prevailed for I was looking forward to the chance to get to know the women better. I knew I should behave with the utmost discretion when transporting the female trainees as I had seen how shy they were and knew that there were men in the area who would be shocked at the idea of a *nasraani* man driving local women.

On the first day I drove Kaatiba, a mother of two and the only still-married trainee, and Salma and Nabiila, two teenage sisters, without exchanging a word. They stared demurely ahead and drew headscarves across their faces as we passed the startled soldiers at the Ahad checkpoint. When it was next my turn to drive Kaatiba and Salma were both ill and my only passenger was Nabiila, a girl of fifteen. I was shocked when as soon as we had passed out of Ahad she brazenly threw back her head coverings and exposed her hair. Such a sight should be for a husband's eyes only. She moved closer to me, reached into her dress for a disco cassette which she put into our player and began chatting animatedly. Everything in England was wonderful. How she would love to find an English husband!

I was horror-struck. I greatly fancied her but would have to put a stop to this madness. I could put myself in grave danger and imperil our whole project. I put my foot down, hoping to reduce the journey time. The Toyota protested as dirt became clogged somewhere in the fuel line. From then on the car could not be persuaded to exceed 20 km. an hour and kept chugging to a halt every few hundred metres. A journey of five minutes lasted an hour. I was fearful lest Nabiila get the wrong idea and think I had engineered the fault. I am not able to talk knowledgeably about cars even in English. I was even more incoherent trying to explain the problem in Arabic. Encouraged, Nabiila said she was longing to learn to drive. Why didn't I come and give her lessons on Fridays, her day off? I protested this was out of the question. What would her father and brothers say? Surely they would worry about her reputation? Not at all, they would not mind in the least. She shrugged provocatively. 'We are independent people. We don't care what people think.'

I soon learned that she was telling the truth and that hers is a refreshingly unusual family. When we arrived outside the car repair shop and junk-yard which is Nabiila's home I thought it my duty to go in and explain our late arrival to her undoubtedly concerned relatives. Her two adult brothers had not even noticed her absence. While one set about fixing the Toyota I was pressed to come in for lunch. I found myself surrounded by three generations of charming people whose scanty dress was much more adapted to the fearsome climate than is thought decent in the area. A score of people lived in one hut and three concrete buildings completely exposed to the gaze of passers-by. Wives of the married brothers carried on breast-feeding while talking to me, displaying none of the modesty which now attaches to this activity elsewhere.

The paterfamilias, who worked as a mechanic in Khamis, returned home and was equally welcoming. Over lunch he told me that all his daughters and granddaughters of school age attended the local school and that they were the only girls who did. He had to fight to get them educated. 'They call my girls prostitutes because we are black and outsiders. They say we are not Arabs and not Yemenis but I was born in this country and my wife left Ethiopia twenty-five years ago. Some people round here don't know Yemen has had a revolution.' His eldest son chipped in with an insulting remark about the sexual organs of their neighbours' mothers. The patriarch told me he had been criticized for allowing Salma and Nabiila too much freedom and told they should be married like other girls their age. His wife broke in. 'I was married at twelve and I can't read and write. My daughters will become civil servants and get married when they want to.' I was delighted with the company of this outspoken family and gladly went back to have lunch and chew *qat* on many occasions. Over time I realized that women from such a rebel family were not the most likely people to win the confidence of local mothers and change their child-rearing habits.

Less satisfactory were repeated visits to Abdul Kariim to try to help him start working. We had drugs and equipment to deliver to him but how could we do so when the building he was supposed to work in had no door? His unit stood exposed just outside a major weekly market and anybody could walk away with his entire drug supply. Dried faeces and hundreds of discarded plastic water bottles lay around the building as soldiers posted to the nearby government *markaz* had been using the health post in the absence of any other sanitary facilities. No one would take responsibility for finishing the unit or offering security. Whenever we mentioned the matter in Nakhwa the officials, who had never visited the area, insisted we were mistaken and the unit had been finished.

To try to end the impasse we went to see the president of the Zahir LDA. Taalib Hussein's fief nestles in the foothills two hours' drive from the government centre. We met him in his fortress which overlooks several villages and a fertile wadi. Taalib Hussein wears several hats. He owns most of the fields of sorghum, papayas and bananas which lay below us. He is also a modern democrat for he is the elected president of the development association for the whole vast district. At the same time he remains a feudalist and has succeeded to the position of *shaykh mashaykh*, the 'sheikh of sheikhs' – the foremost traditional leader over a large piece of sensitive territory touching on the Saudi border. He was dressed scruffily – like many modernist sheikhs keen to show they can mix with the president but not lose the common touch. He lives so far from government that he provides his own. He dispenses justice, has armed retainers who arrest miscreants and even has his own prison. A great many people, some in chains, were hanging around inside and outside his shabby, but massive, *diwaan* in the hope of catching his ear.

We were warmly welcomed and the great man seemed glad to dispense with the hordes of petitioners with their grubby scraps of paper. He made sure we were comfortable and went off for midday prayers in his own mosque, pausing to shout orders to unseen women preparing our food. Generous amounts of *qat* were brought in after lunch but were shared out only amongst a fraction of those present. We chatted about a wide range of subjects. Taalib Hussein turned out to be an avid listener to the BBC Arabic Service and said he had learnt classical Arabic by listening to London. Our conversation ranged over current affairs, world geography, European history, physics and astronomy. So delighted did he seem with my company that the administrative system of his area ground to a halt. The number of supplicants grew as none were being

dealt with. I felt embarrassed as I filled my cheeks and puffed a
water pipe while diverting a man seemingly oblivious to the
irritation he was causing.

Occasionally one of the serfs went too far and shoved a
paper into Taalib Hussein's lap. His geniality vanished. 'Sit
down and be patient or go away! I am enjoying myself.'
During a pause in our conversation, he gave vent to a great
sigh of contentment. 'Ah citizens!', he exclaimed. 'This is just
like being in school. Isn't it wonderful to learn about this great
world Allah has provided for us?' The afternoon vanished in a
trice. So engrossed was he in matters of great moment that he
refused to be led by myself and the patient Abdul Kariim into
discussing the problem of the unfinished unit. He eventually
said he would see if funds could be found to put in doors,
windows and a water tank. Only with difficulty did I manage
to turn down a pressing invitation to stay the night.

Khalid Tahir, a friend of Abdul Kariim's and like him one of
the very few primary school graduates from Zahir, owns the
only pharmacy in the district. I had met him and seen the
inappropriate range of drugs he was stocking. He had grown
wealthy and bought his own Toyota pickup to smuggle drugs
from Saudi Arabia. Although merely an untrained injectionist
he is referred to throughout the district as 'Doctor Khalid'. He
had been befriended by the previous project co-ordinator, the
Australian dentist, and presented as a valuable 'health link
person'.

It was now difficult to refuse his hospitality. Since my
earliest visit with Simon I had felt that to be seen sitting in his
pharmacy was to lend legitimacy to his rapacious 'medical'
practice. He had told me he was about to start building a brand
new three-roomed pharmacy only 100 metres away from the
primary health care unit. This was an unwelcome development
as Abdul Kariim was not regarded as a 'doctor' and did not
have a clientele of injection receivers. We could only hope that
the credit which attached to us as foreign 'doctors' would
somehow rub off on Abdul Kariim and boost his own
prestige.

An incident in an Ahad pharmacy brought home the
magnitude of the task of dissuading people that pharmacy
owners are doctors. I had developed a serious abscess, a

common complaint in the hot and humid Tihama. I thought my conscience would trouble me if I helped myself to the UNICEF-provided ampicillin being stored in my house. A lesser evil would be to give business to a local drug seller. I went to a pharmacy where I was warmly welcomed by the 'doctor' on duty who tried to sell me an imported, overly powerful, antibiotic. I had just persuaded him the much cheaper ampicillin made by the newly opened pharmaceutical factory in Sana'a would do nicely when a Toyota screeched to a halt. Two men entered, supporting a man who was clearly in great pain. One opened a Clinics tissue to reveal the top joint of an index finger. Could the doctor sew it back? The pharmacist immediately sent the men to the hospital. Would he, I wondered, have had a go at surgery if I had not been present?

I was equally unprepared for the shock when Khalid Tahir, looking very pleased with himself, came to see me. He showed me a letter, written by Dr Thaalib prior to his departure for America. Khalid Tahir was appointed to the civil service payroll, Dr Thaalib testified that he was a three-year-trained nurse and authorized him to start work in the Zahir health unit. The document did not mention Abdul Kariim, the real health worker. The letter bore the impressive imprimatur of the governor. Khalid Tahir said he had come to show me the letter and to pass on an order from Nakhwa that we should hand over the UNICEF drugs so that he could start work at once. Could I please give them to him to load onto his Toyota?

8

BATTLING FOR HEALTH

I was stunned by his gall. I had heard of many shortcomings in the health system but had never come across someone completely unqualified in health but appointed to run a government health unit. Dr Thaalib's timing was truly Machiavellian. I imagined him in America, whisky in hand, smirking at the thought of the problem he had caused us. I told the smug injectionist that we had no intention of complying with the order and would complain in Nakhwa and Sana'a forthwith. I sent word to Abdul Kariim and he came to Ahad at once.

We passed a despondent evening. Abdul Kariim unburdened himself of his other problems. He enjoyed school very much and hoped the education service in his district would go on expanding and be able to offer him the chance to get a matriculation certificate. But what was the point of learning so much, he sighed, when he could not share his knowledge and enthusiasm with the person he should be closest to – his wife? He paid out of his own pocket for ten of his daughters and nieces to go to an unofficial class with an Egyptian teacher but wished his wife were still energetic enough to become educated. If only he could have married a literate woman how rich his life would be.

I had heard similar expressions of regret many times. Horizons for men have expanded enormously in a very short time. Educated young men who got married as teenagers to women as badly informed as themselves have seen their lives transformed by schooling or travel in search of work. Sadly, their wives have grown old, exhausted by constant pregnancy and loss of children. Such men often come to believe that

162

women should receive education. When they also acquire, like Abdul Kariim, modern notions of conjugal intimacy and a belief in greater sharing between spouses, a tragic gulf between aspirations and reality is manifest. I tried to share these thoughts with him. He sighed and thanked Allah for his blessings. His daughters' generation would be different.

We left early the next morning and I drove up the mountain recklessly. To calm my anger I played rock and roll cassettes, abusing the forbearance of my tolerant companion. Unknown to us, Khalid Tahir was also on the road, hoping to thwart our protests. I stopped to pick up some passengers, who were stunned not to be charged. They insisted on paying me with some of the radishes they were taking to market. They told me my music was 'terrible', put on a cassette of their own and wanted to know all about me. When they heard I was involved in health and not happy in my work they too started complaining about the local health service and Dr Thaalib. He called himself a surgeon, one man said contemptuously, but had killed many patients. He could only successfully carry out two kinds of operations, for haemorrhoids and for hernias. Both conditions are aggravated by prolonged *qat* chewing and corrective surgery is quick and lucrative. He lined up ten patients at once and charged each a few hundred pounds. Dr Thaalib, they said, had the best house in Nakhwa. He had the only swimming pool in town. Considering Nakhwa lacks a reliable municipal piped water supply this is wealth indeed, an extravagant use of a valuable resource.

I inquired about his family. 'Are they close to the government?' I asked. 'They are the government', one of my passengers snorted. 'But, if God is willing, the president will improve things.' Such faith in the merciful, but distant and televisual, leader, combined with dislike of local officialdom, is very common. Ali Abdullah Salah is undoubtedly one of the few genuinely popular Arab leaders, rivalled only by Yasir Arafat in the general esteem in which he is held by the great majority of his compatriots.

We passed by a construction site below Nakhwa where Indian labourers were building a new hospital. There is a similar Saudi-financed hospital in the town of Sa'dah, another strategic Zaydi tribal area which until recently was only tenuously controlled by the Yemeni government. This hospital is run by an American management company and not by the Ministry of Health. We were worried that the presence of a similar high-tech hospital in our province would make it even harder to persuade people of the benefits of a decentralized system of rural health posts. My passengers' main gripe was that the contractor had preferred to import 'infidel' Indian labourers rather than offer work to unemployed local men.

A shock awaited me on arrival in this beautiful town now tainted in my eyes by its cruel officialdom. As I was going into the health office, a Nakhwa pharmacy owner unceremoniously introduced himself. He said he had just been appointed to supervise primary health care in the province. He demanded to know why we had 'broken the law' by opening an 'illegal unit' in Bani Salim. I was speechless, but pushed past him into the crowded inner sanctum. Dr Thaalib's deputy was ruling the roost in the absence of his superior. Medical consultations were in progress. Despite having no qualifications, the deputy appeared to have also become a locum.

He too immediately berated me as an 'anarchist'. Salah's health post was quite unsuitable and we had no right to open it without his office's approval. I realized nothing was going to come of this conversation and we would have to await the return of Dr Thaalib from America. Before going, however, I wanted confirmation that Khalid Tahir, the Zahir drug dealer, had indeed been appointed to the health post instead of our trained man. Ideally I wanted to get a photocopy of the order so as to show officials in the ministry in Sana'a. I forced myself to smile. Could I please have a copy?

He smiled back at me. 'This is a Yemeni matter, not the concern of foreigners.' 'On the contrary', I beamed. 'We have a responsibility to help in the training of health workers. In the interests of improving co-operation with our Yemeni brothers it is useful for our organization to know of other training endeavours in the province so we do not duplicate your own efforts. We are very interested to hear that young men like Khalid Tahir can become nurses.' The deputy interrupted me. 'He is not a nurse.' I sighed with relief, imagining our stance had caused him to back down. 'He is a medical assistant.'

This was even more far-fetched. In the ministerial hierarchy a medical assistant ranks higher than a nurse and is better trained. By pre-empting us, and presumably offering yet more of his ill-gotten pharmaceutical wealth, Khalid Tahir had further improved his qualifications. I swallowed hard. This was surprising news, I said, for we had understood that only the Health Manpower Institute in Sana'a could train such high level cadres.

Tension between us was mounting and the whole room fell silent so as not to miss the conflict. 'You are again mistaken. We train nurses and medical assistants from this office. Khalid Tahir has completed a recognized course of instruction in our hospital and is a fully qualified medical assistant.'

The ball was back in my court and I pressed on. 'Could we have this in writing? This information does not correspond with that given our organization by the ministry in Sana'a.' My adversary exploded. 'You are calling me a liar! I give you orders, I do not take orders from *nasraanis*. Get out of my office!' I did so, saying we would have to inform the ministry of the unorthodox appointment. The deputy had lost his cool and, in Yemeni terms, lost face by doing so. I had barely managed not to shout myself. Amidst the collapse of our plans I could at least content myself with a narrow moral victory.

Abdul Kariim and I wandered aimlessly down the main street of Nakhwa. He suddenly remembered that he had been told he needed a dozen copies of his photo so that the health office could complete the necessary number of files on him. We popped into one of the many photo studios and while he gravely posed before an improbable Alpine backdrop, I looked at the snaps of previous customers. I saw a beaming Khalid Tahir and asked the studio owner who he was. He told me he was a doctor from Zahir. 'He is not a doctor!' I exploded, 'but a liar and a hypocrite!' Abdul Kariim suggested I cool down and we went off to lunch in Bayt al Baydani. The young serving girl was in tears as she went about her work. That morning she had lost her second, and only remaining, child. No, she had not taken the child to the hospital, five minutes' walk away. The hospital, she said, was not for the poor.

Dead children are sorely missed. Whenever Yemeni parents are asked how many children they have dead infants are included in the total. Further questioning may be needed to determine how many are still alive. However, infant deaths are so commonplace, and women's burdens so great, that there is little time available for them to grieve. Dead children are bundled into the ground with little ceremony, only a very few male relatives attending. It was not surprising to see a bereaved mother carrying on work regardless of her loss.

I returned to our car with the despondent Abdul Kariim. We drove past the sullen soldiers on the outskirts of Nakhwa and I was picking my way round a succession of hair-pin bends when a man popped out from behind a corrugated iron shop and waved us to a stop. He had heard reports that a foreign doctor was on the road and wanted my help. He showed me a plastic bag full of tonics, drips and ampoules of antibiotics and vitamins which had cost him £30. Could I come to his village and inject the boy for whom the drugs were intended? I said I was not a doctor but that my Yemeni friend had experience in health. We got out, squatted on a nearby cliff edge and began unpacking the bag of drugs. We explained how an unscrupulous and ignorant pharmacist had taken advantage of our companion. We were going to suggest he try and get his money back when the man declared himself convinced and suddenly threw the whole bag down the side of the mountain. Such flamboyant demonstrations of trust in our sincerity were repeated on several occasions. It was always highly gratifying.

That evening I telephoned Brian. Having no experience of the wiles of Yemeni bureaucrats, our optimistic co-ordinator seemed to think my account of events in Nakhwa exaggerated. He agreed to go to the ministry to complain about the displacement of the man we had helped train. He rang back the next day and told me that the senior official administering the primary health care department had called Nakhwa and been told by Dr Thaalib's deputy that he could not remember seeing any letter appointing Khalid Tahir. Dr Thaalib's deputy was ordered to search through the register of all correspondence issued from the Nakhwa office and eventually rang back the ministry and confirmed there was no record of such an order. Why then, the departmental head had asked, did the British seem to believe in its existence? He was persuaded the mistake lay in a 'misunderstanding' and told Brian the matter was trivial, a regrettable consequence of my poor comprehension of Arabic.

If the act of one branch of a ministry, endorsed by the governor himself, could be hidden from the central authorities how could we possibly thwart the wily Khalid Tahir? As long as he, and he alone, held the paper he had power and could open the Zahir unit. Abdul Kariim said we had to get hold of a copy of the order and returned to Zahir to speak to Khalid Tahir. Somehow, he persuaded his friend to lend him the letter. He rushed back to Ahad, the nearest place with a photocopier. We immediately sent a copy on to Sana'a.

A further interesting problem arose, necessitating another, but this time more pleasant journey. As yet no Yemeni authorities had paid anything towards the cost of training the nine women studying in Ahad nor taken any official notice of their course. Out of the blue a letter arrived from Sana'a lamenting the fact that it had been reported that the trainees in Ahad were improperly attired. Henceforth the women would be obliged to wear an official uniform. Each would require two sets of trousers, skirt, jacket and veil.

When informed of their impropriety the women were indignant for they were already modestly dressed in terms of local convention. They did not want to have to wear trousers under full dresses and a veil and especially did not want to have to pay for them. An intriguing clash between different Yemeni notions of demure couture had arisen. Tihamis, unlike highland women, are not accustomed to wearing trousers under dresses. They wear longer dresses than mountain women and need no other garment to hide their legs. The aunt of Sayyida, the youngest trainee, sent word it would be highly shameful for her to wear trousers. If she was made to wear them she would be withdrawn from the course.

Much diplomacy was required. I first discussed the problem with Nuriya, Sayyida's cousin, who had worked in the hospital for years. Nuriya, the daughter of a man once renowned for his piety and religious knowledge, was the first woman in the area to complete primary school. As she is now in her mid-twenties, it is unlikely she will ever marry. She insists, as do all such women, that she does not want to and is perfectly happy looking after her widowed mother. When I spoke to her she was feeling miffed that she was not on the training course. She was obviously keen to blame Elizabeth for preventing her studying. I thought it best not to contradict her version of events. For Nuriya can be annoyingly self-willed and over the years had exasperated all project workers and some Yemeni colleagues.

She had recently started reaping benefits from her spiritual capital, the mantle of sanctity inherited from her father. Her work is extremely demanding due to the number of patients she deals with and the mindless bureaucratic tasks imposed on her. Whenever things get too much for her, or she has had an argument with another hospital worker, she stays away from work for a few days. She always sends a note saying she is fasting. Pious women are forever fasting, either to make up for days they could not fast (such as when menstruating) the previous Ramadan, or to earn extra merit through the optional fasts approved in Islam. Nuriya could, like other pious women, work as normal despite fasting but this option was never mentioned. No one dared doubt her right to be off work through fasting. For us foreigners her sudden absences from work were harder to accept. Elizabeth had often been angered to turn up to work on a busy market day only to receive news of another fast.

Nuriya eventually agreed to talk to her mother, Sayyida's aunt and guardian, about the trouser crisis. I pointed out that no one was asking Sayyida to show her legs and suggested that we could perhaps compromise by making her dress slightly longer than regulations prescribed. She passed on these thoughts and word came back that Sayyida could get a uniform as long as she did not have to wear it on a daily basis. This accorded with the preferences of all the other women who wanted to wear it only for their graduation ceremony or to receive important visitors. None wanted to have to wear a veil throughout working hours. The ministry had not offered to pay for the uniforms and after much argument amongst ourselves we agreed to pay for the cost of one suit for each woman, to lend them the cost of another and to deduct money from their monthly stipends for the remainder of the course.

All the trainees were experienced dressmakers and some had been sewing for a living after being divorced or widowed. But none had the expertise to sew such a complicated series of garments. It became clear we would have to go to Hodeidah to a proper tailor. This created much excitement as only two of the women had ever been there in their lives. Sayyida's guardian announced herself scandalized and said under no circumstances could her niece leave Ahad. Problems mounted when Ali Ahmad said he and the two hospital vaccinators would have to come to supervise 'the girls'.

The presence of these unrelated men would be regarded as shameful and would lessen the chances of some of the women getting their male kin to approve of the trip. Acrimonious discussion raged for days. We could have simply measured the women and telephoned the order to Hodeidah but the women had set their hearts on a rare outing. We thought widening their geographical horizons would help to boost their confidence and ability to deal with the male world. Eventually it was agreed that we would take the women in our two cars, that Graham and I would do the driving, and Maryam, the Sudanese teacher, would come as chaperone. Maryam brought all her formidable presence to bear on Ali Ahmad who, until the end, insisted he had to come as he was in charge of the women.

We set off early in the morning with the women jockeying for position in the two cars. I was relieved when Maryam resolutely seated herself between me and the predatory Nabiila. We were making good time along the fast highway when Graham's car suddenly developed a fault. We tied a rope between our two vehicles and proceeded down the highway at a snail's pace until we came to a garage. Spare parts had to be fetched, after which I ferried the women to the hospital in the town where we were stranded. We ended up staying for four hours before the problem was fixed.

While the Ahadi women were entertained by local women employed in the hospital Graham and I had lunch with the director. We had a wide-ranging discussion of health problems. He sympathized with our difficulties having to work with the Nakhwa health office and said how glad he was that his hospital lay just inside the jurisdiction of Hodeidah province. He was obviously well acquainted with the ideas of primary health care and had visited health projects in other

Arab countries. He said that although private pharmacists had a role to play making available drugs not provided by the ministry, they had to be closely watched. By using connections in Hodeidah and Sana'a he had closed down illegal pharmacies and now there was only one outside the hospital gate. The owner knew from bitter experience that if he illegally sold any drug requiring a doctor's prescription he would find himself being escorted to prison by soldiers. I asked the director if supplies of infant vaccine ever ran out. He was hurt and I regretted my gaucheness. 'Of course not! How could I call myself a *mudiir* if I allowed such an important service to be disrupted?' Why, I wondered, had our former programme co-ordinator not investigated this hospital and its director while speeding through the Tihama in search of a likely site for a new project?

The ever suspicious guards at the last checkpoint before Hodeidah looked startled at the sight of two *nasraani* men driving Yemeni women but were re-assured by Maryam's presence and let us pass. I dropped the women at the tailor's and went to do some shopping of my own. When I returned the women were very excited. The police were after me! A patrol car had just called in response to a report that a *nasraani* had kidnapped a group of Yemeni women. The shy Ahadi women had not dared to try to disabuse the police of this notion. The police had my registration number and had gone away to look for me. Fortunately we made a quick getaway and went to hide in the *suq*.

Shopping was the real reason for our trip and the recurring topic of conversation all day. As bidden, I dropped the women off outside a row of goldsmiths' shops. They were reluctant to move off although Maryam had firmly told them they had to hurry as they only had a short time to do their shopping. After much whispering, one of the bolder women stepped forward. Could I lend them all a few hundred rials against their next stipend? I had foolishly not anticipated this request and had not brought much BSDA money. I handed over my own cash and was naturally concerned to remember exactly how much each had borrowed. I had only just learned all their names and identification was hard now that all were dressed in the hideous all-enveloping black *sharshafs* they had borrowed.

Thus, pen in hand, I stood in one of the main shopping streets of Hodeidah counting out hundred rial notes for a group of veiled Yemeni women while the bolder ones teased me for my inability to identify them. This created an enormous crowd of passers-by and I was greatly relieved when the women finally went off to shop.

A few weeks later the women had to wear their uniforms as Dr Thaalib, back from the USA, sent word he would be passing through Ahad. Maryam set the women to scrubbing their room and removing all the litter which had gathered round the rest of the still uncompleted mother and child extension. Dr Thaalib and his entourage swept into the room, intimidating the veiled women. He began quizzing them about what they had learnt. He asked one what she would do in the event of a woman requiring a caesarean. When she replied she would send the woman to Hodeidah Dr Thaalib rolled his eyes in horror and told us how stupid the woman was. Her answer had been quite correct. The journey to Hodeidah is straightforward and painless. There are no facilities for carrying out surgery in Ahad and our experienced BSDA midwives had never dared attempt a caesarean in the chaotic and septic environment of the Ahad hospital. Dr Thaalib went on to ask how malaria was caused. A woman replied that mosquitoes were the vector, a fact not known by the great majority of Tihamis. The doctor was dissatisfied. 'Yes, but what kind of mosquito?' None of the women knew the word 'anopheles'. 'They will have to work much harder', he told Maryam sternly.

I had dysentery and a fever when another group of flying visitors arrived shortly afterwards. The deputy director of the hospital rang my bell to tell me two Americans had arrived and wished to speak to me. The Americans were in a hurry and I had to come at once. I dressed quickly and had an exhilarating motor-bike ride across town. I came into the *mudiir*'s office to find a man and a woman dripping sweat and having their words interpreted by an Adeni woman. I apologized for my lateness and explained I was ill. The Americans looked worried they would catch something nasty and asked what the matter was. When I replied that I thought my fever was probably not malarial the man was relieved.

'Oh, if that's the case, I can shake hands with you.' Bewildered by this response, I accepted the woman's card and was further confused to find she was a health systems adviser. I felt quite inadequate not having a flashy card of my own to brandish. Her colleague, she explained, was a development economist. This left me no wiser and the woman had trouble explaining herself. She appeared in a daze. I later learned she used a lot of valium.

She told me of a great advance in community health in Yemen. The US Agency for International Development had proposed to the YAR that AID assume a managerial role in the development of primary health care in the five of the country's ten provinces which did not already have foreign health teams. When they mentioned which provinces, it seemed no coincidence that all were provinces either adjoining the sensitive borders with Saudi Arabia or South Yemen or areas in which the government was still fighting with tribal leaders to establish its legitimacy. Why, I cynically asked myself, if the Americans wished to gather intelligence about these strategic areas, where their presence would otherwise be regarded with great suspicion, did they not send more astute people than these two?

The new programme, tentatively entitled the Child Survival Program, would be the largest American project in the country. High level committees would be set up and two training centres in each province would train male and female primary health care workers. The Americans would pay for everything. The Ministry of Health was sure to approve and, in the meantime, the directors of health in the provinces concerned were each being taken to America for English language and administration courses. The Americans were travelling round the country visiting possible training sites as part of a 'base-line survey'. They had come from Sana'a specially to see us.

This was the first we had heard of the scheme. Why, I asked, were USAID contemplating working in Ahad if they wished, as they had said, to add to, not compete with, other assistance programmes? The Americans smiled knowingly at each other and gave me no answer. They asked about my colleagues and our work. I began to answer but soon noticed

the woman appeared to be taking little in. They glanced at
their watches and said they had to be off. It was still not half
past ten in the morning and they had been in the town for only
half an hour. I suggested that they, together with Ali Ahmad,
might like to come to our office where we could talk more
comfortably and freely. They allowed themselves to be
persuaded but said there was no need to take Ali Ahmad along.
We got into their air-conditioned 4WD vehicle and drove to
our house. When I noticed that the driver was staying in the
vehicle, I invited him in for some tea. As he began to get out
the Americans said he would be happier where he was. The
Adeni woman was told to instruct him to stay put.

Caroline, my new colleague, came back from her visiting
but was equally unable to get information from the Americans.
How, she asked, would our endeavours fit in with the
Americans' plan? This would be determined 'at a higher level'
following an 'in-depth' analysis and 'demographic studies'. I
tried to explain the basis of our discontent with the Nakhwa
health office and why people in the Tihama felt similarly
estranged. What, I asked, was the benefit of sending people
such as Dr Thaalib to the United States for extensive periods? I
was told our adversary had greatly benefited and this had been
demonstrated in the course of an 'intensive de-briefing'
following his return from his previous trip.

Having gathered all the relevant facts, our visitors got up to
go. They left us wondering about our futures and we were to
remain in suspense for months. It became clear that factions in
various Sana'a bureaucracies were opposed to the new
American scheme while others were enthusiastic in their
support.

While these intrigues went on above our heads, work had to
go on. Another trip became necessary as Abdul Kariim and
Salah, six months after their graduation, were still not on the
civil service payroll. Officials in Nakhwa had not even passed
on their files to Sana'a as they were obliged to do. My
colleagues in Ahad agreed it might be worth seeing if I could
achieve anything by accompanying the two men to Sana'a. I
could also continue the fight against the appointment of the
usurper in Zahir. I set off, feeling that all I was doing in
Yemen was to spend time on fruitless drives listening to the

many bootleg music cassettes I had bought since arriving in the country.

Neither man had ever been to the capital before and Abdul Kariim had never left the Tihama. I greatly looked forward to the privilege of sharing their reactions as they first saw the diversity and beauty of their own country. However, in Nakhwa I almost had to turn back in disappointment as a soldier became convinced he had spotted a flaw in my pass from the security authorities. He interpreted it to say that I was entitled to travel from Sana'a to Ahad, but not to do the opposite journey. I was arrested and taken to the security headquarters where I was grilled as to the purpose of my journey. When I foolishly said I was going to Sana'a to help my colleagues secure employment, I was told this was none of my business and I was to return to Ahad at once. In future if I wished to leave Ahad for any reason I had to apply for permission and list my reasons for wanting to leave my place of employment. A plain-clothes officer was detailed to make sure I headed out of town in the direction of the Tihama. He rifled through the cassettes in the glove box and put some in his jacket. He asked me where his *qat* was, a clear hint that if I gave him money I would be allowed to go on to Sana'a.

I surprised him by suddenly pulling up outside the health office. As he lunged across to grab me, I opened the door and leapt out. A fierce argument ensued inside the health office. The security man alleged my residence permit had expired and I was in the country illegally. I replied by accusing him of theft and demanding bribes. Eventually, after losing my temper in a most unseemly manner, I was told I could continue my journey if I got another permission. This involved a visit to several offices and took two hours. After several drafts a piece of paper was finally made out which authorized me to go to Sana'a whenever I wanted as long as I was driving the Daihatsu Rocky, the registration number of which was written down. I was sent to the commander of the Nakhwa garrison to secure a final stamp to validate this new permission. A colonel from the south of the country took one look at the document and burst out laughing. He spoke rather good English. 'These people here are crazy. I have no authority to endorse such a permission. In any case there is nothing wrong with the other one. You can go.' I continued using my original permission and handing out photocópies at every checkpoint. I often wondered how many trees have to be felled to provide paper for the masses of photocopied permissions handed over to bored young conscripts manning the many checkpoints on the highways of Yemen.

After Nakhwa the road descends to 1,000 feet above sea level before beginning an awesome climb to almost 10,000 feet. Neither of my colleagues had ever been to such an altitude and grew fearful as our ascent seemed never to end. They whispered together, wondering whether they would be able to breathe and were relieved when we emerged on to the plain of Amran. Alongside the road a husband and wife were working together in a field, a sight which is not common in the north Tihama. Abdul Kariim drew Salah's attention to this strange occurrence. What could it mean? 'Perhaps they don't have any bulls here', suggested Salah, 'and have to use women instead.' They were buzzing with excitement when we reached Sana'a. We went at once to see Tahrir Square, the centre of the modern city. Like other visitors from the countryside, they had Polaroid snaps taken of themselves standing stiffly beside the tank which began the 'glorious and eternal revolution' of 26 September, 1962. They stopped in amazement in front of a neon sign and spent several minutes marvelling at the alternation of letters and images.

The next days were frustrating. Each man had in his possession six identical files containing multiple photocopies of everything known about them by the state. Yet they were sent from office to office, from ministry to ministry, by officials who themselves appeared not to understand the system. They eventually heard a rumour that, as an economy measure, the president had ordered that no one be admitted to the civil service list, no matter how pressing their claim, for another six months. Salah was told not to raise his hopes at all for he would never be employed as he did not have a primary school certificate.

On Friday we went on a *dowra*, an expedition-cum-picnic to enjoy the beauties of the countryside around the capital. As we walked through villages and fields local people were, as always, congenial and happy to chat. Abdul Kariim and Salah, still farmers as much as health workers, were delighted to learn about the different grains and fruits of the region and to discuss differences in their own agricultural almanac and star calendar. We stopped while Salah and I chewed *qat* before wandering back in the direction of our car. On the way we were waylaid by a group of veiled women returning from a tiring journey to fetch water. When they saw my *qat* bulge they stopped in amazement. With much giggling, they began to tease me. 'You should be ashamed of yourself! Educated 'experts' should know better! Yemeni men, like your worthless companions, are lazy enough as it is without foreigners encouraging their *qat* habit.' In vain did I plead it was Friday and that chewing is a justified pastime provided it is not indulged in on a daily basis. Salah laughed at my discomfiture. Abdul Kariim, a resolute opponent of *qat*, was at pains to assure the women he completely agreed with them.

Another matter detained me in the ministry. The Ahad hospital had run out of road to health cards just as local mothers were beginning to see their importance, look after them and to regard them as important legal documents which would safeguard their child's rights. The provincial office seemed unconcerned and we had debated whether to have the cards printed. Individuals in our other projects accused us of the error of 'back-stopping', covering the deficiencies of the ministry. The matter had been earnestly discussed at a six-monthly conference. Eventually we were given grudging permission to have 5,000 printed. This we had done, and now wished to have at least tacit ministry approval. Clearly the Yemenis did not wish to have the shortcomings of their state pointed out, but then neither did we wish to be in a position to be accused by our enemies in Nakhwa of taking matters into our own hands. The director of the mother and child health department, the only female departmental head, had to be informed. Finding her was not easy and only on my third visit to the ministry did I spot her as she rushed along a corridor. I raced after her, trying, in competition with several groups of her colleagues, to catch her ear. I thought I had succeeded when her door was slammed unceremoniously in my face. We decided not to bother seeking permission.

A conflict arose with Brian, the Sana'a co-ordinator, and

Hassan, his newly-appointed Yemeni assistant. We had heard of a 'fixer' employed by the American health project in Hodeidah who might arrange for our men to get on the payroll. The co-ordinator was adamant that to pay bribes would encourage corruption. It would, he insisted, 'set the wrong example'. Again the moral self-righteousness of developmentalism came home to me. The idea that the actions of our tiny organization were noticed by anybody was improbable. None of our Yemeni counterparts in the other projects had ever become salaried without powerful inter-mediaries pulling strings or paying money. I argued hard and eventually it was agreed that our project could give a limited amount of money to our two health workers on condition that they decided how best to spend it to get their salaries. Such sleight of mind kept consciences clear and avoided the heinous sin of 'interventionism'. I gave Salah and Abdul Kariim the fixer's number and they went round to see him.

They were unused to the sophistication of city life. When the fixer said, euphemistically, that he would like some *samn wa 'asl* (ghee and honey – both highly prized and expensive *baladi* foods) they took him at his word. Probably he wanted money, but they shopped round for bottles of ghee and honey which they took to the Sana'a office of the Hodeidah project. They thought, as I did, that the offering should be discreetly hidden in a plastic bag and slipped under the fixer's desk. They told me, however, that the fixer had asked for the bottles to be put on his desk, a visible demonstration to his American and Yemeni colleagues of his power. He took their files and said he would be in touch.

Before leaving my colleagues in Sana'a I secured an interview with the director of the primary health care department. I presented a letter of complaint about the Zahir pharmacist, clipped to which was a copy of the order from the Nakhwa office appointing him. The departmental head rang Dr Thaalib. For my benefit, he berated him for defying the national health policy and appointing such an unsuitable person. He hung up and assured me the matter was solved. I asked if we might have this in writing and was told this was not necessary. Dr Thaalib was a good friend of his and a loyal servant of the ministry.

On my return to Ahad I learned that the extension to the Ahad hospital was finally ready to really be opened. But how were the rooms to be allocated and a system of patient flow arranged? Another meeting in my room was convened. As before, *qat* and melon seeds were abundantly consumed and I was left with a difficult cleaning up job. Graham, the increasingly embittered co-ordinator, insisted on opening the meeting, and trying to remind those present of the basis on which BSDA had solicited money from funders. He could not make himself understood and eyes turned to me as the speaker of more comprehensible Arabic. I said we hoped there would be a room in which Nuriya could register and weigh children and give health advice, a vaccination room, a room for ante-natal check-ups, a delivery room and a doctor's room. Especially important was that a room be allocated to dehydrated children so that they could lie under a fan for a few hours, receive oral rehydration solution and gather strength for the journey home.

Everyone seemed amenable to our proposals except for Ali Ahmad to whom we had earlier outlined our views. He surprised us by insisting that he should have an office in the new building. He was the supervisor of the *murshidaat* (female health guides) and had to be near them. Space was short and there were not enough rooms to be able to afford the luxury of a rehydration room. He would set up his office alongside the ante-natal examination room.

The implications of his sudden claim were absurd. How could a man, without any health training, be in charge of the nine women? How could he have an office, which would no doubt soon be filled with idle men, at the end of a building which had been designed specifically to allow women to come to the hospital without undue embarrassment? I did my best to explain this to the meeting and sought allies amongst the women present. They agreed it would be difficult to persuade local women to come to the hospital for ante-natal checkups and deliveries if there were strange males milling about. Ali Ahmad countered. 'We are all one family in this town. We all know each other. Foreigners can not be expected to understand this.' Women would come to the new facility in droves. Susan, who for months had been hearing of the social obstacles

preventing women from coming to the hospital, was rendered
speechless.

The discussion dragged on for hours. We knew Ali Ahmad
was trying to consolidate his ambiguous position in the
hospital hierarchy by acquiring the status conferred by having
an office of his own. We were prepared to humour him in his
belief that he commanded the women. As a compromise, we
proposed that he set up an office in an out-building which
Uthman and Lutf, the vaccinators, would be vacating when
they moved into the new building. This appeared to satisfy
everybody, but the resilient Ali Ahmad fought back. He had
just been ordered by the provincial office, so he told us, to
earmark this room for food aid. His resolution was implacable.
We talked for hours and hours but reached no other item on
the agenda. Discussion became aimless and the meeting broke
up. Another was arranged for a few days hence.

Relations between us and Ali Ahmad deteriorated from this
day onwards. He blamed me, as the spokesman for our team,
for having thwarted his ambition. The next day he came to see
me in the evening just as I was unwinding from another hot
day and writing letters on my word processor. His arrival
meant I had to quickly turn off the computer which was being
hidden from those in the town who might maliciously report
us as spies to the security authorities. Ali Ahmad chews a great
amount of *qat*, probably equivalent to four times his nominal
salary. At this time of day habitual chewers can become
depressed, loquacious and often rather incoherent. Ali Ahmad
rambled on about how sad he was that he did not enjoy such
good relations with us as he said he had had with our
predecessors. I suggested that differences were inevitable now
that we were trying to implement things, not just planning and
talking as before. No, he sighed, the problem was much
deeper than this. I was an imperialist, sticking my nose into
matters which were not my concern. We had no right to take
drugs up to Salah's unit. This was his responsibility. I should
not be going out of town into the countryside without him
and without his permission.

I protested that he was a very busy man, occupied twelve
hours a day handling the huge correspondence generated by
the health centre and its constant budgetary problems. I had

very little to do and, thanks be to God and to Ali Ahmad's help, could now speak enough colloquial Arabic to make myself understood. Also, though of course we would keep him informed, no one had told us we needed his permission in advance to go out of the town. It was not clear that he was in charge of primary health care for this was the responsibility of trainer supervisors appointed by the ministry.

He was not impressed. I eventually got rid of him but two days later he came back in the same whining mood and repeated himself. I began to be both angered by and sorry for him. Here was an undoubtedly intelligent man from a humble family in the grip of overweening ambition. In trying to aggrandize himself, he was alienating his peers. He had no real friends, merely those associated with the hospital, or aspirants for hospital jobs, who flattered him as they would any other sheikh-on-the-make. His pettily dictatorial acts were highly annoying. He allowed no one else to draft correspondence as he claimed their classical Arabic was deficient. Whenever he was not present in the hospital he locked the telephone into a filing cabinet, thus preventing both incoming and outgoing calls. He displayed his authority by carrying an unwieldy bunch of keys attached to the belt which supported his ever-immaculate sarongs or ersatz safari suit. We, and his Yemeni colleagues, were always searching for him to get doors and cupboards opened.

To prepare ourselves for the next meeting, we discussed how to seal the breach with Ali Ahmad. Realizing we would have to abandon hopes to use the end room as a rehydration centre for children, we agreed on a compromise. Ali Ahmad did not get his office but neither did we have our way for the room was given to Yahya and Yusuf, the Ahadi nurses on whom we had pinned our last desperate hopes of starting a training course for men. In pique, Ali Ahmad claimed that the keys for the room had been lost so I bought a padlock and screwed a bolt to the parts of the door frame not yet eaten by termites. We kept a key, the nurses kept one and one more was added to Ali Ahmad's impressive bunch.

We took the opportunity of this get-together to try to tackle the issue of language. I had now been at many meetings and was becoming slicker in Yemeni rhetorical performance. I was learning to litter sentences with buzz words such as 'co-operation', 'co-ordination', 'planning', 'progress', 'cadre', 'cit-izen', 'unity', 'revolution' and the English word 'routine'. 'We must improve co-ordination and co-operation between us', I began. 'We must speak one language in order to explain primary health care to the citizens. All cadres, including ourselves, should stop calling the trainees *binaat* (girls, virgins) or *qaabilaat* (midwives).'

These terms are often pejorative and I suggested we try to use the official term *murshidaat*, a word redolent with Islamic connotations. By referring to primary health care units as 'hospitals', or allowing the citizens to do so, we encouraged unreal expectations of the services about to be provided. I said we should popularize the phrase 'health unit' and use the same terminology to describe the health services as people hear on television. The *murshidaat* and the young men were enthusiastic and talked together about the issue. After much teasing, they began to use the new terms. However, the befuddled old *mudiir* had not the slightest idea what we were on about. Primary health care was none of his business.

We hoped that a system of health talks could be arranged to take advantage of the fact that scores of adults had to hang around waiting to be seen by Caroline, our doctor. The building had been designed with a large verandah for such a pedagogic purpose. We offered to buy benches to provide seating for patients and to keep them from crowding into the doctor's room. Would it not be best, we suggested, if those in the hospital took turns to try to educate this captive audience? We suggested that Ali Ahmad prepare the roster and the list of subjects to be talked about.

Ali Ahmad immediately spoke up on behalf of the *murshidaat*. 'Our women are too shy to do this. It is not part of our tradition for women to speak in public.' 'But', I replied, 'all over the republic, thanks to the revolution, ideas of what women can and cannot do are changing. You yourself have seen how in the Ibb hospital women stand up in front of strangers and teach them how to bring up healthy children.' He was not impressed and succeeded in blocking the idea. It was agreed we could buy the benches and I arranged this with a local carpenter. No one in the hospital would help me carry them across town to the new building so Susan and I put the benches in place. The seating was used by those waiting to have their children examined but also provided display place for those we had not wished to encourage: the young girls who, rather than attend school, hang round the hospital peddling chocolates, chewing gum, biscuits, crisps, sweets and other undesirable items of the modern diet we had hoped to dissuade people from regarding as nutritious.

Diplomacy was called for when it came to putting up posters round the new building. From visiting other health centres in Yemen we knew that colourful pictures with succinct captions would best draw the attention of hospital users. Somehow we also had to respect the views of those unused to pictorial representation and heed the conviction amongst the educated elite that refined language and immaculate calligraphy is the best way to interest and uplift their compatriots.

None of the men in the health centre seemed interested in covering the blank walls so I bought timber and put up some noticeboards in the new building. Nuriya, now increasingly resentful of the authority being claimed by the *murshidaat*, had very fixed ideas on what was required in her room. She put up a large picture of the president and produced a poster she had been working on for weeks. Under a stylized eagle, symbol of the Yemen Arab Republic, were thousands of tiny hand-written words, all in classical Arabic. It was a summation of the knowledge she had gained, a proud, but sad, display of her erudition. As a visual aid to stimulate parents to learn about health, it was useless.

A better-presented series of posters were drawn by Zaynab, a new arrival in the hospital. Zaynab was born in Mecca to parents from a small village an hour's drive from Ahad. She had studied for nine years in Saudi Arabia and had left her family behind to come home because she wished to 'serve my country' and become a nurse. Her achievements and abilities eclipsed those of the Ahadi women and especially threatened Nuriya. Fortunately, we had sufficient wall space to put up both Nuriya's and Zaynab's posters, together with the best of those collecting dust in our office.

Ali Ahmad looked through our posters about bilharzia and

announced his preference for one produced by the ministry over others made by a German aid organization. The Yemeni poster lacked pictures, explained nothing of the cycle of the bilharzia schistosome and was little more than a series of stern injunctions, implying that women, as water collectors, were responsible for the continuation of the disease. The series of German posters were very eye-catching, explained bilharzia in simple language with clear diagrams and contained the single most important piece of advice to prevent the illness: if water drawn from a polluted source is left untouched for twenty-four hours then it may safely be used. We compromised and put up both.

The posters soon commanded interest. Some were horrified by the graphic representation of a man squatting to defecate alongside a stream from which water was being gathered, while others applauded its frankness and told everyone present to take heed. A UNICEF collage showing mothers from a dozen countries happily breast-feeding their babies was much admired. Interest among men did not flag even when Nuriya felt compelled to stick some tape over the breasts of an unclad Indonesian. Groups also gathered in front of the International Baby Food Action Network poster and stared at the pathetic sight of a marasmic, bottle-fed baby. I watched as younger literate men read the caption and told their astonished companions, that the waif at death's door was a Yemeni.

On the direction of my medically qualified colleagues, and with help from Salah, I had been preparing brief leaflets, using local colloquial language, on a number of subjects. These we also stuck up. I was proud of the malaria leaflet. It had an eye-catching picture of a mosquito to reinforce the idea that it was the bite of this insect, and not eating particular foods, which caused malaria. It had a picture of a repellent mosquito coil to correct the belief that Indian incense sticks, recently arrived in some shops, were specifically designed to deter mosquitoes. The leaflet used all the words by which the illness is known in different parts of our catchment area and tried to correct the widespread belief that malaria and hepatitis are the same illness. We advised people to try to cover themselves at night and to keep chloroquine tablets to hand, explained dosages and said that injections were hardly ever necessary.

Chloroquine is a relatively benign medication and we suggested that whenever children exhibited malaria symptoms during the winter mosquito season they should give them tablets. Doing so was in violation of ministry policy which impractically insists that no medication can be prescribed if a blood test has not been done. It was as absurd as the regulation that no one was to be treated for rabies unless they came to hospital with the head of the dog which had bitten them. Our health centre was sited many hours away from most of those who depended on it. Many visitors came to the hospital only because they thought they or their children had malaria. Some could not take tests ordered for them because of the large amounts of money which the hospital administrators demanded. We thought it good advice for people to diagnose and treat themselves, for in almost all cases malaria, if treated, is not life threatening.

Simon and Elizabeth had had strong views about malaria and had called me 'irresponsible' for refusing to take prophylactic doses of chloroquine. Their rather exaggerated fears of malaria seemed typical of doctors who had never had the disease, nor lived in areas where it is endemic. I saw the same attitude displayed by foreign-trained Yemeni doctors from highland areas where there is also no malaria. They saw the answer to malaria in persuading people to take permanent prophylaxis. I had had four progressively less severe attacks of malaria, despite prophylaxis, and believed that I had acquired some immunity and that the dangers to my liver and kidney from repeated prophylaxis were greater than the risks of getting malaria. Fortunately Caroline, who had studied tropical medicine, had a more questioning attitude towards the received ideas of her profession.

Ali Ahmad was unimpressed with the malaria leaflet, saying that no one could understand it as all the Arabic was 'wrong'. Hassan, BSDA's administrative assistant, came to Ahad on his first visit. He was also shocked by the grammar and syntax and spent two hours 'correcting', and greatly lengthening, the leaflet. My efforts to persuade this sophisticated urbanite that rural people could barely read and should therefore be addressed in simple, albeit graceless language, were quite in vain. In contrast, Dr Tawfiq, the sympathetic Somali, was impressed by the information and persuaded his Sudanese colleagues to stick up this leaflet in their part of the hospital and to hand out copies. The next day, however, all the leaflets had disappeared. The advice contained in it was directly threatening one of the main sources of income for pharmacists and their friends in the health centre.

A crisis in our relations with Graham was imminent. He had been showing signs of depression as his two-year period of employment drew to an end. He hinted he would like his colleagues to recommend an extension. The London office pressed us to either decide to do so, or to draft a job description to assist the search for his successor. Again and again Caroline, Susan and I dodged the unpleasant issue while Graham sat at the computer and tinkered with the fictional document describing his untenable role. All the diversionary activities which his predecessor had dabbled in were once more dutifully listed. Psycho-babble was added to describe the co-ordinator's role in 'personnel management', 'group management techniques' and 'project orientation'.

The problem had to be faced. None of us wanted Graham to continue in the project after his contract came to an end. We had decided that the 'strengthening of the health centre', at least in terms of rubber-stamping receipts and negotiating the hospital's annual budget, had to be dropped. This was Yemeni business and our involvement in it was sending all the wrong signals about our objectives. Having reached this decision we went on to look at the gallimaufry of non-existent tasks detailed in the job description and came to the conclusion that a viable job did not exist. We decided not to seek a successor but to abolish the post when Graham left. A few weeks later our colleagues in Kahima made the same decision. Their blow to Helen's morale was even greater as they refused to allow her to use the title of 'co-ordinator' or speak on their behalf for the months remaining of her contract.

On the surface, Graham took the decision well and bravely argued that it was a conclusion which he himself had reached. At a deeper level the effect on his morale and general health was harder to judge. For some time he had been intermittently unwell and thus at first we were not unduly concerned when he came down with a mysterious fever. After a few days resting in Ahad he started taking chloroquine but his condition did not improve as we all prepared to go to Sana'a for another six-monthly conference. He was exhausted by the rough journey and in Sana'a complained of acute sensitivity to light. We drove to the Thawra hospital and Caroline introduced herself to the over-worked receptionist in the casualty department. She explained Graham's symptoms. Due to the risk of meningitis and cerebral malaria a blood test should be done at once.

The receptionist asked for 6,000 rials (£600) before Graham could be attended to. We knew the Thawra was expensive but were staggered that patients could be expected to carry this amount of cash with them. We counted our money and found we had only 3,000 rials. Around us unattended accident victims sat shivering. There were no blankets except for the one we had brought for Graham to huddle into. Other patients and their relatives were in a similar situation. They had to decide whether they could raise enough money, or whether their patient was up to being taken to the less prestigious, but cheaper, hospital funded by the Kuwaitis.

I pressed forward and pleaded with the receptionist. I used obsequious and non-Yemeni phrases of the kind being picked up and used by young men who have worked abroad or watched Egyptian soap operas. Could the esteemed gentleman admit Graham and authorize a blood test while I returned to collect the rest of the money? The official was not unkind but could not relent. 'The rules say that you have to pay the full amount. I have no authority to change them.' At that moment a Czech neurologist happened to pass by. He glanced at Graham and endorsed Caroline's diagnosis. He spoke to the receptionist and learned that only the hospital director or his deputy could give permission to admit a patient without full payment in advance. Someone had to act as guarantor that the patient would eventually pay the bill. Though the Czech knew nothing about us he immediately offered to do so.

We set off together in search of the deputy who was said to be somewhere in the building. We ran up and down many dimly lit corridors of the administrative wing. The deputy was not in his office, nor in other places we were sent to. Officials we met gave the Czech conflicting reports of the great man's whereabouts. After ten minutes we gave up and sprinted back to the casualty department. The Czech resolved to test the limits of his authority in the hospital. He scribbled his acceptance of responsibility for the rest of the bill and sternly told the receptionist to admit the patient.

The poor man was put on the spot. He would love to agree but had to have someone more senior be responsible for this breach of normal practice. He gave us the name of such an official whom we found reading a magazine. We presented our request. The official had an un-Yemeni arrogance peculiar to a few young bureaucrats from important families. The Czech's patience in dealing with the insolent teenager was impressive. It took half an hour to draw up the guarantee a second time and we returned to the casualty department. By dint of bullying, Caroline secured one of the few examination rooms so that Graham could have relative quiet out of earshot of groaning fellow patients.

It was noted on Graham's forms that because of the risk of contagion he should be isolated from other patients. He was taken up to a ward and met by immaculately dressed Indian and Filipino nurses. No single rooms were available unless we paid more money. This seemed an insurmountable hurdle and Graham was wheeled into a darkened room with three already occupied beds. We were told that each patient had to have a minder, a person who would listen to the dosages and treatment ordered by the doctors and ensure that the nurses carried out instructions at times specified. As my eyes become accustomed to the dark I noticed that below each bed a friend or relative was sleeping on the floor.

Clearly I had no choice but to be minder. Fortunately, by virtue of my race, the nurses accorded me special privileges. A camp bed was brought in and a blanket was found. I passed a restless night, imagining myself catching meningitis and fearful of being asleep when I should be checking the nurses. When a new shift of nurses arrived in the early morning the state of each patient was summarized by an Indian sister. She spoke only in Hindi so I, my fellow minders, the three Filipino and the one Yemeni nurse in the deputation, were all hampered in our various supervisory tasks.

Graham stayed in the hospital for three days. He did not

have malaria and when his spinal fluid was finally cultured the Thawra said he did not have meningitis. He had, nevertheless, been extremely ill and required prolonged rest. He took advice to return home.

9

FACING FRUSTRATION

The six-person team I had joined in Ahad had now been whittled down to three. Susan left for a richly deserved holiday, leaving Caroline and me to return to Ahad and the denouement of our long tussle with Mohammad Ali, the secretary-general of the local development association. The women had almost completed their course and he was still refusing to pay their promised stipends. We had lent the *murshidaat* some of the money owed them and would only be repaid if we could force Mohammad Ali to pay up. After much complaining in Sana'a Graham had been given a cheque and an order to deduct 50,000 rials (£5,000) from the account which the Ahad LDA maintained in the only bank in Nakhwa. Mohammad Ali got wind of this development and asked the bank not to honour the cheque. When I had tried to withdraw the money in Nakhwa an embarrassed clerk politely passed the buck to the bank in Ahad. We now had a further order from Sana'a to present with the cheque but still did not expect it to be honoured. However, to our surprise, the Ahad bank handed over cash from the LDA'S account. We quickly passed the money on to the nine women and ensured that each wrote out a receipt. In trepidation, I searched for Mohammad Ali to present him with the receipts.

I found him lounging in a café. For several minutes he refused to acknowledge my presence. When he spoke he was rudely antagonistic. 'Why have you stolen our money? Why are you interfering in our affairs?' Bystanders gathered to hear our objectives ridiculed and our organization slandered. A Yemeni would not have tolerated such insults for a minute. As a foreigner I had little choice but to do so. My attempts to explain to the crowd that we were only trying to see national health policy implemented were useless as Mohammad Ali continually interrupted. I felt most alone. I gave him the receipts and left.

A week later a senior official from the headquarters of the local development movement arrived unexpectedly. He told me he had received a letter complaining that the Ahad LDA was being forced to pay money to women who did not live in Ahad district. It was further alleged that the two black women, Salma and Nabiila, were Ethiopians and thus not eligible to be studying. We went to see Maryam and the *murshidaat* and the official soon established that the charges were baseless. He was angry that he had been brought down to Ahad on false pretences and dispatched Ali Ahmad to fetch the secretary-general. While we were waiting he apologized to me for the inconvenience caused us and the discourtesy shown by the Ahad LDA. I was flabbergasted. I could have hugged the man, so delighted was I to meet an important civil servant showing understanding of our frustrations.

Once again Mohammad Ali proved elusive. We sat for an hour as various hospital employees were sent scurrying round town to look for him. He was variously reported as being in Saudi Arabia, Sana'a, ill or as having simply disappeared. The official soon realized that the wool was being pulled over his eyes and suspected Ali Ahmad of being party to the deception. He later confided that one of the more annoying aspects of his job was the difficulty of meeting LDA officials when he had the chance to tour the country. He eventually lost patience and we all got into his car to go and seek help from the *mudiir an naahiya*.

We found the prefect on the way back from his midday prayers and he agreed to send soldiers to search the town. An embarrassing silence ensued as our party waited to hear a sincere, not simply perfunctory, lunch invitation. The *mudiir* did not vehemently oppose our first refusals so the Sana'ani visitor knew we could not dine with him. We took our leave.

The big man was in the embarrassing position of having nowhere to eat. He asked me to recommend a restaurant and we all went up the road to Tawiil's. When important men eat lunch there is conspicuous over-ordering of food and this was no exception. I was nervous, feeling we should be offering hospitality in return for the help being given us, but also knowing I did not have enough money on me to pay for all the food needlessly ordered. The official noticed my predicament and sent a minion to settle up with the Tall One. At that moment the secretary-general, accompanied by other development association officials, swept theatrically into the restaurant. Mohammad Ali took the offensive in this very public place. 'You have deeply shamed me by not dining in my house', he declared reproachfully. 'Why', he asked me, 'did you not bring my brothers to my house where I was awaiting them?' He was mortified that we had had to make do with the poor food in the restaurant when he could have given us the very best. He appeared particularly solicitous of my welfare. Would we make amends by doing him the honour of chewing *qat* in his house?

The charade of *bonhomie* continued for the next few hours as the association's money was spent on providing us with *qat* leaves. We all agreed that the problems between BSDA and the LDA had been a terrible misunderstanding caused by problems of communication. Of course, the women deserved their stipends and Mohammad Ali would help them, and future male trainees, whenever he could. From now on we would meet regularly and all would be well. The Sana'a official had done his job. The requisite display of amicability had resulted from his visit, the foreign experts had appeared to be placated. He could go back to Sana'a. Life went on as before. Mohammad Ali continued to snub us whenever we ran into him.

Further gratifying news was the return of Abdul Kariim and Salah after weeks in Sana'a. Each had paid 1,000 rials, a month's salary, and been given letters admitting them to the civil service. They had not presented their hard-won papers in Nakhwa on their way back to Ahad, fearing they would be asked to pay more bribes if not accompanied by me. So once more we drove up to Nakhwa. We found that Dr Thaalib was away on another sponsored trip, this time a three week 'study tour' of Egypt. His deputy was again diagnosing and dispensing in his stead. Surprise was expressed that Salah had not closed his 'illegal' unit.

Salah and Abdul Kariim politely presented their hard-won letters ordering the Nakhwa office to start paying their salaries. I passed on a similar letter from the ministry asking that Yahia and Yusuf, the two Ahadi nurses, start receiving their salaries from Nakhwa. The deputy professed great surprise. The provincial health budget had no provision for primary health care. Surely it was the responsibility of BSDA to pay the salaries of primary health care workers and their trainer-supervisors?

I refrained from asking why he had not mentioned this during the many months spent preparing the two men's files in the Nakhwa office, and changed the subject. Fearing the worst, I again mentioned the case of the usurper, Khalid Tahir and learned the situation was unchanged. Dr Thaalib had told him that Abdul Kariim could work alongside Khalid Tahir in the health unit if he wished, but would have to take orders from the 'more experienced' man. I saw no point in a further debate about Khalid Tahir's qualifications. I realized just what we had taken on. We were embroiled in a fundamental, and public, conflict and were challenging a principle vital to the maintenance of power structures in this backward and atypical province. If someone who had paid to join the civil service was seen to get nothing because of protests at a higher level, then who, in future, would pay money to the dispensers of patronage? Dogged resistance was only to be expected. I once more returned to Ahad in a gloomy mood.

Salah stayed the night and I drove him home the next morning. Before climbing to Bani Salim we continued along the wadi to visit the uncompleted 'official' unit in Suq as Sebt. Salah had a headache and asked me to pull up in front of the only pharmacy in the entire government district. The owner is a brother of the director of the personnel department in the provincial health office. Salah returned to report that the drug-store owner had refused to sell him any paracetamol and said he did not want his custom. We went in together and I said I had a headache and would like to buy a packet of the cheap generic paracetamol now being produced in Sana'a. The pharmacist was very civil to me and refused payment. Salah and I had a quick look round his pharmacy and noted several drugs labelled as UNICEF or ministry supplies. Salah convinced me it would be futile to make an official complaint. We should discredit the man by telling others what we had seen.

After his enforced idleness in Sana'a Salah threw himself into his work. Caroline and I started going to see him once a week. These visits soon became the highlight of my week and, for a few months, a reason for carrying on. Caroline enjoyed the respite from the pressures put on her in the hospital. Naturally, the presence of the foreign doctors (for, no matter what I said, I was taken for one) was a great draw card. Because the unit was on top of a hill our car could be seen for miles around. Salah suggested we park at some distance from the health post to avoid this problem. We also adopted the habit of only spending a short time in the unit before moving off to visit villages, thus thwarting those who had set off on foot on hearing that the foreign doctors had come.

Salah's unit was more than a health amenity. In a society without any cafés, shops or other foci it was a valued meeting point. Men hung round during the morning listening to the patients and, at the same time, acquiring from Salah some knowledge of health. To further the process we handed out to the few literate people in the district some Arabic copies of the key text on primary health care, 'Where There Is No Doctor'. Salah's eagerness to share his knowledge was a welcome contrast to that of almost all our other counterparts.

One of the keenest attenders was a good friend of his, Ibrahim. He had been working in Saudi Arabia for years and, like many other Yemenis, had somehow picked up literacy in the process. At this time of year he was, like many men, at a loose end, recovering his energies before another period of enslavement to the despised Saudis. Because he had a wide vocabulary, and could switch away from the local dialect, I found talking to him a pleasure after the great difficulty of understanding the other men in Bani Salim. Ibrahim told me how local men earned money by smuggling qat, livestock and illegal immigrants across the Saudi border and of ruses adopted to fool the gullible Saudis. He told me of brothels in Jeddah and how members of the Saudi royal family imprison their subjects for up to fifteen years for chewing qat but themselves are known to enjoy the innocuous leaf. He entertained me with hair-raising tales of acquaintances who had driven back into Yemen through a hail of bullets, laden with electronic goods, as the Yemeni army tried to halt their flying Toyotas.

Ibrahim impressed me as an intelligent man receptive to the ideals of primary health care. He read 'Where There is No Doctor' and I imagined we had made a convert. I was not too concerned to learn one day that his wife had lost a lot of blood during childbirth. Salah had diagnosed anaemia and suggested iron tablets. His friend was doubtful about the advice and asked Caroline and me to see his wife. While I waited outside, Caroline went in to examine the woman. Ibrahim's wife spoke only broad dialect and Caroline's Arabic was still minimal. She could not explain matters to the wife but asked me to speak to her husband. I told Ibrahim his wife was gravely anaemic. It was imperative that she begin taking iron tablets at once. If she did not she might die. Salah provided Ibrahim with iron tablets and explained their use.

Anaemia is a major problem for rural Yemeni women. Women's work load, tending animals, fetching water and wood, cooking and child-bearing is never-ending. As there are few dark green vegetables in the traditional diet, and women are given less meat than men, few receive sufficient iron. Prejudice against taking iron tablets is strong. Many pregnant women believe that they will increase the size of the foetus and cause difficult deliveries. We learned over time not to stress that iron tablets would make the baby big and healthy, but that they would ease delivery. Salah's task in persuading women to take iron tablets was further complicated by a belief that foods rich in iron such as papaya, molokhia and a local spinach-like plant, themselves cause malaria.

Ibrahim did not believe his friend's advice. Nor did he believe our opinions. How could medicine and advice given for free be of any utility? His wife did not take the tablets. He borrowed a Toyota and bumped her down the fearful track to Ahad. She was not taken to the hospital, but to a pharmacist in whom he placed trust. She was injected with the usual cocktails of vitamins, calcium and powerful antibiotics. She still felt weak but as they have no relatives in Ahad had to set off home. On arrival, her husband had to lift her out of the Toyota. She died shortly afterwards.

By chance, we arrived the next morning and heard the news. Ibrahim was, as usual, sitting in the health post. It is not considered seemly to grieve in public for the loss of a wife. Ibrahim had lost his previous wife in similar circumstances a few years earlier. We offered no condolences and tried to chat normally. Only once did I catch an expression of horror crossing his face. Was he regretting his failure to question his assumptions about health and its practitioners? Perhaps he was lamenting the fact that his years in Saudi Arabia had been in vain? All the labour required to get together the high bride prices demanded in Yemen would have to be repeated yet once more. A few weeks later he set out to Saudi Arabia once more to begin working towards his third wife. Would she fare better in the perilous business of bringing Yemeni children into the world?

Ibrahim's wife did not die in vain. The story of how Salah's advice had been spurned spread quickly. Children were sent to Salah to ask us to come to see pregnant women. We spent the rest of the day visiting a number of tiny hamlets, drinking endless cups of tea and fighting off further offers of food. Whenever we stopped all the mothers and children gathered to speak to us. We were kept busy all afternoon explaining about anaemia, how to identify it by examining the finger nails and the eyelids and how to avoid it by eating local foods rich in iron. We weighed children and explained the road to health card. Salah kept handing out iron pills and sachets of oral rehydration solution. Suddenly the barriers of doubt had been burst. Perhaps a life had had to be lost to achieve this. It was a tiring but highly rewarding day.

In subsequent weeks Ibrahim's child struggled for life. Ibrahim asked his own mother, who had not had a child for a decade, to breastfeed and to our surprise she eventually produced some milk. Why, I asked, was the child not suckling from another recently-delivered mother? Such wet-nursing is, after all, enjoined by the Koran. I was told that mothers used to feed the children of those who died after giving birth but that it is no longer thought modern to do so and the practice has been abandoned.

Salah arrived unexpectedly one evening to report an epidemic of measles. Several children had died in one hamlet and the illness had also broken out in neighbouring villages. He wondered if it would be possible for one of the hospital vaccinators to come up to Bani Salim to provide an emergency vaccination service in affected villages. It seemed a reasonable request and it was supposed to be part of the duties of a primary health care worker to gather children for vaccination. However, the Ahad vaccinators had never ventured outside the town and the old *mudiir* said they could not do so without permission from the provincial office in Nakhwa. Uthman phoned Nakhwa and was told a formal request in writing would have to be made. Days were lost while Ali Ahmad wrote a sufficiently flowery letter and got the old hospital director and the government prefect to sign and stamp it. It was sent up to Nakhwa and word came back a few days later that such a visit was not permissible. Vaccines given to the Ahad health centre could not be used elsewhere. Children from the area would have to be brought down to the health centre.

Some children whose families could afford transport were brought to Ahad but the majority were not immunized. If there is not a sufficient degree of coverage of a population at risk from measles even some of those vaccinated may contract the illness. If not properly treated (and few fevers are properly treated in Yemen) they may die. More children passed away, one of whom had, indeed, been vaccinated. Thus was Salah's patient work explaining the importance of vaccinating infants undone.

These and other frustrations were preoccupying the BSDA team. We were forever questioning our curious roles. None of us was doing the job for which we had been recruited. Much as we tried to take troubles in our stride, to laugh at the farcical situation we were in, we were regularly losing our tempers with Yemeni colleagues. I was allowing myself to be riled by the youth of the town who had changed my name from Abdullah because of my apparent resemblance to an American wrestler seen on television. My protestations merely increased the taunts. We all began to crave the kind of privacy impossible in a small town. We could never escape from our problems as visitors could arrive at any time. We ranted and raved to each other about our problems. Fortunately, perhaps for the first time in the history of the project, we honestly tried to share our fears, sympathize with other's difficulties and bolster our morale and egos. In place of the much-vaunted 'rigorous use of ongoing self and group assessment techniques' prescribed by Eze-Vu – which had done nothing to bring our predecessors together – we tried to judge the time to listen, to stay silent and to talk about anything except our continuing crises. Night after night we played Scrabble, mention of our problems prohibited.

Susan's relations with her colleagues were excellent and her morale relatively good for, alone amongst us, she had a realistic job to do and was achieving results. She was, however, sorely handicapped by her Arabic training. Every day women with severe labour complications were brought to her by their male relatives. Often she had to press men to take women to Hodeidah as quickly as possible. Sometimes they showed great reluctance to do so, sought second opinions or first went to have lunch or buy *qat* for the journey. Susan's inability to berate them in fluent and convincing Arabic was understandably frustrating. She was also annoyed that the *murshidaat* showed little desire either to get out of the hospital and visit women in their homes or to take the opportunity to educate the crowds swarming round the doctor's room. She was upset they did not follow up the health of new born children in the first months of life and that Maryam, their trainer, did not encourage them to do so.

Maryam's position was difficult. After prodding from UNICEF the ministry had accepted that female primary health care workers should not simply learn about delivering babies but should also know how to prevent and cure the illnesses which rob Yemen of half its children in the first five years of life. Yet the ministry had not issued a new syllabus and textbook, and Maryam was obliged to follow the old guidelines in preparing students for exams. I had to mediate between the two hard-working, respected midwives, some-times sadly divided by culture and language.

A crisis erupted when, on a busy *suq* day, Susan grabbed one of the trainee *murshidaat*, pulled her to her feet and told her to go and speak to the patients besieging Caroline. Nuriya and Ali Ahmad exacerbated the unintentional affront and a meeting had to be called to allow us to fulsomely apologize. Soon afterwards a newly arrived male doctor, the first Yemeni doctor sent to work in Ahad, burst into the delivery room without knocking. As local women wailed in horror, Susan slammed the door in his face. Inured as she was to the frustrations of working in the National Health Service, she both surprised herself and felt guilty at the raw anger she expressed.

Caroline was also dissatisfied with the curious role she had been forced into. In the hospital she was practising bad medicine, inundated with patients whose children could, in almost all cases, have been treated by the *murshidaat*. Because she was popular and did not charge, she saw as many patients as the other four doctors in the hospital put together. Children sent for blood and stool tests did not return because their parents could not pay the large amounts illegally demanded of them. Others were hijacked by her fellow doctors and their parents persuaded to pay for dubious medication. The hospital pharmacy was emptier than ever. Caroline was especially irritated when time and again she referred children to be vaccinated only to be told supplies had run out. Even when vaccine was available the old *mudiir* and the Yemeni doctors upheld ministry policy and prevented even moderately ill children from being vaccinated. In the West such a precaution is justifiable, but in a situation where epidemics are commonplace and adults are unlikely to bear the expense of bringing children to hospital except when they are ill, the ministerial dictate was medical absurdity.

Susan kept hearing how vaccine could be bought from the two vaccinators if they were visited after working hours. Our suspicions were aroused when Ali Ahmad called a meeting, unbeknownst to us, to discuss the problem of vaccination. Garbled accounts from the *murshidaat* led my female colleagues to suspect that a deal had been struck. The women could start vaccinating children when Uthman and Lutf were absent in school. They agreed to be more prudent in collecting money from patients likely to complain. They would not provoke the Nakhwa office by joining us in demanding more vaccine.

A UNICEF employee, resident in the country for many years, had told us UNICEF had provided sufficient vaccine for the province. We had now visited many health centres and seen that even those which lacked basic drugs had sufficient supplies of vaccine. Caroline was adamant that we had to take a strong stand to ensure that Dr Thaalib's nephew be forced to keep the Ahad hospital supplied. We explained that all we wanted was for him to observe the national supply system and provide each health centre with 125 per cent of the amount of vaccine used in the previous month. This was a litmus test of the health office's commitment to preventative medicine. I phoned Nakhwa several times without achieving anything.

Only Salah's progress still gave any hope. As his confidence grew, so did his wish to expand his knowledge of ante-natal care, a subject he had not studied during his course. At first only his closest female relatives would allow him to examine them. Salah asked if some of the women being trained in Ahad might accompany us on our weekly visits. Maryam, their teacher, was immediately supportive. The ministry did not approve of male health workers learning basic midwifery but the experienced and pragmatic Maryam saw the need to boost Salah's knowledge and his credibility among women. Like us, she realized that the *murshidaat* led such sheltered urban lives that they knew very little of the lives, health problems and diet of the peasantry in neighbouring districts. The *murshidaat* were very eager to widen further their horizons and there was much competition to be placed first on the rota of visits which Maryam drew up. Once more Sayyida's aunt forbade her to leave Ahad.

Maryam said the women were to wear their uniforms on visits and at first they all did so. She chose the most confident of the *murshidaat*, Amina and Katiba, the only married woman on the course, to be the first to go. The day before our planned trip a marital dispute between the volatile Katiba and her husband threatened the expedition. I had met her husband and been impressed by his liberalism. Most men would not have allowed their wives to leave children and home every day in order to go off to study. I was thus surprised to hear that he had ordered her to stay in her village and cease her studies.

Maryam and Susan went to visit Katiba on the first conciliation mission. The background to the dispute emerged. In the course of a slanging match Katiba's husband had angrily walked out of their hut. Katiba had pursued her husband and, in full view of neighbours, swatted at him with a broom. Naturally, he had lost a great deal of face and had to be seen to be taking a firm line. Maryam asked me to come with her and Susan on a further placatory mission. She sat with Katiba and female neighbours and relatives while I sat sipping tea with her husband and other men. While doing research a few years earlier I had acquired experience as a marital intermediary when sent by a friend to his estranged wife's father to negotiate the terms of her return to the marital home. But this time I had not been briefed and had no idea what was expected of me. I drank glass after glass of tea and chatted inconsequentially as we watched World Cup football on a flickering television inadequately powered by an ancient car battery. Fortunately, the real negotiation was going on elsewhere. Maryam popped her head into the men's room to say she wanted to speak to the husband. They went out of earshot and came back to announce the problem had been solved. It seemed that my presence had been necessary simply as affirmation of the seriousness of the affront done to the husband's honour.

For the *murshidaat*'s first visit to Salah's health unit there were not many women to be seen. We sat round waiting for patients and eventually went off to Salah's hamlet for lunch. The women seemed not the least bit abashed to be in the company of strange males. Conversation flowed freely, subjects ranging from the mercenary attitude of pharmacy owners, corruption in the provincial health office and the poor quality of grain donated by the World Food Programme. This was a slack time in the agricultural cycle and many men, attracted by the spectacle of chatting with educated women, came from nearby hamlets. The nature of Islamic marriage, the qualities to be looked for in husbands and wives and the ideal relationship between them were earnestly discussed. I sat quietly, imagining the outrage of the Muslim Brothers if they could see such relaxed dealings between strange men and women, encouraged, if not instigated by, *nasraanis*.

Local women sent boys to request visits from Katiba and Amina. We spent a busy afternoon going from village to village. I squatted outside with men talking about health issues while Salah, Caroline and the two midwives went inside huts to examine women. I talked for half an hour to a particularly benighted old man forever belittling Salah and the women and praising pharmacy owners. I had tried to be patient in combating the old man's prejudice and respect for any one wearing white coat and stethoscope. When Amina came out to join us I told her that the old man's wife was soon due to deliver and that he planned to take his wife down to the Suq as Sebt pharmacy so that the 'doctor' could give her an oxytocin injection. Amina let fly. 'You senile old fool! What's the matter with you? Still living in the days of the Imam? Don't you dare make your wife suffer!' The man was roundly ridiculed in front of an amused crowd. Local women gawped with stunned admiration at the power of the strange looking women in white.

Over the next few months all of the women, except Sayyida, visited Bani Salim. Initially some had the airs and graces of disdainful urban ladies. Khayzara on her first visit made herself up, tottered round the rocky terrain on absurdly high heels, refused to eat the 'dirty' food, touched local women and babies with obvious repugnance and complained about the 'incomprehensible' local dialect. A word with the redoubtable Maryam led to a stern telling-off. Khayzara, like the other *murshidaat*, dropped her arrogance and soon established excellent relations with the local people. The trip up to Bani Salim became the highpoint of the trainees' lives.

The women learned what foods were available in the area and tailored their nutritional advice accordingly. They and I were stunned to find that local people regard tinned kidney beans, a basic staple of the diet everywhere else in Yemen, as a great and unaffordable luxury. Numbers of local women had the road to health card patiently explained to them. Several showed me, with pride and admiration, how their child's weight had shot up after being visited by the *murshidaat*. Locals competed to offer us hospitality. More than once we found people arguing amongst themselves about who had prior claim to our presence at lunch. People pressed into, or onto the roof of, our car in order to share the excitement. We were always overloaded and in danger of overturning on the sharp rocky bends. At times passengers had to nimbly jump out and sit on the bonnet when we seemed about to topple over. Men were always getting me to stop and jumping out of the car to scramble through the scrub to fetch wild plants, and particularly henna, wanted by the women.

Confidence in Salah grew and he was increasingly allowed to examine pregnant women. The bonds between Salah, Caroline and myself were strengthened as we all had knowledge to exchange. Salah blossomed into confident manhood, eager to know more of the wider world. On every visit he bombarded me with questions. When told of China's vast population he shook his head in wonderment: 'I always thought my country was a big place but I suppose in relation to China we are no more than a tiny village.' He was equally surprised to find that planets and suns are different kinds of celestial bodies. He asked me if Poland was part of Britain and I gave him a map of the world which he devoured. Like other Yemenis he showed a disarming ability to find his own lack of knowledge a source of continual merriment. When I pointed out that the blue sections on the map represented oceans he chuckled at his ignorance but was soon able to place the continents and began teaching others the rudiments of world geography. When his wife became pregnant he started sporting the prominent curved dagger, the symbol of the *qabiili*. When worn by Salah, it somehow did not seem macho. He remained modest about his achievements, ever at pains to share his knowledge and assure grateful beneficiaries of his service that he was not a doctor.

The threat to his work seemed to have receded, but we were still fearful. On one occasion we were returning from visiting Salah when we almost collided, in pouring rain, with the car of the obliging local *mudiir an naahiya*. He called me over to his car. Our chat had to be brief for we were both concerned to get out of the wadi before a wall of water descended from the hills. A horde of frogs – miraculously arisen from months of subterranean rest – provided a cacophonous background.

The prefect did not look well and had lost weight since assuming his post. His diet, he told me, was lousy. Isolated in his government enclave, he had only tinned beans to eat and was longing for fruit and vegetables. I reported that officials in Nakhwa had described Salah's unit as 'unofficial'. When the prefect expressed determination to protect Salah and his work I risked an outrageous request. If an order came from Nakhwa could he first check that it had the authority of the ministry in Sana'a before acting upon it? We went our separate ways.

Meanwhile, Abdul Kariim, our other trained health worker, was getting nowhere in his struggle for credibility against the wily 'Doctor' Khalid Tahir. I paid several visits to Zahir but negotiations with the local development association and the prefect produced no results. We again swallowed our pride, months after we should have done, and agreed to put up the money ourselves. I found a carpenter and a metalworker who agreed to provide a door, door frames and bars over the windows. When the work was done Abdul Kariim formally wrote to Ali Ahmad requesting permission to equip the unit. Ali Ahmad came with us on his first visit to the area and supervised the unloading and registering of the drugs and equipment. All was ready, yet Ali Ahmad refused to allow Abdul Kariim to start work before an official opening party.

We heard that the governor himself might be coming to the area on 26 September, the anniversary of the republican revolution. It seemed most unlikely that this luminary would spend such an important day in an isolated place lacking in amenities, but we were assured he would. Rural Yemenis are always prey to rumours that the governor or even the president himself is about to pay a surprise visit and it is not for foreigners to gainsay them. A week before the great day the Nakhwa health office made their first contribution to the work of the unit – an ornate board was sent down to Ahad with orders it be erected as soon as possible next to the Zahir unit so that the governor would see it. We were presented with a bill for the board and its carriage. We refused to pay and the local development association was lumbered with the unnecessary expense.

On the great occasion we went to Zahir and found only Abdul Kariim and a few friends in attendance. It was clear the unit was not going to be officially inaugurated. Ali Ahmad tried to close the building and shoo away those who, attracted by our presence, trickled in to be treated. Abdul Kariim insisted on working 'temporarily' until the ceremony. Caroline and I started visiting him once a week without official blessing. In the end the health post was never 'opened'.

It was soon apparent that the unit had been insensitively

sited. It lies between an important local market, several
hamlets, a government *markaz* and a school. All except the
lowest status *akhdaam* women were deterred from coming to
seek help in such a public place. Men, however, seemed to
welcome the new building as a multi-purpose leisure facility.
For those drawn to the area by commerce, litigation or
curiosity and with time to kill, the unit was a cheaper, more
entertaining place of rest than any of the ramshackle corrugated iron cafés in the *suq*. One could sit round in the shade,
smoking Rothmans and chatting without being chivvied to
buy soft drinks or water pipes. School students, many of them
young adults, wandered in and out of the unit all the time.
Motorists coming in from distant districts stopped to pick up
news. Police wandered over from their nearby checkpoint and
soldiers squatted with litigants rehearsing the accounts they
would present when summonsed up the hill to testify to the
haakim (judge) and the prefect.

Because of the masculine ambience of his workplace Abdul
Kariim only got to see women when we went on home visits.
These were few and far between as Abdul Kariim was keen to
be seen attending his unit. Being right under the prefect's nose,
he feared that if he was not present when soldiers were sent to
him his absence would be construed as dereliction of duty. If a
negative report were sent to Nakhwa he might never receive a
salary.

A constant stream of male hypochondriacs attended the unit,
many simply suffering from headaches or constipation induced
by *qat*. They clamoured for attention and were disappointed
when Abdul Kariim did not take their ailments as seriously as
the opportunist pharmacist Khalid Tahir and would not offer
injections on demand. One such wheedling old man turned out
to be Khalid Tahir's father. He is a lively character and his
bawdy presence attracted others. He regaled me with improbable stories of derring-do during his days as a soldier for
the Imam while pleading for 'strong medicine' to restore his
potency. He seemed interested in learning about health and
Abdul Kariim tolerated his rifling through the cupboard of
medicines. He came across a box of condoms we had
provided, unknown to Ali Ahmad, and perhaps contrary to
ministry regulations. He was immediately intrigued. I began to

explain their use as best I could. A look of incredulity crossed his face and he started guffawing. He could barely contain himself. 'Surely', he whispered, 'you are not going to tell people about these? They could destroy marriages. Everyone will be getting off with everybody else. The Muslim Brothers won't like it!' The prospect seemed to delight him and I was at pains to look sincere as I assured him condoms were purely for use in marriage in order to prolong intervals between births. He took some away for his own use. I ran into him again a week later and he drew me aside. He had had a wonderful time! Could he have some more?

The long struggle against his son produced unexpected results. By repeated complaint we goaded the ministry into writing an order to Nakhwa, stating that only Abdul Kariim could work in the Zahir unit. Dr Thaalib's deputy, fearful of an investigation of why Khalid Tahir was receiving a state salary, was forced to act. He issued an order, once more stamped by the governor, stating that Khalid Tahir, the 'medical assistant', was to work in the Ahad hospital.

This prospect was frightening to all parties. Our avaricious adversary did not want to work in a place where the drug market was already sewn up and came to me to parley. We hammered out a compromise. If Khalid Tahir stayed in his pharmacy and promised neither to endanger the health of patients in the Ahad hospital nor show his face in Abdul Kariim's unit then we would not complain about his getting a salary for doing no work and would turn a blind eye to his nominal employment in Ahad. He gave us his word. On successive surprise visits we only once found him in Abdul Kariim's unit. As soon as our Toyota approached he climbed out of a window.

Caroline and I wondered what we were achieving by our visits. The bulk of my time was spent trying to persuade the hangers-on of the difference between private medicine and primary health care. Success was hard to determine as many patients were clearly trying all avenues of health care open to them. It was not uncommon for men to have taken a sick child to a writer of amulets, to someone who cauterizes the sick on parts of the body believed efficacious, and to Khalid Tahir's pharmacy before coming to us.

Only once was I confident of the value of my intervention. A child weighing 2.5 kg., half the weight for its age, was brought in. Abdul Kariim and Caroline were occupied with other children and left me to explain the use of sachets of oral rehydration solution. I showed how ORS should be mixed and filled a plastic bottle with water from the water filter we had provided the unit. At first the child refused to take the water offered by spoon. I told the father he had to be patient for the child would soon want the liquid. He went away but came back an hour later to complain his son had had a drip in the pharmacy but was still not better. Again I explained and again the man drifted off. Two hours later when he returned once more the level of liquid in the bottle was slightly reduced. He complained that the child was still poorly. I went through the information again, gave him extra sachets and told him to keep giving the liquid for three days. I thought my time had been wasted but was delighted when I met the man a week later. He was most grateful and had come specially to show us his child. When we weighed him we found he had increased his weight by two-thirds.

Our success in taking women on day trips to help Salah emboldened us. Caroline and I conceived an audacious scheme – we would see if we could take Nuriya, and Amina and Khayzara, the best two of the nine *murshidaat*, to visit other mother and child health centres in the country. We had little hope of getting permission to drive round Yemen with local women but our determination grew as a consequence of our other setbacks. We discussed our plan with Ali Ahmad who approved but was hurt that he was not also being invited. He telephoned Nakhwa and was told the trip was out of the question. We had anticipated this difficulty and had spoken to the female doctor heading the ministry's mother and child department. She supported the idea but, conscious of her precarious position in the ministry, declined to put her approval in writing. I rang back and lied to Dr Thaalib that we had ministerial permission. Caught unawares, he could think of no objection and told the fearful old Ahad *mudiir* that the trip could go ahead provided the guardians of the women agreed and the prefect was notified.

Caroline came down with malaria, and Susan was, as ever,

busily visiting the infants and mothers of the town, so it was
left to me to get permission for the women to travel. Maryam
accompanied me to the compounds of the three women.
Mystery surrounded the identity of Amina's male guardian but
eventually we traced a man who appended his thumb-print to
our piece of paper. Nuriya's mother, the guardian of Sayyida,
was once more hard to convince. Three times in the course of
the day I returned to try to overcome her resistance. The ever
mercurial Nuriya spent most of the day saying she did not
want to come. She was just a clerk who knew nothing about
health. At the advanced age of twenty-five she was too old to
learn. Others would benefit more from the trip. I pretended to
lose my temper and said her attitude was shameful. As the first
woman in the whole region to have obtained a primary school
certificate she was an inspiration to others. It was ridiculous
that ten years later she had stopped expanding her knowledge
and allowed other women to surpass her. She owed it to the
less fortunate women of the town to go on this trip and to
continue studying. She eventually came round, agreed to go
on the trip and soon bullied her mother into submission. I was
later very pleased that she returned to school after her long
absence.

It was now late in the evening and endorsement of the
guardians' approval had still to be gained. The old *mudiir* had
fallen off a motorbike while riding pillion and been taken away
to hospital in Hodeidah. His deputy was even more fearful of
permitting such a novel enterprise, but was eventually
persuaded to send his son to the hospital to fetch the official
stamp. We thought the hostile Ahad *mudiir an naahiya* might
still throw a last minute spanner in the works. Lutf, the wilier
of the two vaccinators, offered to himself go to the *hakuuma* to
give the prefect a copy of the permission after we had
successfully got away.

Our departure the next morning was delayed by Nuriya
again being capricious. A group went to find her and
eventually persuaded her to come on the journey. A crowd of
some fifty women, all no doubt highly envious, came to see
the women off and implored Allah to return them safely. As
we left town we could hardly believe what we had pulled off. I
stopped at Khamis to make multiple photocopies of our hard-
earned permission before setting off for Hodeidah.

We reached there at lunchtime to face an obstacle we knew would have to be overcome. The women had announced that during our trip they would live off biscuits eaten in the car rather than face the shame of eating in public. Caroline and I spent the best part of the journey from Ahad telling them of a restaurant in Hodeidah which had a family section where we had seen women from the best families in the city eating. Unfortunately, when we arrived there were no female customers and Nuriya promptly refused to get out of the car. I asked a waiter to draw a curtain round the tables in the family section and eventually Nuriya was persuaded to come in. Caroline and I asked the waiter what was available and a fairly extensive list of foods was rattled off. We asked the women what they wanted but got no response. We realized they had never been in a situation where they could chose what food was to be put in front of them. They were frozen with indecision so we ordered for them. Though no one could see us, Khayzara refused to uncover her face and precariously raised each spoonful up and around her veil, a messy procedure.

After lunch we went to look for the unfortunate old hospital *mudiir* languishing with a broken femur in Hodeidah's Republican Hospital. We had some difficulty explaining ourselves to the Chinese staff who run the hospital as the nurses we found spoke neither Arabic nor English. Eventually we found the old man and presented him with the Chinese tinned fruit which is the usual gift to the sick in Yemen. A long journey was in front of us, so we had to take our leave. We stopped briefly to buy *qat* and when I got back to the car Caroline told me of a problem we had foolishly failed to anticipate – the women needed a toilet.

There are no public lavatories anywhere in Yemeni cities. Men can squat wherever there is relative privacy but for women there is no escape from the burden of retaining honour. It would be out of the question to be seen entering one of Hodeidah's posh hotels and using the facilities we ourselves patronized. We racked our brains and eventually remembered an employee of the USAID-funded health project. Fortunately she was in, and obligingly made the women welcome. She told us that her project was coming to

an end and that she was to leave soon. She feared that the
health workers the Americans had trained would desert their
posts as they would receive no money once the Americans left.
We left her to her gloom. The Ahadi women were stunned
that a single woman had an air-conditioned flat with three
toilets all for herself.

Once we had passed out of the city and through the
checkpoint the women visibly relaxed. They dispensed with
veils and began chewing *qat*. Cassettes of Yemeni male singers
were produced and their respective merits discussed. Khayzara
surprised Nuriya and Amina by pulling out a packet of
Kamaran cigarettes. As they all lit up, they alternately revelled
in their naughtiness and allowed Nuriya to chide them for the
prayers they had not done. Whenever we passed through a
town the cigarettes were extinguished and the veils came
down.

We stopped for a rest in the historic city of Zabid. The
women were keen to see the sights and we started walking
round the walls of the old town. We immediately attracted a
crowd of curious youths who started following us. When one
boldly engaged the women in conversation the whole pack
came forward. Caroline and I were put on the spot. We had
gravely sworn to the women's guardians to protect them at all
times. We were *in loco parentis*. Were we not obliged to tell the
boys off? But would not this be both 'paternalist' and
'interventionist'? We bundled them into the car and resumed
our journey.

The women had had enough shocks for one day and we
thought it best not to force the issue of putting them in a hotel.
Thus we drove through Ta'iz and on to Ibb where Khayzara
had relatives. We reached there late at night thoroughly
exhausted after the long drive. After leaving the three women
Caroline and I went off to find a hotel. In the first we came to
there was only one room left. Oblivious to local sensibilities,
we decided to share it. The hotel was full of soldiers with
glazed eyes. From behind every door wafted the sweet smell of
the marihuana for which Ibb is noted.

In the morning I again visited the Ibb mother and child
health centre. Since my previous visit the Norwegian Save the
Children Fund had ceased funding the centre. Hopes that the

ministry would pick up the burden of supporting the project
had been confounded. Salaries had been slashed by two-thirds
and many employees had left to work with other foreign-
funded projects. Still, for the time being, and in comparison
with Ahad, an impressive service was being offered and our
women spent a busy and informative morning. We drove back
to Ta'iz, nervous whenever we passed through checkpoints.
However, in this most liberal part of Yemen no one seemed
concerned at foreigners travelling with Yemeni women. We
were also relieved that the hotel we chose in Ta'iz raised no
objection to the women staying, as would have been the case
elsewhere in the country.

We visited the Swedish clinic I had seen a year earlier. After
being shown round we were introduced to a very articulate
male health educator. I spoke to him, in English, and he
impressed me as a highly modern secular intellectual. He
agreed to speak to the women. We all sat spellbound for half
an hour as he discussed ways of persuading people to amend
their health practices. He cast aside his modernism. The whole
thrust of his message to the Ahadi women was couched in
terms of religious and patriotic obligations. Again and again he
quoted the Koran to back up his arguments. Islam enjoined all
believers to ceaselessly broaden their knowledge, but it also
condemned those who hoarded knowledge and took pride in
their superiority. One must be vigilant to avoid the sin of
pride. The only way to bring about change was by listening to
the people, learning the circumstances of their lives, talking to
them in their own language and showing respect for their
beliefs.

Nothing he said to them was new. In my own clumsy
manner I had been trying to get across similar concepts. The
same messages from an impressive, and handsome, fellow
Muslim were far more convincing. For days the women
discussed both his ideas and his eligibility as a marriage
partner. Nuriya occasionally remembered to rebuke them for
their un-Islamic immodesty but, nevertheless, enjoyed Amina
and Khayzara's bawdy fantasies.

The women were keen to visit one of Yemen's major tourist
attractions, the palace used by the despotic Imam Ahmad. The
palace has been left exactly as it was in September 1962, a

tribute to the restraint and historical sense of the revolutionary mobs who chose not to loot it but to leave it as a monument to tyranny. Yemenis from all regions of the country were visiting this shrine. In the entrance lobby the women looked at the ghoulish photos showing the early martyrs of the republican cause being decapitated. A museum attendant, who explained that he had been one of Ahmad's footmen, showed us the bedroom in which the old man had finally died. He had survived several assassination attempts, and was in constant pain from shrapnel which could not be removed from his body. Today Ahmad is routinely depicted in school textbooks and the media as a degenerate drug addict. Crowds of Yemenis were keen to see the syringes with which he injected morphine in his last painful years.

We were shown the extraordinary collection of consumer bric-à-brac Ahmad collected at a time when the import of any kind of western manufactured goods was totally banned. We saw his vast collection of perfumes, patent medicines and quaint art deco electrical appliances. We stopped to look at pictures of the former royal family and our guide spoke fondly of the young men he had known who are now in comfortable pensioned exile in Kent and Saudi Arabia. At the end we rewarded our elderly guide for his trouble with a few rials. I gauchely asked if he kept in touch with any members of the former royal family. He looked shocked, as did the Ahadi women. 'Certainly not! I am a son of the revolution! The Hamid ad Din family kept us in backwardness!' There was no doubting his sincerity.

The next morning we set off for Sana'a. The women were unwinding more with each passing day and kept making us stop to take pictures of them posing against the stupendous mountain backdrops. There was much giggling about whether they should ask to have their photo taken with me, with Khayzara egging the others on. She struck a flamboyant pose, her hand resting on her provocative hips, but then became concerned that we not tell her family and to show the photos only to her. Later when I heard Amina praising the people of Ta'iz for their liberal attitudes I butted in to suggest that she marry a Ta'izi man. This produced howls of laughter and merriment for several days. I learned that she was already notionally married. After her first husband and her two children had died there was much pressure for her, still in her teens, to remarry. Rather than compromise her family by defying convention, she agreed to be married to an elderly relative (the elusive guardian I had searched for) but only on condition they not live together and the marriage not be consummated. For years she had been content with this arrangement. Yemeni women, especially widows and divorcees, are not without resources in negotiating the terms of their marriages, whatever travesties of Arab marriage in the western media may suggest.

We arrived in Sana'a late at night. We had assured the Ahadi women and their worried families that we had space to safely house our guests and after much argument persuaded BSDA to drop objections to putting them up. The social mores of Sana'a are years behind those of Ta'iz. To have taken the women to a hotel would have been to brand them as prostitutes, and subject them to inconceivable harassment.

The women were excited by Sana'a and the prospect of shopping but felt nervous in the capital, finding themselves bothered by men in the streets in a way they had not been in Ta'iz. They were acutely embarrassed when Caroline and I took them to a public lecture on primary health care at the Yemeni Medical Association. We found the talk was for men only and were asked to leave. After this rebuff the Ahadi women found it less stressful to remain indoors and we were obliged to do their shopping and provide for them. Amina asked me to get her a bra – a garment mostly bought by men in Yemen – but I coyly passed the commission to Caroline.

The women went out only to visit the various mother and child health centres in and around Sana'a. This was informative and enjoyable, except for a jarring experience when we turned up at a clinic formerly financed by the West Germans. We were refused admittance on a pretext that our papers were not in order. It was again clear that resentment against *khubaraa* was spreading.

Yusuf and Yahya, the two Ahad nurses whose fight to be allowed to work in their home town had caused me such aggravation, were in Sana'a. They were about to complete a six-week course to enable them to become trainer supervisors of primary health care. On ministry instructions BSDA had already paid them a stipend for the course, set by the World Health Organization, which temporarily boosted their salaries by 500 per cent. The Ahadi men found, by chatting to other nurses sponsored by foreign organizations, that colleagues were getting even more out of their *nasraanis*. They asked me for more money, complaining how expensive *qat* was in Sana'a. BSDA policy not to pay such top-ups was of long standing and I repeated it to them. Naturally, they were not satisfied. Eventually it was agreed that Brian, the nurses, and I would meet with the director of the training department in the ministry to discuss the matter.

When we did so, we exchanged small-talk for a while before coming to the point. The departmental head made it clear that the ministry would greatly appreciate a long-term commitment to top up the salaries of the two men and reminded us that all other foreign organizations aiding the training of health workers did so. I said nothing, expecting Brian, the pro-gramme co-ordinator, to reiterate our policy. I had not reckoned on his need to make himself popular. He agreed that the Ahad project might pay them more money. BSDA gave him no authority to spend the funds of particular projects, but the damage had been done. Our colleagues in the other projects agreed that our stand against paying such salary increments had to be upheld. When this was later explained to the two nurses they were bitterly resentful, comparing my 'meanness' and 'lack of understanding' to the generosity of our nice 'director'. I was furious at the position Brian had put me in.

Before going back to Ahad we took the women on an outing to Marib, the most important city of pre-Islamic Yemen. Yemenis believe that Bilqis, the Queen of Sheba, founded her kingdom in this far eastern region which adjoins the Empty Quarter. They are intensely proud of the achievements of their countrymen during the *jaahaliyyah*, the 'age of ignorance' prior to the coming of Islam. The National Museum in Sana'a is always filled with tribesmen and their families marvelling at the artefacts of the vanished civilizations centred round Marib. The Koran relates how the Marib Dam collapsed shortly before the advent of Islam, a catastrophe credited by Yemenis as condemning their inventive ancestors to a migratory existence. In all probability, this 'collapse' is a metaphor for the increasing desiccation of the area in historical times.

As we descended from the central mountains of Yemen a vast desert lay before us. We passed groups of nomads who looked so different it was hard to believe we were still in Yemen. Until a few years ago the population consisted of small groups of semi-nomadic tribesmen only intermittently under the control of central government. In the days of the Imams raiding parties used to seize youths from important sheikhly families and take them to Sana'a where they were held prisoner to guarantee the loyalty of their tribes. On a previous visit to Marib I had been put up by one such former royal hostage who had spent six years imprisoned in the capital. Eventually, his father negotiated with Imam Ahmad for another son to be held in his place and my host fled the country. He walked for three months through the wastes of the Empty Quarter before reaching Mecca. He worked as a houseboy but found he did not like Saudis so moved on to Bahrain. During his wanderings he acquired five different nationalities and played football for the national teams of three emerging Gulf mini-states.

His first schooling was acquired while working for British Petroleum in Qatar. He told me of his absolute astonishment when he read a history book and realized that he came from an area of outstanding archaeological significance. He spoke movingly of the deep shame he had felt at belonging to a backward country whose rulers allowed their subjects to remain in such ignorance of their own heritage. He developed a voracious interest in archaeology and with the outbreak of the revolution in 1962 was able to return home and be reunited with his family. He joined the republicans, became director of antiquities in Marib and eventually obtained a postgraduate degree in archaeology from a British university where I had met him. On the way back to Marib I was saddened knowing we would not meet again. Like other Yemeni friends I had made he was dead – a victim of the car accidents which today cut down large numbers of Yemenis in their prime.

Since 1962 representatives of the republican state have only entered this area at the invitation of independent sheikhs. Now, with the discovery of petrol, much is changing. We passed construction teams laying the pipeline which will carry Yemen's new-found wealth to the world. Accompanying the oil men were large numbers of soldiers brought in to deter local tribesmen from sabotage. The pipeline was being sunk deep into the ground to make it harder for local tribes to hold the state to ransom once the army had moved on.

We arrived in all that is left of the old town of Marib. The impressive six and seven-storey mud houses built on a mound obscuring the earliest settlement were already succumbing to the ravages of time when bombed by the Egyptian air force in the 1960s. We climbed to the roof of one of the more intact abandoned houses. An elderly soldier, once in the employ of the Imam but now a convinced republican, showed us round the town. To her surprise, Khayzara discovered that the man was a distant relation. I was reminded how small a country Yemen is, despite its incredible diversity of landscape and culture. Our guide went to perform his noon prayers whereupon bored young soldiers, obviously resenting being sent to this bleak hardship post, came up to chat with us. Khayzara and Amina were all for accepting a lunch invitation from strange males until Nuriya brought them to their senses.

We drove on to see the new Marib Dam completed a month before thanks to the largesse of Shaykh Zayid, the paramount ruler of the United Arab Emirates. Zayid's family aggrandize themselves by claiming descent from the illustrious Arabs who built the original dam. Rainfall in the area is only a fraction of what it was 2,000 years ago and the new dam is probably an expensive white elephant. It looked impressive but was holding back only a relatively small amount of water.

Of more interest were the remains of the old dam. We settled ourselves in the shade of a massive sluice gate and ate our lunch. The women threw all discretion to the winds and abandoned their veils even when other parties of visitors came close to us. We sat on the historic site chewing *qat* for the better part of the afternoon. Local youths took a break from herding camels and goats to come and join us. The women chatted unashamedly. However, being from the far west of Yemen, they found the dialect of the far east difficult to follow. I was gratified that I was able to help sort out some of the linguistic misunderstandings which arose.

We returned to Ahad on a Thursday night, our spirits raised by the trip, but were soon brought back to earth. Caroline's electricity had been cut off in her absence. She had paid all her bills and I went over to the electricity office to complain. Officials examined the records and agreed she should not have been disconnected. No one, however, bestirred themselves to reconnect her supply. The *mudiir* said it would be done on Saturday, after the day of rest. An over-the-top, and hopefully entertaining, protestation of outrage was called for. 'Shame on you!', I told the director. 'Is this any way for Muslims, deservedly renowned for their noble generosity, to welcome a poor defenceless foreign woman into their community? The doctor is weeping, wondering what to tell her mother when she asks if she is being well looked after.' The audience began smiling at the *mudiir*'s discomfiture. He eventually relented and I accompanied the 'engineer' who would reconnect the supply. As he did so, I talked with one of the *murshidaat* who was Caroline's neighbour. She told me the hospital had completely run out of all kinds of vaccine the week before. I was glad of her help in fighting off demands for a £5 reconnection fee.

I walked home, longing to rid myself of sweat. I entered my black hole of a kitchen and perspired freely all over the meal I threw together. I washed with water stored in a metal roof tank – water which was only cool enough to use in the evening. I had just turned on my feeble air-conditioner – which at full blast brought the temperature down to a balmy 32° – and settled down to eat when a messenger came from the hospital. A delegation had arrived unexpectedly from the provincial office in Nakhwa. I had to come to the hospital at once. I walked over and met Ahmad al Saydali, the primary health care director for the province. He showed me an order, written by Dr Thaalib and endorsed by the governor. Salah's unit was 'illegal' and to be closed at once. His drugs and equipment were to be handed over to the Nakhwa office. Our assistance in this task was required.

10
THINGS FALL APART

Arriving by dead of night after the weekend had begun, was definitely below the belt. As we sat on beds placed in the middle of the hospital compound Susan, Caroline and I suspected our visitors had assumed we would not be in Ahad. We were all angry, but our fury, broken Arabic and intemperate body language did not help us put our case. Dr Tawfiq, our Somali ally, tried to encourage conciliation but, as insults began to fly on all sides, gave it up as a bad job. We offered no compromise but kept insisting Salah's unit was official and that we had no intention of handing over the remainder of his drug supply. We stayed for an hour of fruitless exchanges and left.

We were up early and set off to take the bad news to the people of Bani Salim. Salah was not surprised to hear his unit was to be closed down, but his countrymen were astounded. On their insistence, we drove off to spread the news and were soon joined by other Toyotas. We picked our way from settlement to settlement, stopping at high places while men bellowed the news to inaccessible hamlets. More and more men clambered on board. They poured curses on the heads of those responsible, declared their support, and seemed not to know what to do next. Everybody wanted to climb onto the overloaded vehicles to join the protest. Salah showed his new mettle by ordering silence. Only the local sheikh or headman of each community was to join the delegation. In some hamlets this policy worked, in others it provoked discussion as to whether there was a universally acknowledged headman. By the time we came to the village of Nasar Mohammad, the former president of the local development association, we were a crowd of sixty. We had earlier heard that Nasar Mohammad was ill and resting. He reacted to the news like a roused bull. He cursed the new LDA president whom he immediately blamed for this underhand move. His successor would regret picking a fight. The people of Bani Salim were not friendless. The governor's deputy and his family originally came from the area and would intervene. The citizens must gather and go up to Nakhwa to protest. He armed himself with his rifle, short wooden club and a grubby, but expensive, *kufiyya* (woven hat). With no further preparation for the journey he strode out and got into the vehicle at the head of the convoy.

Half a dozen Toyotas, some with fifteen men on board, lurched their way down the rocky slopes. Drivers began racing each other along the sandy wadi bed, passengers cheering them on and jeering rival crews. There was a carnival atmosphere. Men seemed pleased to be uniting in a common cause, responding to a 'summons' and acting 'with one voice', just as the ideology of tribalness ordains they must. I had wondered at their lack of the structures of authority possessed by the valiant tribes of Yemen against whom they unflatteringly compared themselves. Now they had ceased to be cardboard boxes, passive recipients of fate. I wondered if we were going to drive all the way to Nakhwa in this festive mood. Could all these men abandon their concerns and leave home at a moment's notice?

On arrival in Ahad, a score of men trooped off to Ali Ahmad's house while the rest remained with the vehicles. All three levels of beds in Ali Ahmad's best hut were soon filled. Ali Ahmad's measured words were like a damp squib on the mood of shared revolutionary endeavour. Precipitate action now would provoke the authorities in the Nakhwa office. It would be counter-productive if the men went en masse to Nakhwa. This was not the *tariiq al nidhaam*, the path of order, the modern way to resolve differences. Instead, they should commission him to write a letter. In a few days they might send a small delegation.

The Bani Salim men perched uncomfortably on their tiered beds, torn between a bureaucratic approach to conflict resolution and a more traditional faith in robust democracy.

The men talked for hours and came to no agreement. Many seemed to feel they had shown they were not the tribesmen in search of a tribe they might appear to be. They had publicly expressed how seriously they took the affront to their communities and now looked to their leaders to continue the fight. As the others drifted off Nasar Mohammad and a dozen supporters stayed on, still determined to go up to Nakhwa in the morning.

It was unwise for us to be seen in the phalanx of aggrieved citizenry and Susan, Caroline and I made our own way up to Nakhwa the next morning. We knew we were in for a long confrontation when Dr Thaalib took the unusual step of clearing the front stage, ordering curious hangers-on out of the office. His deputy, and Saydali, the other pharmacy owner who ran the primary health care department, flanked him. Conversation with the doctor was in English with only occasional asides to the minions. Over tea we discussed the delights of Disneyland and Dr Thaalib's admiration for the *nidhaam* (order, political structure) in the United States. Eventually we got down to business.

'I am a sad man today', he began histrionically. 'We always had such good co-operation between your famous organization and my office. I have been honoured to work with the British in Ahad.' He listed the names of all our predecessors, or at least the males amongst them whose names he had learnt. 'With them I had deep personal friendship. I want to be friends with Doctor Tim, Doctor Caroline and with . . . ' He looked momentarily flustered. 'Sorry. I can't remember the name of your middy wiffy.' Susan spluttered. He had met her half a dozen times.

'Now we have these problems of . . . what do our American friends call it . . . mismatch. My deputy tells me that one of your colleagues, I think Mr Graham, was insulting to him. I find this very hard to believe.' He turned to the deputy and switched to Arabic. 'It was Mr Graham who insulted you, wasn't it?', he asked disingenuously. The deputy glowered. 'No, it was that one who is called Abdullah', he said, pointing to me. Dr Thaalib was astounded. He simply could not imagine such a mild person as Dr Tim behaving in this way. What a truly tragic misunderstanding!

We broke the ensuing silence by explaining that 'Mr Graham' had been invalided home. Dr Thaalib was insistent on knowing who would now be in charge. Efforts by Caroline to explain that we had no leader and should all be consulted were undermined by Brian's silence. We argued at cross purposes for two hours. Saydali was insistent that every health post in the country had to have three rooms and a bathroom. I replied by hoping he would have the chance to visit the provinces of Ta'iz and Ibb where the greatest progress in advancing primary health care had been achieved. He would then be able to see that the majority of health posts were one-roomed locally-financed structures similar to that built in Bani Salim. Dr Thaalib's deputy again became abusive. Foreigners should not dictate to Yemenis. His government's policy was crystal clear. Any health post with less than three rooms and a bathroom had to be closed.

Reaching no agreement, we tried to raise a number of other issues – the inadequate supply of vaccine and basic drugs, non-payment of salaries, absence of a budget for primary health care, vagueness of plans for a training course for men, lack of interest in starting the process of securing salaries for the *murshidaat* – but got nowhere. Whenever he was on the verge of having to commit himself, Dr Thaalib nimbly steered the conversation to another topic. Our words were only sporadically and inaccurately translated. By sticking to English Dr Thaalib was able to keep face while backing down from his initial insistence that Salah's unit had to be closed until funds became available to enlarge it. The mismatch between the concessions he made and the triumphant smile playing about his face was apparent only to us, the English speakers.

After several parties of intruders had been rudely dispersed, a more determined group forced their way into the room. At their head was the prefect of the district which includes Bani Salim. Sheikh Nasar Mohammad, a dozen other local men and the prefect's retinue of soldiers trooped in in his wake. The *mudiir an naahiya* did not beat about the bush. 'What's this I hear about the hospital in Bani Salim being closed? The citizens want to keep it and I want to know how it can be regarded as "un-official". I opened it.' Dr Thaalib was startled by his brusqueness, we by his audacity in not only refusing to execute an order signed by the governor himself, but in heading a protest delegation to the provincial capital. Dr Thaalib's resolve collapsed in the face of such opposition. When Nasar Mohammad proposed a compromise he agreed willingly. Salah could continue working in his area for five days a week, would work once a week in the UNICEF unit in Suq as Sebt, would receive a motorbike and start getting a salary. He and Abdul Kariim were to return with me the next week to receive their salaries and motorbikes.

It was now lunch time. Dr Thaalib used the lateness of the hour to rush the gathering to a close. When Brian said we had not discussed the project's other problems the director reluctantly agreed to meet again the following week. He made us appear distrustful. He exuded magnanimous *bonhomie*. Amidst avuncular hand-shaking and back slapping, he announced in Arabic that 'all our problems, our needless misunderstandings are over'. We were being fobbed off and Brian asked if the agreement could be put on paper. Dr Thaalib had been pushed too far. He wound up the meeting and easily brushed the request aside. The basis for future violations of the agreement was laid.

Dr Thaalib invited the whole delegation to lunch in his house. Either the *mudiir an naahiya* judged the invitation insincere, or he did not wish to obligate himself by acceptance of hospitality. The others followed his lead and we left the health office for a victory lunch in Bayt al Baydani. We were joined by the proprietor and by those who had been hanging around, awaiting the verdict. One of the Nakhwa officials who had sat silent through the morning's altercations slipped into the party. The prefect ate with relish, pleased with the outcome. The Bani Salim men were fulsome in their praise of the prefect and 'our brothers, the British'. The bureaucrat, who had been charged with closing Salah's unit, showed he was no interloper by saying the order had been wrong. So grateful were all parties, that a furious argument had to be fought, and many hundred rial notes thrown about, before the *mudiir an naahiya* was allowed to pay the bill for the whole party. We bought *qat* for the journey. As mist settled over the town we set off and discussed the day's events as we chewed. I asked the name of the Nakhwa official whom, I had learnt, was in charge of the ministry storeroom in Nakhwa. I told Salah I had been impressed by his honesty. Salah laughed and told me the man's name was Abdullah Hanash. Hanash, he explained, is a word for 'snake' and was most apt.

Days passed and still no vaccine came down to Ahad. On a Thursday Caroline gave notice she would go on strike the next week if new supplies were not available. Ali Ahmad thumped his chest and told her she was only a doctor and should not interfere in Yemeni concerns. Caroline retorted that to be a modern man he had to show respect for women and their achievements. A slanging match flared up which brought people from throughout the hospital. On the Monday the situation was unchanged. Caroline refused to work in her usual clinical capacity and instead went around the town with the *murshidaat* visiting mothers and children. I negotiated terms with a Toyota owner prepared to transport the two motor-bikes to Ahad and two days later drove up to Nakhwa with Salah and Abdul Kariim.

On our way into the health office we were waylaid by the furious director of the personnel department. He told us we should be ashamed of ourselves, spreading lies about his brother, the pharmacy owner in Suq as Sebt. His brother was a qualified nurse and had obtained all his medical supplies legally. He was probably going to be appointed as the primary health care worker to operate the Suq as Sebt unit. We were warned not to repeat the slanders.

Despite our appointment Dr Thaalib was not free to meet for long. In his habitually unctuous manner he told us he could only stay for half an hour. He weaved and dodged on all matters of substance. Brian told him that if progress could not be made we would be obliged to write to the ministry listing our complaints. We were urged to be patient. All our mismatches would be settled the following week when he would come down to Ahad for an inspection tour of the Tihama areas of the province.

Before he disappeared we asked about vaccine. He appeared unconcerned when Caroline told him she had gone on strike. 'If you want to take a little holiday instead of doing your work that is up to you.' Caroline swallowed her anger and Dr Thaalib passed the buck by telling us to see his nephew in the hospital. We eventually found the vaccination official in his pharmacy and were told to mind our own business. He would come to Ahad in his own good time.

We returned to the health office to find the personnel director had authorized payment to Abdul Kariim of one month's salary, but had told Salah there was no money to pay him. The two men had also learnt that one eighth of their salary was to be creamed off by the personnel department, that they would have to live off less than 1,000 rials (£100) a month and would receive no money for petrol, motorbike repairs and running expenses for their units.

We went, as arranged, to the health department store but had to kill two hours before Hanash, the man we had dubbed 'the snake', finally showed up. Without a word of apology he informed us of an unfortunate clerical error. On checking his inventory, he had found there was only one UNICEF bike in the store-room. This was the one ear-marked for Abdul Kariim. Salah would have to do without until UNICEF sent a new batch. Could we move the crated motorbike out of the store as he was in a hurry?

We had only a quick glimpse into the store room as we lugged the motorbike into the street. We stood round in the drizzle watching Abdul Kariim assemble the machine to make sure none of its parts had been stolen. Salah was despondent, surprised the Nakhwa officials had taken such immediate and cruel revenge on the people of Bani Salim. He revealed that Hanash had told him he could solve all the problems surrounding Salah's work if the citizens gave him one of their best quality kufiiyas. These woven hats, made from a type of bamboo imported from India, are very expensive. The best ones made in Bani Salim cost £3,000. Their manufacture is very time consuming and the fine needle-work takes its toll on the eyes. I had met several half-blind kufiiya makers eking out a miserable living.

Salah urged me not to mention the demand for a substantial bribe at this stage. I said we would write a letter to the ministry complaining of how Salah had been treated. We would state our grievances in the light of information we had learnt from our friend, the supply officer in the UNICEF office in Sana'a. UNICEF had provided a motorbike, an electricity generator and a water pump to every primary health care unit in the country. The ministry could not deny having received them. I told Salah that UNICEF were far from satisfied with progress at implementing North Yemen's primary health plan and had announced to the Yemeni government that they would be drastically scaling down their help. It was going to be up to the Yemenis to devise means of funding units and providing drug supplies in the future.

Our friend in Sana'a had spent years in Yemen and, unlike his colleagues, had learnt Yemeni Arabic. He knew that in certain provinces a large amount of UNICEF material was being purloined. Like me, he believed one gained respect in Yemen from plain talking and not disguising dissent. Once he had so offended a powerful provincial official that the security authorities were persuaded to throw him out of Yemen. He remained only because more informed Yemenis pointed out that UN personnel could only be expelled with the agreement of their employers.

In some cases provincial health authorities co-operated and allowed the UNICEF officer access to storerooms to check the distribution of UNICEF aid. This was not the case in Nakhwa. A few months previously he had come to Nakhwa by appointment with the health office. Only junior clerks were in the health office as everyone with responsibility had gone into hiding for the duration of his visit. He had not even been able to locate the storeroom and left Nakhwa furious at being so crudely duped.

We prepared ourselves for the meeting with Dr Thaalib in Ahad. Hoping for advantage on a home pitch, we arranged the cushions in my room and discussed how we should seat ourselves for maximum benefit. To honour our guests we bought crates of soft drinks from my landlord's shop. We provided thermoses of cold water purified by the filters we were trying to promote in the hospital. However, our campaign against the notion that clean water only comes in expensive plastic bottles was undermined by Ali Ahmad who routinely refused to drink our water. He was keen to offer his own obeisance to Dr Thaalib, to Saydali and to Hanash. He distributed a carton of litre bottles of water.

I proposed that the meeting be held in Arabic to avoid 'misunderstandings and problems of translation'. Hanash replied by saying that our Arabic was too bad, allowing Dr Thaalib to squash the idea. Once again he refused to commit himself and nothing was written. Any concessions wrung from the director were not translated for the benefit of his minions. Brian seemed content with the assurances given, but I objected there was a 'mismatch' between our conversation and the impression given in Arabic. Our co-ordinator and Dr Thaalib both rejected such an uncharitable interpretation. The meeting broke up with the usual hastily-contrived display of accord when a man came to fetch the whole party for lunch.

When I learned the identity of our host, the owner of a local pharmacy, Susan and I wondered whether we should obligate ourselves by accepting the invitation. Susan, together with Maryam, the Sudanese trainer, had been collecting evidence from pregnant women about the man's malpractice and his violation of the law by injecting valium, oxytocinon and Depo-Provera. We felt that accepting the invitation might make it harder to present this evidence in an official complaint. Our ever genial co-ordinator brushed our fears aside. It was vital that we show Dr Thaalib and his party our goodwill. My arguments that Yemenis themselves often find pretexts for turning down invitations, lest their freedom of action become circumscribed, fell on deaf ears. While awaiting a sumptuous feast we were forced to watch a video of American wrestling. I suggested to those near me that the bouts, though skilfully choreographed, were obviously rigged. A lively debate ensued as this improbable notion was considered.

After lunch Dr Thaalib returned to Nakhwa, leaving behind Saydali and Hanash. Fortunately Brian delayed his return to Sana'a and was present the next day to see our 'agreement' unravelled. We arrived at the hospital in the early morning to find our two adversaries taking charge of the primary health care room in the new building. With them was a man with a tape measure. We asked what they were doing. 'Dr Thaalib has asked me to set up a primary health care pharmacy', replied Saydali. 'We are going to build a dispensary hatch into this wall. These drugs have to be distributed to the mothers and children who need them. Patients will receive drugs from this room.' We were told we had to hand over the rest of the drugs we had brought from Sana'a.

I replied that the drugs were given by UNICEF on condition that they be used only by rural health posts and not as a solution to the problem of supplying hospitals. 'We have informed UNICEF we are storing them to ensure their distribution to the specified beneficiaries. Yesterday Dr Thaalib confirmed his understanding of this policy. We agreed that cartons of UNICEF drugs are to be delivered unopened to health centres for distribution to earmarked units. We also agreed that this room will be used only by the two trainer supervisors as an office and storeroom.'

Saydali feigned amazement at our misunderstanding. I was long inured to these absurd conversations, but the effect on Brian was dramatic. The scales fell from his eyes as Saydali went on to list the drugs he had to confiscate. 'They have passed their date of expiry and are dangerous.' They had collected bottles of chloroquine syrup and cartons of multi-vitamin tablets and antibiotics, all popular UNICEF-provided drugs profitable to private pharmacy owners. Some had expired but most had not yet done so. We argued about each expiry date. So ill-educated are the two officials that they could not understand the expiry dates stamped with the unfamiliar numerals used in the West.

The confrontation turned heated when we categorically refused to hand over the medicines being stored in my house. We appealed to Ahmad Ali as a witness that we had never agreed to help set up a pharmacy in the hospital. He sided with the men from Nakhwa which emboldened Hanash to threaten to go to the government prefect and have us arrested if we did not give up the drugs. We called his bluff and stormed out. We agreed to hand to the ministry the hard-hitting letter complaining about the failure of the Nakhwa health office to implement the national primary health care plan. Brian would get it translated. I took him up the road to catch a taxi for the first leg of the arduous journey back to Sana'a.

A long argumentative day was only just beginning. The Nakhwa delegation had an early lunch at Ali Ahmad's then startled us by pulling up outside Susan and Caroline's house and tooting their horns until I popped out to see the cause of the commotion. I was curtly invited to join an inspection tour to see existing units and select sites for new health posts. I knew this was an absurdly ambitious programme for an afternoon but had to humour the officials as we had done three years previously when a flying motorcade, led by Dr Thaalib himself, had 'selected' sites. Unfed and resentful, I got into Rocky and was glad Caroline jumped in to lend support. We drove out of town at high speed, trying to keep up with our tormentors.

We had no idea where we were going but soon realized our first destination was Zahir. When we arrived the men stopped not at Abdul Kariim's primary health unit, but at Khalid Tahir's pharmacy. He welcomed his old friends who, it transpired, had come to 'inspect' his premises prior to upgrading his licence from that of pharmacy to clinic. Caroline and I pointed out the drugs illegally smuggled from Saudi Arabia and others supposedly banned in North Yemen. We noted he was selling costly, brightly-packaged aspirin with 'added vitamin C' but not the much cheaper aspirin produced in Sana'a. We could find no Yemeni-made drugs. 'Is it not the duty of ministry officials', I asked, 'to encourage pharmacists to stock drugs produced by the Yemen Drug Company, instead of foreign drugs? Has not the brother the president repeatedly urged cadres to encourage Yemeni industry?' Our remarks were brushed aside. Khalid Tahir was a medical assistant and what he sold in his pharmacy was not our concern.

We went on to the unit. Saydali looked through Abdul Kariim's register of patients and pronounced himself dissatisfied. During the inspection a patient with a dehydrated child dared to come in. Saydali explained the use of ORS sachets in hectoring tones until the man disappeared. Hanash rummaged round and I was relieved Abdul Kariim had prudently removed the condoms and contraceptive pills we had provided. Unfortunately he found something even more incriminating. With a triumphant grin he brandished a stethoscope.

According to ministry policy, stethoscopes are not supposed to be used by primary health care workers. Caroline had proposed that we quietly ignore this ban. If pharmacy owners have stethoscopes as props to their credibility why should real health workers not have them? We had bought stethoscopes from a pharmacy in Hodeidah. Salah, and to a lesser extent Abdul Kariim, had shown immediate competence in using them to diagnose a variety of respiratory complaints. Saydali pounced on us. We had broken the law. Only doctors were allowed to have stethoscopes. It was his duty to confiscate this illegal equipment and report us to the ministry. Only with great difficulty did I refrain from mentioning that we knew stethoscopes were on sale in his own pharmacy in Nakhwa.

Darkness was already falling as we set off to visit Salah. The Nakhwa men insisted on taking the most direct route through the mountains and Ali Ahmad claimed to know the way. Only we had done the journey before, yet when we came to crossroads and dithered over directions our suggestions were not adopted. We were soon completely lost and drove round aimlessly in the gathering gloom. Whenever our Rocky was in the lead Hanash impatiently tooted his horn and taunted me for my 'unmasculine' driving.

By accident we found ourselves in the wadi below the fortress of the *mudiir an naahiya* and Saydali decided to go up to visit him. A further slanging match ensued in front of the embarrassed prefect. Saydali told us we were not authorized to meet either prefects or officials from any of the LDAs in our area. We were in Ahad solely to provide staff to the hospital. Primary health care was not our concern. We had no business to leave the town except to go to Nakhwa and Sana'a, and then only with permission from the Ahad prefect.

Ali Ahmad did not contradict this travesty of everything we had been trying to achieve for four years. Neither did he take our side when Saydali said that we had agreed that Salah had to work three days a week in Suq as Sebt. The *mudiir an naahiya* growled disagreement at this act of bad faith and expressed gratitude for the work we were trying to do. He was further angered when the visitors mentioned they wished to pop in on the president of the local development association, whose village 4 km. away could be reached in another half an hour. I had no wish to see the reclusive president whom I had only met once and who had disappointed us by joining the alliance trying to close Salah's unit.

With relief I heard that the LDA president had gone to Nakhwa to complain to the governor of the indignity suffered when the *mudiir an naahiya* had arrested him and tried to dismiss him from his post. The right of the prefect to do so was far from clear and triggered a prolonged period of uncertainty. For months the feud between the two most important men in the district, arising, at least in part, out of the dispute over Salah's unit, brought official business to a standstill. Both men left their posts to lobby potential allies in Nakhwa and Sana'a. When honour is at stake between determined Yemeni males, no expense or effort is too great.

Despite the lateness of the hour, the delegation was still determined to reach Salah's unit and the whistlestop tour resumed. Around midnight we found ourselves at a crossroads near Bani Salim. Caroline and I took stock. We had spent a hot, exhausting and fruitless day being insulted while we trailed behind the Nakhwa officials. We had no power to limit the damage they were doing to our work. We were fed up and decided to return to Ahad.

We met Ali Ahmad in the hospital the next morning. We asked what had happened and were told of a brief inspection visit to Salah's unit. We were thus unprepared in the *suq* when we met excited cloth merchants from Bani Salim. Had we heard the wonderful news? The party from Nakhwa had arrived at a late hour and talked at length with sheikh Nasar Mohammad and the citizens. They had stayed the night and announced their willingness to help the area. Salah's unit was going to be temporarily closed while it was upgraded and converted into a hospital. When the work was done a foreign doctor would be posted to the hospital, together with a midwife.

I had enough and my anger reached new heights. There was not the slightest chance of such scarce personnel being sent to such an isolated and powerless area. What was the point of our continuing to explain the nature and the limitations of primary health care if no one helped us deflate people's unreal expectations? Caroline tried to restrain me but I insisted on returning to Ali Ahmad. Again I asked him what had happened the night before and again he fobbed us off with the same reply. Why, I asked him, did he accuse us of not sharing information and responsibility with him, yet not tell us of staying the night in Bani Salim and the decisions made about the unit? He bridled, saying his reputation as an honest man was unassailable. When, he demanded to know, had he ever done anything dishonest?

Like a fool, I did not let the challenge pass. I mentioned the decor of his hut. Months earlier he had tiled his main reception hut with the same tiles he had bought for BSDA to complete the new hospital building. He started swearing and I insulted him, albeit mildly in Yemeni terms, by calling him a 'person of little politeness'. He replied that we were 'imperialists'. He could do without our stipend. 'I don't need your miserable 300 rials a month. I chew *qat* worth more than that every day!' He puffed out his cheek to indicate his wealth and independence.

War had been declared. A sense of gloom gripped us in the days ahead. We knew we could not go on working at such cross purposes with determined officials. We had allies and friends – the *murshidaat*, the hospital vaccinators, the women of the town, Abdul Kariim, Salah, the people of Bani Salim and their obliging local prefect. We were shown respect and hospitality when we visited rural areas. Yet none of this could compensate for the stress of having to cope with calculated discourtesy and enmity from hypocrites professing to share the philosophy of primary health care. No cycle of meetings could resolve this.

Hope was fading fast. It seemed most unlikely that we would ever see the training course for male primary health care workers which, according to our original agreement with the Yemenis, should have started three years previously. Yet we could not afford to be seen to be the first to abandon this goal and had to maintain a sense of keen urgency about the recruitment of students for the course. We knew that Yahya and Yusuf were far from being ideal trainer-supervisors but they were all that we had. Since returning from their brief course in Sana'a they had shown no interest in putting their supposed newly-acquired skills to use. For financial reasons they continued to wield syringes rather than disabuse people of the notion that tablets are invariably 'weak' medicine. They had not acted on hints that they should come out into the countryside to publicize the course, explain the benefits of a local health post and to seek candidates for training. They preferred to stay in the hospital making money. We decided to press them and, to our surprise, both men eventually agreed to come up to visit Bani Salim.

Salah was expecting us and showed the utmost patience as the two nurses ponderously explained knowledge he had long since acquired. Yusuf and Yahya had never visited a primary health care unit and did not realize how few people actually come to such health posts. According to the national plan, the thrust of the health worker's efforts should be in preventive work and home visiting. Many units only register a dozen people a day as recipients of medication. The real success of such primary health care is unquantifiable. To a bureaucratic mentality, to those indoctrinated into a system investing the collecting of statistics with a farcically inflated importance, Salah was failing in his work. He was now recording up to thirty people a day and dutifully noting down their names, addresses, ages, sex and the amount of medication prescribed. The two newcomers still thought this insufficient.

A sumptuous meal was arranged in honour of the two men. The people of Bani Salim are generous and no doubt wished to secure Yahya and Yusuf as allies in the conflict raging about the unit and the hospital they hoped would replace it. As dishes of chicken and lamb were placed in front of us, I doubt whether the nurses realized just how much money was being spent on them. Meat is a very great luxury in the area and, unlike in many parts of Yemen, quite beyond the means of most households on any regular basis.

Yahya and Yusuf are both habitual qat chewers. Having finished lunch – and scorned the water-pipes laboriously prepared in our honour – they lit up Rothmans to calm the anxiety which is characteristic of determined chewers not sure where the afternoon's leaves are coming from. The astute Salah diagnosed the cause of their concern and assured them that a car had been sent down to Ahad to buy qat. When bunches arrived the lion's share was given to Yahya, Yusuf and myself.

It was the least enjoyable qat chew I ever attended. Yahya and Yusuf added to the damage done by the Nakhwa officials and undid much of Salah's patient work. The tone was set when I casually mentioned that we had just received a new consignment of the Arabic version of 'Where There Is No Doctor'. I suggested it would be useful to give copies to young men who might wish to become health workers. The two nurses were not pleased. 'Such books are dangerous', declared Yahya. 'People will start pretending to be doctors.'

Yahya and Yusuf did so throughout the afternoon as a succession of hypochondriacs gathered about them. Many complained of nervous disorders, using the word *mitnervos* which has only just come into Yemeni Arabic via the medium of television. Salah, had he been alone, would have explained the use of aspirin, advised such men to chew less *qat* and sent them packing. The two nurses pandered to their fears. They talked of the great advantages of valium and of the benefits they had personally obtained. I described the problems caused by excessive use of tranquillizers in the West and of restrictions on the use of intravenous valium. Yusuf interrupted with a pointed question: 'Are you a doctor? Have you experience of treating nervous disorders?'

My intervention was also pooh-poohed when a man suffering from insomnia, a common complaint among *qat* chewers, was advised to try intravenous valium. When he replied that he had already had a series of injections in Nakhwa the nurses advised him to try electro-convulsive therapy. I was surprised to learn that ECT is available in Yemen. Both men talked of benefits they had seen from its use in the Hodeidah hospital where they had trained.

That evening we rang Brian and were told that Dr Thaalib had agreed to meet us again, this time in Nakhwa. We went, in great trepidation, to give Ali Ahmad this news. We eventually found him in the pharmacy where an air-conditioner had just been installed. Ructions had surrounded use of this machine, the only air-conditioner in the hospital. It had formerly been in the X-ray room but as there had been no X-ray service for over a year the Sudanese nurses had started living in the delightfully cool room. Ali Ahmad, now staking out a populist position opposed to the foreign staff in the hospital, arranged for the air-conditioner to be moved to the pharmacy. The pharmacy was as poorly stocked as before. Ali

Ahmad and other young men were chewing *qat* with piles of account books and school text books lying in front of them. The air-conditioner was on full blast and the window was wide open. Such profligate waste of power is common when it is the government which has to foot the electricity bill.

We greeted Ali Ahmad and coldly shook hands for the first time since our very public altercation. 'I have spoken to Dr Thaalib and to the governor', he told us, 'and asked for a meeting. The governor has ordered you to go to Nakhwa tomorrow.' We saw little point in disputing his interpretation of events and instead made the suggestion that we take the *murshidaat* up to Nakhwa with us. They had all just passed their examination, and the ordeal of gaining official recognition as health workers could now begin. As a first step to joining the civil service payroll all needed to be issued with birth certificates, identity cards, good behaviour reports from the police, security clearances, certificates of good health, education certificates and other documents with mysterious Arabic titles I could not understand. Lutf, the unpaid vaccinator, immediately asked if he could also come in order to pursue his own salary claim. Ali Ahmad agreed and we arranged to meet and travel together.

At seven the next morning a large party milled about outside Susan and Caroline's house. Sayyida's aunt had agreed, much against her better judgement, to let her go on the trip but had come to check she would be well guarded. Maryam solemnly swore to look after her. Another of the *murshidaat*, a neighbour of Caroline's, was with a delightful little boy who suffered from a urinary tract condition. Dr Thaalib had offered to do the surgery which he, but not Caroline, considered necessary. Car space was at a premium and there was much jostling for position. At the last moment Ali Ahmad came over to me with what seemed a reasonable request. Some goods had to be delivered to Nakhwa but the hospital Toyota was full. We offered assistance and I helped load sacks of charcoal and sorghum and half a dozen new, and obviously smuggled, car tyres onto our roof-rack.

Confusion surrounded our arrival in Nakhwa. Soldiers at the final checkpoint were suspicious of foreigners driving Yemeni women. We all had to get out and Maryam, Ali

Ahmad, the *murshidaat*, Lutf, Caroline and I displayed our various permissions. Maryam was offended by the soldiers' rudeness and expressed her anger by addressing the women on the subject of Islamic good manners. How, she asked pointedly, could the soldiers be Muslims when they behaved in such boorish ways to strangers? The soldiers were unmoved and ordered us to follow escorting army vehicles up to the security headquarters.

We had to pass by the health office where Caroline and I switched off our engines and jumped out. I announced we would go no further. The resulting rumpus blocked the street and brought officials out from the health office and bystanders from nearby shops. I asked Dr Thaalib to confirm that we were in Nakhwa on official business at his invitation. He declined with great amiability saying he was no more than a humble civil servant. I agreed to go to the security head-quarters, taking Lutf as a witness, provided that Caroline be allowed to proceed and deliver the sick boy. As this was being negotiated, Ali Ahmad quietly moved the goods into the now empty hospital vehicle and sped off. Caroline took the ill child who was to be lodged in Dr Thaalib's magnificent house and to be operated on in his own private theatre. She turned up just as an embarrassed Ali Ahmad was unloading the last of the tribute we had helped carry to his liege-lord.

We were already in a foul mood by the time we met up with Brian. Dr Thaalib tried a new tactic, picking off our most tractable colleague. 'Can I speak alone to Mr Brian for two minutes?', he asked sweetly. Caroline and I were upset at Brian's acquiescence but filed out with meek obedience. After a quarter of an hour sitting round with other petitioners at the doors of power we returned uninvited. 'Give us five minutes more. Mr Brian and I are solving all your problems and will tell you of our decisions shortly.' I replied that our organization did not give the co-ordinator such powers. Caroline added that we had been invited to a meeting to discuss our jobs and had a right to be present. Brian, like our adversary, looked angry, and we had no choice but to withdraw.

The snub was not without consequence. More than our pride was hurt. Everything we had said about the non-hierarchical nature of our organization was being publicly contradicted. Our powerlessness was made obvious. Brian was undoing years of effort to impress our collective working practices on Yemenis. In the past there had been occasions when the entire staff of the BSDA programme attended crisis meetings in the ministry. Brian's predecessor had never arrogated such authority as to be sole representative at a meeting.

We sat around growing more agitated as Saydali, Hanash and the director of the personnel department addressed snide remarks. After an hour and a half we had had enough and left the building. We had not had breakfast and were famished. We were still eating when a messenger sent by Dr Thaalib came to fetch us. We took our time finishing our meal.

Ali Ahmad and the minions were also awaiting us in the inner sanctum. Dr Thaalib took the floor. 'Dr Caroline and Dr Tim, I have had a long report on your activities which is very damaging to your honour. The governor has read the report and is very worried. He wishes to see you both.' He tantalized us by holding a copy in front of him but not telling us of the accusations it contained. Caroline broke the silence by asking who had written the report but Dr Thaalib only smiled. It was left to Brian to fill us in. 'Ali Ahmad has written a letter to his excellency the governor and to Dr Thaalib.' The nature of the complaints only slowly became clear. In his three page letter Ali Ahmad accused us of espionage, indolence, insubordination, theft of drugs and political agitation. Dr Thaalib spoke as if he gave credence to the charges. 'Why have you travelled to the Saudi border? Why have you left Ahad without getting permission and informing the authorities? You have been using your Daihatsu for private purposes and not for hospital business and we will have to report the matter to UNICEF. You have told people that my health office does not wish to help them. You have insulted Ali Ahmad's honour.'

Brian sat in silence, unable or unwilling to come to our defence. His culturally inappropriate spinelessness suggested to those present that he believed the charges and could not rebut them. Caroline and I were dumbfounded and protested our innocence but with little effect. Dr Thaalib interrupted with the remark that it would be a great shame to bother the busy governor with 'our little mismatches'. If we apologized to Ali

Ahmad the matter could be forgotten. I replied that of course I was sorry that we had had a disagreement with Ali Ahmad but felt it fair we be shown a copy of the letter he had written. Brian again looked displeased, a silence ensued and Caroline and I obligingly debased ourselves further. We apologized and shook hands with Ali Ahmad. He smiled smugly, not reciprocating with a word of regret for the persistent discourtesy and ill-temper shown us in previous months.

Ali Ahmad's diatribe and its aftermath had taken up the whole morning and again Dr Thaalib was able to plead another appointment and slip away. With difficulty our own leader fixed another meeting two days hence. When we got outside into some welcome fresh air Brian, to our great surprise, announced that he too had to leave as he had arranged a meeting in Sana'a with a fellow expatriate. Caroline asked him to stay so that all the charges against us could be discussed, future action by the security authorities anticipated, the letter of complaint to the ministry finalized and a strategy for the next encounter prepared. Brian was adamant that he had to return to Sana'a. He drove off, telling us to ring him that evening.

Our spirits were not raised by having to continue chaperone duties for the *murshidaat*. We drove down the main street of Nakhwa, attracting much attention from the purely male passers-by. We parked and argued over what to do next. The women had not got far in chasing papers and would have to return the next day. This had not been anticipated by the Tihami women, some of whom had unrealistic expectations of the swift machinery of Nakhwa bureaucracy. A few were all for driving back down to Ahad immediately, without even pausing for lunch. Others wanted the men to fetch food from the *suq* and to eat in the vehicles. Ali Ahmad, Lutf and I tried to persuade them of the impracticality of going back to the Tihama only to return early the following morning. Maryam spoke sternly to the women, telling them they had to stay and see the business through. She then departed to stay with Sudanese colleagues, leaving us to continue wrangling. Sayyida, fearing her aunt's wrath, was especially reluctant to remain and Katiba was worried about the reaction of her husband and mother-in-law.

Caroline's intervention proved decisive. She had heard enough bickering and told everyone to get out and go to Bayt al Baydani where they would have lunch and stay the night. To our surprise, her impressive display of controlled anger worked wonders. Amina, out of earshot of the bustling Ali Ahmad, complimented her on her decisiveness. Ali Ahmad, with whom we were desperately trying to be amicable, led our party into Bayt al Baydani and arranged for the women to be given the biggest room. Our large party was eventually served lunch. Lutf asked to be recompensed for various informal, thus unreceipted, expenses he had incurred in the course of the morning. We also paid the *murshidaat* for their food and accommodation expenses and took our leave.

We walked aimlessly round town, still simmering with anger at Brian. Near the hospital we ran into an Indian who was so delighted to find fellow English-speaking non-Muslims he immediately invited us to tea. We learned that he and another male laboratory technician, together with six female nurses, all but one of them married, had already been in Nakhwa for nine months. They were under instructions from Dr Thaalib not to walk around town without reason and to observe a curfew from 8 p.m. to 8 a.m. They had been recruited by a labour contractor in Kerala and led to believe they would be earning good money in Yemen. On arrival they found they were to receive only 50 per cent of the money promised them and in the course of the next few months the Yemeni rial slumped against the dollar, further reducing their incomes. They were now earning the same money they could have got working at home and living with their families. They were desperate to leave, but Dr Thaalib had impounded their passports and was insisting they see out their two-year contracts. They were not allowed to leave Nakhwa. The Indian women accepted their uncertain fate with irrepressible humour and grace. They showed us pictures of the children they had left behind. We invited them to come to stay with us in Ahad, visit the sea and witness a friendlier aspect of Yemen. It remained unsaid, but we all knew they would never get past the first checkpoint on the road down to the Tihama.

Our own problems paled into insignificance. We could always resign and leave and had both contemplated doing so.

We were mobile and free to travel where we pleased. The prospect of staying the night in Nakhwa depressed us intensely and we decided to drive on to Sana'a to have things out with Brian. We hit the road, playing the rock and roll we both fortunately enjoyed. To the sound of Jimmy Hendrix we prepared our arguments for the confrontation ahead. A hapless passenger we picked up gritted his teeth at the cacophony but politely tried to take an interest in our culture. 'Stoned free. Free as a breeze. Free to do as I please', sang Hendrix. 'What did he say?', asked the Yemeni. My translation was economical with the truth.

We arrived in Sana'a at an unfortunate time as Brian's young children were being put to bed. Brian was surprised to see us and suggested we meet him an hour later in the British embassy club. It was the weekly drinks night and the place was filled with expatriates, enjoying pay and conditions superior to those at home, yet drinking too much in order to drown their sorrows. All my colleagues had been accorded honorary club membership and all but a few came to the club to play tennis, swim and drink.

A visitor to Yemen, a fellow employee of the agency on holiday from Latin America, was much struck with the 'expat' atmosphere of BSDA after being taken to the club. In an unofficial report he wrote of 'the besieged feeling which manifests itself in gathering round the embassy pool'. For making such observations, and for expressing envy that we were well paid, well equipped and generously financed in comparison with our colleagues in other countries, the report was buried. Its author did not receive the courtesy of an acknowledgement when he submitted it to the London office.

We had no desire to talk to the expats and huddled round the empty pool. I was inadequately-dressed, shivering and ill prepared for the sudden change of altitude and climate. We had all had a long tiring day and were on a knife edge. Tension immediately exploded. Caroline and I expressed our disquiet at the way the morning's meeting had been handled. Brian bridled. He insisted he had done his best and had nothing to reproach himself for. We complained at being humiliated and his failure to defend us. We had a right to know what had been said and should not readily believe Dr Thaalib's assurances the matter would go no further. The practice of presenting a united, and at least vaguely non-hierarchical, image to the Yemenis was important and should not be abandoned. There was a difference between displaying necessary politeness to Dr Thaalib and his staff and Brian's un-Yemeni lack of forthrightness.

The argument grew heated and personal, Brian becoming flustered and I in my weariness choking back tears of frustration and rage. Neither made allowance for the problems of the other. Brian insisted we had misunderstood the organization's authority structure and told us of new discussions in London giving more authority to country representatives. He was shortly to go to London for a three-week long conference of programme co-ordinators which would formalize the new policy. The meeting broke up.

The next day brought news from London of a possible replacement for me as Ahad 'facilitator'. The London desk person described him as an 'ideal candidate' – an American Muslim, a former Peace Corps volunteer who had worked with the YAR Ministry of Health and spoke excellent Arabic. The desk person urged us to accept the American to work in Kahima or Ahad. My hopes of being able to leave the Ahad project without the trauma of resignation were instantly raised.

Caroline and I looked through the American's cv and his interview notes. The candidate talked of his great friendship with Yemenis who were 'natural people'. He could get on well with them, whereas in the West he had hardly any relatives and, he admitted, no friends. Was this, we asked, the kind of balanced person able to cope with the tensions we had all been under? Worse still, was the candidate's silence about his previous stint in Yemen. He had listed no referee able to assess his work with the Peace Corps. No one who had interviewed the American in our London office had commented on this omission.

Our suspicions were shared by our two Arab colleagues from the Kahima project who also happened to be in Sana'a. By phoning round to the Peace Corps, and to half a dozen Yemeni officials who remembered the prospective recruit, they soon established that he spoke next to no Arabic and had been flown home early by the Peace Corps on the verge of a nervous breakdown. In the course of fifteen unhappy months in North Yemen he had worked in no less than five places because he found it so hard to get on with Yemenis. Some of the officials he had met were so horrified at the thought of his return to their country that they vowed to pull strings to block his entry papers.

Defying recognized procedures, my colleagues relayed this news back to London. The head of the agency's overseas programme was incensed. Our information was 'mere gossip' we had had no right to collect. Once more we were being asked to believe in the infallibility of an interview process run by people who, for all their proclaimed expertise in development, had never shared our experience and who would not have to live twenty-four days a day with what looked to be another severely depressed person being recruited for the wrong job in the wrong place.

I broached with Brian my transfer to the Rahbaan project. Sarah had been discussing my problems in Ahad with Mujahid our diligent Yemeni counterpart. The Rahbaan director was concerned that some of the outlying health posts were not being visited sufficiently often. Having seen that I had the knowledge and enthusiasm, and the makings of sufficient Arabic, to convey the ideas of primary health care, he wished to recruit me. My lack of precise medical knowledge would actually be beneficial as I could complement the Yemeni health worker without undermining his authority. Mujahid envisaged me going out on week-long walking trips to visit two or three units, show the health worker he was not forgotten, publicize oral rehydration solution, infant vaccination and growth monitoring and generally lend to the health workers the credibility which, whether we liked it or not, attached to us as foreign 'experts'. The director and my colleagues in Rahbaan agreed to offer me such a job provided I would commit myself to staying for the six months which remained of my two-year contract. I had accepted willingly. The thought of going to work in a project where our most important counterpart not only knew that I was arriving, but had himself thought out a viable role for me, was exciting. I was thrilled at the idea of again working amongst gregarious highlanders. However, Brian did not share my enthusiasm and indicated such a transfer from one project to another could not be decided without the approval of BSDA management. I would have to wait and see.

We were shown Hassan's translation of the letter we had drafted to the ministry. Even without the benefit of an Arabic dictionary, it was clear the letter had been radically expurgated. Caroline and I asked Hassan why he had decided to change our letter. 'This is my country. I know how to speak to my people', he replied. 'Some of the things you said are very rude.' We took his point but said that the letter was not a communication between Yemenis. It was not a criticism of the Yemeni government, or the Ministry of Health, but an implied rebuke to certain provincial officials. We were facing serious difficulties and they needed to be ironed out before we could decide to keep our project going. Hassan was greatly hurt at the implied denigration of his abilities as a translator and left the office in a huff. We agreed that I would take the letter to be retranslated and would hand Dr Thaalib a copy before submitting it to the ministry.

I took the letter to an Egyptian doctor, employed by AFJAD to work in a clinic set up to benefit the ostracized *akhdaam* garbage collectors of the capital city. She raised no objections to the firm, but polite, tone. For our funders, under a new director, had adopted a less pussy-footing attitude than that of BSDA. In attempts to iron out difficulties impeding her project the Egyptian had helped write even more hard-hitting letters to various ministries. She dictated a better translation and I went straight back to the BSDA office. Lest Hassan make changes when typing, I myself sat down in front of the unfamiliar keyboard and laboriously typed out the letter.

Brian told us of decisions made in London. Hassan, he said, was no longer to be regarded as an administrative assistant but as a candidate for national deputy co-ordinator. A new administrative assistant would work under him. Hassan, he had decided, should come with us to Nakhwa for our next encounter. He had to learn more of our work and to meet those we worked with. This was the first time we learned that yet another person was going to be recruited to our already over-staffed office. Caroline and I protested that Hassan knew little of health needs in rural Yemen, nothing of our project and its problems and should not be thrown in at the deep end in the midst of a crisis. His previous experience had not equipped him for the role of mediator which would, because of his nationality, fall upon him in any confrontation with Dr Thaalib. Our arguments fell on deaf ears. Caroline and I drove back to Nakhwa in no better humour than before.

Our fears were borne out. As Dr Thaalib read our letter a smile played about his face. Before he had read very far he asked Hassan, in Arabic, how he thought our 'little problems' could be solved. Did he not agree that sending such letters to the busy ministry officials was so unnecessary? Surely he could use his intermediary position to explain to his British friends the need for patience, co-operation and co-ordination? Hassan willingly became his victim and began to propose his own compromises to problems he had only just learnt about. He was put in an impossible position, forced to prove his fidelity to a powerful compatriot and be seen to try to resolve misunderstandings. Brian allowed him to ramble on, as the morning wasted away. Again we presented a completely disunited image.

I broke in to reply that we could not go on wishing disagreements out of existence. Months and months had gone by without us doing anything to help the citizens whose need for a comprehensive health service was so great. Our understanding of the national primary health care plan was fundamentally different from that of the Nakhwa health office. We urgently needed to clarify rights and responsibilities. Which geographical areas were covered by our project? Did we have the right to visit freely in these areas? Were we authorized to speak to officials of the local development association and to government prefects? Who was to choose candidates for a male training course and sites for health posts? Was it accepted that a health post would be regarded as 'official' even if it did not have three rooms and a bathroom? Who was to pay for training, construction of buildings, and salaries? When would the provincial office prepare a budget for primary health care? How were UNICEF drugs to be distributed and how could arrangements be made to secure community participation in raising funds for primary health care once UNICEF drugs ran out?

None of these issues were even touched upon. The letter remained unread and was tucked away underneath a wadge of papers. Dr Thaalib once more played for time, saying he had to go to Sana'a on important business and could meet us there in a week 'to finally solve our mismatches'. When we pointed out this would involve meeting on Christmas Day he agreed to meet on Boxing Day. We arranged to meet with Brian on Christmas Eve to discuss our strategy. Our co-ordinator then returned to Sana'a with Hassan. The *murshidaat* and Lutf had got as far in their pursuit of employment documentation as could reasonably be expected after only three days. I returned to Ahad, my journey quite without success.

Over the next few days we prepared a document expressing our understanding of primary health care and the role of BSDA, LDAs and citizens in its implementation in the north Tihama. The document grew and grew as we tackled all the obstacles strewn in the path of developing a relevant community health service. Susan, who had hoped to go with us to the capital for Christmas, was disappointed when word came that the governor might pass through Ahad on Christmas Day and would hand out certificates to the *murshidaat*. She quite rightly felt it would hand our enemies a trick if none of us were present and seen to be taking an interest on such a public occasion. Caroline and I, less diligent and self-sacrificing, left as planned. On past experience we doubted whether the governor would really turn up. The Sana'a showdown with Dr Thaalib had to take priority.

The governor's motorcade did in fact arrive in Ahad on Christmas Day and in a hasty, unpublicized ceremony the women were given their certificates. Dr Thaalib, supposed to be in Sana'a, was in the entourage. Instead of speaking to Susan, he sent a note in his execrable English to say that he would not be able to meet us as planned as he had been ordered to accompany the governor on his tour. When Susan relayed this news by phone we realized we had been out-manoeuvred once more, duped into going to the wrong part of the country and powerless to monitor events.

On our return to Ahad a few days later a barrage of bad news awaited us. The *murshida* who was Susan and Caroline's neighbour, and whose nephew had been operated on by Dr

Thaalib, was in tears. The boy had survived the perils of Dr Thaalib's operating table only to die the following day. Dr Thaalib had written no post-operative instructions and the boy died from the effects of an inappropriate injection administered by a nurse in the Nakhwa hospital. Dr Tawfiq, our Somali ally, came round to visit us and was not surprised to hear of this latest fatality. He described operations performed by our adversary which he had attended. Gloves or masks had not been worn. Anaesthesia had been haphazardly administered by those Dr Thaalib had 'trained'. He told us how Dr Thaalib had contrived to prevent other specialists working in his province. A few years previously a Yemeni surgeon, and his respected East German gynaecologist wife, had been expelled from Nakhwa by the security authorities at Dr Thaalib's behest.

Dr Tawfiq told us what had happened in Ahad in our absence. Without any consultation with us, the local development associations or local communities, another five-year plan for health development had been hastily cobbled together in the course of a *qat* chew and approved by the governor. Male primary health care candidates had been hurriedly chosen. The governor had signed an order approving the choice of candidates and sites for 'hospitals'. Each year during the five-year plan one hospital, financed by UNICEF and the Ministry of Health, was to be built in each government district. We learned that in one small village four men had been selected for the training course for health workers. In another, three men were chosen. Several of the candidates were drug-sellers who, according to our Somali friend, had openly talked of buying a place on the course. They had no intention of attending but would pay to pass the exams, seeing a health worker's certificate as a valuable business investment. Dr Tawfiq advised us to stop being so naïve, leave Ahad and go and work in an area of Yemen where the ethics of medicine were not a complete dead letter. He was surprised we had not realized the error of our ways in coming to Ahad a long time before.

When we went to the hospital there was great confusion as a new shipment of food aid was being unloaded. We heard from the *murshidaat* of further grim developments. Ali Ahmad, who had been de facto hospital director for the past few months while the old incumbent was side-lined with his broken femur, had been replaced. Dr Thaalib and the governor had appointed one of the newly arrived Yemeni doctors as the new director. He had immediately demoted Ali Ahmad, ousted him from the office and told him to work as a vaccinator. In pique, Ali Ahmad was staying at home, refusing to come to the health centre.

The new director had further decreed that there was no need for the nine recently graduated *murshidaat* to come to the hospital. They did not have sufficient training or experience to become salaried health workers. He, or other doctors, would in future deal with delivery cases. The women were to stay at home and come to the hospital only if called for assistance. Some had obeyed this order. Others, encouraged by Ali Ahmad, were holding their ground and still reporting for work.

We met Lutf, the vaccinator, who told us of a further devious propaganda stroke from the resourceful Dr Thaalib. There had been an announcement on national television the previous evening. Viewers were told that after a rigorous selection process, supervised by the governor of Nakhwa, excellent cadres had been selected to begin training as health workers in Ahad. Their course would start in ten days' time.

Dr Thaalib was leaving us precious little time to protest. But should we play into his hands and do so? He was inviting us to make fools of ourselves. If we tried to block the course Dr Thaalib would be able to point to the perfidy of the British who had spent years in Ahad failing to start the course they had promised to begin within months of their arrival. He could give the impression that vigorous Yemeni officials had had to act unilaterally to set a much needed course in progress because the dilatory British had conspicuously failed to do so.

In the *mudiir's* office we found the new incumbent talking with Sheikh Taalib Hussein, the president of the Zahir development association. While he cordially greeted 'us the doctor pointedly refused to acknowledge our presence. Chairs were vacated and we sat at the back of the gathering. When I heard the director saying that UNICEF would build a hospital in Zahir and promising that the British would pay the stipends of those on the course, I broke into the conversation. 'It has been understood for four years that we would be part of the committee selecting candidates for training. It was agreed there would be an entrance examination to assess suitable candidates. We do not understand why these men have been suddenly chosen and are certainly not prepared to pay to train more than one man from any particular village. We know from UNICEF they do not intend to help build rural hospitals or provide them with drugs. It would be irresponsible to promise the candidates for this course that they will receive anything from our organization before we discuss these very surprising developments in Sana'a.'

The new director heard me out. With withering contempt he said we were obligated to pay for the cost of training. Selection of candidates, choice of sites and details of the course were none of our concern. We were 'imperialists' and 'lacked respect'. We should stop 'interfering' in the administrative and political concerns of Yemen.

Over lunch we discussed developments. Furious though I was, I was relieved. Surely even our most optimistic associates in London and Sana'a could no longer suggest that we give Dr Thaalib the benefit of the doubt? We decided to go to Sana'a and announce our immediate withdrawal of support for male primary health care. Dr Thaalib's actions were so blatantly in violation of the national health plan we imagined we would have no difficulty justifying our decision to the ministry.

We resolved to hand over the Daihatsu Rocky, the primary health care vehicle, to the Ahad health centre at once. Thus we would show we were in earnest, deprive Dr Thaalib of ammunition and prevent his cronies from expropriating the car for their own gain. As a snub to the new hospital director we decided to pass control to Ali Ahmad. He was no more likely to look after the car than others who might claim the vehicle. We feared that the Rocky would in future be used only to carry *qat* from the Khamis market to the empty air-conditioned hospital pharmacy.

We handed the keys to a grateful Ali Ahmad. Without rancour we discussed how to voice our complaints in Sana'a. Ali Ahmad was now allied with the *murshidaat*, in struggle against a common enemy. Whether he had really shed his misogyny, and acquired respect for the role of trained women, or whether it was merely bureaucratic vicissitudes which had brought him to their side, mattered not. It was a considerable relief to again find ourselves ranged alongside this intelligent, headstrong and frighteningly ambitious young man. Affinities in our characters could be recognized. In a happier mood, I set off once more to the capital. I imagined I would be returning to the cauldron of Ahad only to pack the rest of my belongings.

11

PACKING IT IN

The dismissal of the *murshidaat* was such a gross violation of ministry policy that it was reversed within days. Ali Ahmad was restored to his ambiguous position of administrative assistant but his adversary was also appointed as head of technical services in the Ahad health centre. The new doctor continued to claim that part of the responsibility of this post was the supervision of the mother and child building. We learned that there was no such post as technical services director, except in the very largest metropolitan hospitals. The doctor had obvious scope to further scupper our work but there was no more we could do.

In Sana'a we discussed with Brian how to present our decision to withdraw from male training in the most favourable light. We drafted a letter stressing the successful aspect of our work, the training of women. We decided not to list our grievances, but merely to note that the Nakhwa authorities had shown an ability to organize a training programme for men without our assistance. We wished this course every success, but regretted that we did not have the means to support it. On receipt of our letter the deputy minister acted with uncharacteristic alacrity. He declared that a committee would be sent to Ahad to investigate the problems.

This was bad news indeed. The sending forth into the countryside of a committee is often no more than a face-saving bureaucratic reflex, an attempt to wish problems out of existence rather than solve them. Such investigatory committees come back reporting the complete success of their reconciliation mission while the distant conflict rumbles on as before. I tried in vain to persuade Brian to go back to the

248

ministry to suggest that the situation could best be dealt with in Sana'a or Nakhwa rather than put everybody to the trouble of going down to the Tihama.

We returned to Ahad arriving shortly before Dr Thaalib and his committee. They spent much time incommunicado with the *mudiir an naahiya* before coming to the hospital where we, Ali Ahmad, his doctor rival and a horde of the curious were all anxiously awaiting them. It was immediately apparent that Dr Thaalib had convinced Dr Ansar, the director of the primary health care department, and Dr Kawkabani, another high official, that all our problems had to do with Ali Ahmad. He began the meeting with a lengthy peroration on the import-ance of co-operation, communication, dialogue, and trust between Yemenis and foreigners. Ali Ahmad, he announced in English and Arabic, lacked all these virtues and had caused a very serious crisis. He told the committee how Ali Ahmad had written a series of lies to the governor and had gone through all the wrong circles. Dr Ansar took up the same themes. When he flagged, Dr Thaalib returned to the attack. Members of the committee were prevented from hearing any of the evidence they were supposed to collect. We could not get a word in edgeways.

Once again I was forced to admire the Machiavellian guile of our adversary. He had shifted the whole focus of discussion to his own ground. I repeatedly tried to interrupt to put the view that, though we had problems with Ali Ahmad, these were now solved. The heart of our disquiet was that we and the Nakhwa office did not share a common interpretation of primary health care. Brian did not back me up in these endeavours. Dr Ansar was able to wind up the meeting by saying he was glad he would be able to report to the minister that the difficulties of the Ahad project had been overcome.

While the others rushed out of the room Dr Kawkabani stayed behind. In Sana'a I had presented him a letter of introduction from a mutual friend in London. He had studied in Britain and had, so I had been informed, shown progressive sympathies. We had chatted several times in the ministry and I took this opportunity to speak frankly about our problems. I spoke in English, and we were by now alone in the room. 'To be honest, and between ourselves, the heart of our problem in this project is that there are people in Nakhwa whose commercial interests are threatened by the arrival of primary health care.' Brian stepped heavily on my foot. For a moment I could have punched him. If one was not allowed to make such a generalized comment to a man who may well have been sympathetic, or at least forgiving, then there seemed no point in staying on.

Clearly nothing had been resolved, no matter what kind of congratulatory report was presented to the ministry. Our exercise in extrication had to go on. We drafted another letter to the deputy, expressing appreciation of the devoted efforts of the conciliation committee, but regretting that our decision to withdraw from supporting male training was unchanged. Brian took this back to Sana'a where it produced an immediate result. Another meeting was convened which would be attended by all four of the senior doctors in the ministry, those outranked in the hierarchy only by the minister and the deputy.

Our crisis was now reaching the highest possible levels and it was important that we present a united front. We adjourned to Sana'a once more to discuss tactics. With some reluctance, Brian agreed not to immediately present our proposed document setting out terms and conditions under which we could continue helping male training. We would stick to our guns and show it only as a last resort if the entire project were threatened with closure. We did not have it translated, as we assumed it would stay hidden in Brian's briefcase and not be needed.

We arrived in the office of the congenial director of the ministry's international relations department at the appointed time. While waiting for his colleagues to arrive, we chatted about the sports he had enjoyed while studying medicine in Britain. After half an hour the other senior officials had still not come and our host grew restless. He picked up the phone and began ringing round the ministry. Dr Ansar, who was supposed to be with us, was nowhere to be found. 'I can fully understand your frustrations', he told us, 'having to work with such a man as Dr Ansar. It is a crying shame that such an important department is headed by a man who is not at all interested in primary health care.' This, and further plain

speaking, encouraged us to reciprocate and we began talking of
our difficulties with the Nakhwa health office. The official said
it was a pity that we felt we had to stop helping the training of
men but appreciated the work we had done and understood
our decision.

Eventually, Dr Ansar arrived without a word of apology.
With him was Dr Khowlan, the third most important man in
the ministry, and his deputy, Dr Kawkabani. Dr Khowlan
shook his head and in his magnificent patrician English begged
us to reconsider. 'Can you honestly look into your hearts and
not admit you might have acted hastily? I hope you will reflect
on your decision. Should you abandon men? Why are all our
foreign friends so concerned to help the ladies in our country?
Are not men equally deserving? Social relations are still very
primitive here. We are a very backward country. It is
foolhardy of foreigners to pin great hopes on the training and
encouragement of women. One cannot fight the great weight
of tradition.'

We remained immune to his cajoling and did not offer to
rethink. Eventually, Dr Khowlan accepted our intransigence
and, in a spirit of some resignation, said we were, of course,
free to offer whatever help we wished. Our efforts would be
appreciated and our previous assistance would never be
forgotten.

Dr Ansar then made his first and only contribution to the
meeting. 'Our primary health care programme is concerned
with the training of men and women. You are obliged, by the
terms of your agreement with the ministry, to provide help in
training both sexes.' I sat back, confident Brian would not be
swayed by these half-hearted objections from the least senior
official present. Our project agreement was such an anodyne
document that it did not specify our training obligations. I
expected Brian to point this out but, unfortunately, his resolve
cracked.

To my horror, he pulled out our draft agreement. It
provoked great excitement and a collective sigh of relief.
Copies were given to all those present. Silence ensued for
several minutes as it was read. The head of international
relations was the first to speak. 'This is a truly excellent
document, specifying the responsibilities and obligations of

our foreign friends and their Yemeni counterparts. This is fully in line with our ministry's policy. I wish every foreign project in Yemen could produce such a clear document. I can see no objection to our recommending this to the deputy minister as soon as an accurate translation is produced.'

Dr Khowlan endorsed his subordinate's opinion. 'We must, however, take account of the personal feelings involved in your problem with Dr Thaalib. Obviously, we do not want him to feel bullied into agreement. I would like you to first discuss this agreement with him as he will be one of the signatories. On a few aspects of wording, or translation, it might be necessary for you to meet some of his objections. We have to allow him to save face. Do not worry. I shall speak to him and make it clear that the draft meets with our approval and that only minor changes can be made.'

The meeting broke up with requisite amicability. Hopes were expressed that after Dr Thaalib had given his approval, the document could be translated and submitted to the deputy minister to be signed within ten days. In the meantime, the course would not begin in Ahad as announced and candidates and sites already selected would be reconsidered. Brian informed the officials he was going to Britain for a month and that in his absence any member of the Ahad project could sign on BSDA's behalf.

I tried to put a brave face on this frustration of our hopes. More time was going to be lost on another round of meetings. The only bright point was that senior officials had tacitly accepted that local communities had a financial role to play in building health posts and providing them with relevant drugs. Now it was important that the ministry not be allowed to backtrack on their provisional agreement. To try to prevent this, we drafted another letter to the deputy describing the approving comments of the officials we had met. We rang Nakhwa and arranged to meet Dr Thaalib in three days' time. John, the new director of AFJAD's Yemen programme, who had been attentively following our crisis, said he would like to come to get to know Nakhwa in order to judge whether further funding could be justified.

On the morning of our departure for Nakhwa the document had still not been translated. We went in search of Hassan and eventually found him at home. He had only translated the first page and that in a bowdlerized fashion. We handed Dr Thaalib a trick, and were made to look foolish, by having to postpone our meeting for a few days. John asked the Egyptian doctor to translate the document properly.

A different kind of futile meeting took place the next day. Brian laid great stress on liaison with other non-government organizations (NGOs) working in development in Yemen and spent much of his time in the company of fellow expatriates. He had invited them along to an informal get-together in our office. UNICEF had reluctantly agreed to send a representative but no Yemenis were invited to join this discussion of the future of health care in their country. Representatives of several of the agencies, especially the commercial organizations dependent on keeping the goodwill of the ministry for the length of their lucrative contracts, showed great unease. They introduced themselves by stressing that the meeting was unofficial and not, in any circumstances, to be reported to the Yemeni authorities. Key officials had warned NGOs not to meet together outside the portals of the ministry.

For some time the meeting debated whether to constitute an official negotiating body on behalf of NGOs. I suggested that we had a duty to the Yemeni people to do so. Despite a promising start, the system of primary health care was collapsing around the country. We should not encourage avoidance of this fact or discourage discussions of new ways of providing support. Supplies of drugs and funds for building health posts were running out and the ministry had to be prodded into allowing community funding of health facilities and made to realize that foreign largesse could not be guaranteed in perpetuity. There was no support for this idea, least of all from my own embarrassed director. Each organization, our own no less than the others, was determined to hold onto the slice of the development action granted it.

After being prodded, the UNICEF man acknowledged what we had unofficially heard many months before. UNICEF had decided not to fund the construction of any new health posts and to give no more equipment. A quantity of drugs sufficient for only ten health posts would be given to North Yemen in the coming year. The director said this was not a sudden decision. UNICEF had informed the ministry five years previously that its support for primary health care was only pump-priming and that responsibility had to be eventually assumed by the YAR, as it was by other national governments with whom UNICEF worked. Yemen had already been given ample time to show whether it was interested in establishing a primary health care network on a sound financial basis. The government was not as poor as it made out to aid donors.

A Dutch representative reported an experience identical to my own. He had been repeatedly assured – at health centre, province and ministry level – that UNICEF's continued commitment to total provision of drugs and funding of units was guaranteed. The UNICEF representative said this was not the first time he had heard this, but there was nothing he could do. If the Yemenis chose not to pass on information unequivocally relayed to them there was nothing the United Nations could do. Though pressed, he said that he could not provide written confirmation of UNICEF's decision to scale down its aid for us to present to ministry officials. 'Think of my position. I sympathize with your difficulties, but I really should not be at this meeting at all.'

After the inconclusive gathering broke up relations with Brian further deteriorated when we again disagreed on Hassan's role in solving our project's difficulties. Fortunately, with backing from Caroline, Susan and John, the AFJAD director, Brian was persuaded not to bring Hassan along to again complicate our discussions. We drove together to Nakhwa and pulled up outside the health office, steeling ourselves for another round of barbed niceties. I feared the consequences of having to blood another neophyte not yet immune to Dr Thaalib's charm.

A surprise was in store. Sitting in Dr Thaalib's fine leather chair was his infant son. With him was the deputy who joked that the boy was testing the chair for the day he would succeed his father. We learned that Dr Thaalib had had to pop out as the president had decided to pay an unannounced visit. His helicopter was due to land at any moment. The deputy and the heir apparent were both keen to join the crowds gathering in the streets, and left us alone in the office. To lighten the mood for the confrontation to come Caroline and I also took

turns sitting behind the massive desk. Our lese-majesty
extended to putting on the great man's sunglasses and having
ourselves photographed against the impressive framed map of
health facilities in the province. By now I had realized that
many did not exist and some had phantom staffs drawing
salaries from the ministry. The map's only purpose was to
impress visitors from Sana'a or Washington.

When Dr Thaalib returned he found John unseduceable. It
was immediately clear the representative of our funders was in
no mood to be messed about, but insistent on changing the
rules of engagement. I had told John of the disadvantage we
had put ourself in by allowing Dr Thaalib to continue speaking
noncommittally in English and of my discomfiture at Brian's
acceptance of this. John speaks classical Arabic more profi-
ciently than most educated Yemenis and far better than the
ill-educated men Dr Thaalib surrounds himself with. Though
Dr Thaalib tried to speak in his usual cloying English, John
persisted in speaking Arabic.

With a great sigh, Dr Thaalib acknowledged defeat and the
conversation remained in ostensibly polite, acidly refined,
Arabic. When Dr Thaalib tried to repeat Ali Ahmad's
aspersions against Caroline and myself, John's counterblast
was withering. 'How dare you impugn the honour and
integrity of our colleagues in Ahad! As the funder of the Ahad
project, we wish to make clear our absolute confidence in the
professional abilities and moral character of our friends in
Ahad. We are convinced they are an ideal team to implement
the goals of primary health care and are not prepared to enter
into discussion with anyone who suggests otherwise. If there
had been equal goodwill from your office they could have
achieved far, far more than they have.' I was delighted by this
vote of confidence, as were Caroline and Susan when I
provided a whispered translation of as much of his flowery
language as I could understand. A greater contrast to our own
pusillanimous director could not be imagined.

Dr Thaalib then surprised us by producing the piece of paper
signed by BSDA four years previously, pledging support for
training men throughout the province. How he had laid his
hands on this document, considering the general chaos of the
filing system in his office, was a mystery. He pressed his

advantage by brandishing the latest version of our project agreement. We found for the first time that the final draft signed by Graham, our erstwhile co-ordinator, obliged us to provide a doctor, two midwives and a project co-ordinator. (I noticed that my job was not even mentioned – a reminder of the low priority Graham had accorded to primary health care). Dr Thaalib said we had no right to change the terms of our assistance unilaterally.

Caroline brought the meeting back to our problems by virtually accusing Dr Thaalib of deception in drawing us away from Ahad on Christmas Day and suddenly choosing candidates and sites. He smiled, offered no apologies and said that the final selection still had to be made. I expressed surprise as I had seen a letter, bearing his signature and stamped by the governor, listing the names of successful candidates.

John said months had been wasted with fruitless negotiations. The patience of funders was not limitless. The members of the Ahad project had better things to do than attend meeting after meeting if nothing resulted. Could we please hear from Dr Thaalib what he objected to in the proposed document? Could we go through, clause by clause, to reach a consensus?

We began with the first section which stipulated our rights to travel freely in the three government districts surrounding Ahad and to hold informal meetings with citizens, development association representatives and government prefects. Dr Thaalib said we were talking to the wrong man. These were questions for the security authorities. If they saw fit to limit our mobility, there was nothing he could do. I reminded him that it was his own officials who had imposed these restrictions. Our adversary smiled and looked at his watch. There was, he said, insufficient time left to discuss the agreement. He suggested we come back the next week.

For the first time we stood firm against his delaying tactics. John said it was out of the question. Brian was going to Britain the next day and we had all been instructed by the ministry to reach agreement as soon as possible. John said we should not leave Nakhwa without doing so. So firmly was Dr Thaalib pressed, that he agreed to meet us in the afternoon, time normally given over to seeing private patients. We adjourned for lunch.

I went to our project Toyota and was annoyed to find we had a puncture. I looked round and saw that every car in the street had a more serious problem – two or three flat tyres. I spoke to a man resignedly rolling two tyres along the road in search of a tyre repairer. I learnt that the report the president was travelling by helicopter had been merely a ruse to throw would-be assassins off guard. Several helicopters – 'father of the fan' in colloquial Arabic – had landed, but the president had not been on board any of them. Instead, he had come up to Nakhwa by the dusty Tihama road. Before his arrival his nervous security men had deflated the tyres of every vehicle in the centre of the town to prevent anybody shooting out into the middle of the presidential motorcade. This did not seem a way for a leader to court popularity, but my informant assured me it was normal practice and was surprised to learn we did things differently in my country. Such vigilance has enabled Ali Abdullah Salah to survive longer than any of his ill-fated predecessors who fell victim to assassins. As I struggled to change the large and heavy tyre, I was thankful that the security men had made a concession on recognizing our special foreigners' plates, and only let down one tyre.

Over lunch, John started translating the document yet again, trying to make it shorter and less intimidating without jeopardizing the rights we wanted. His efforts were wasted for when we sat down again with Dr Thaalib he came up with a novel objection. He had, he said, rung friends in Sana'a for advice. They had warned him it was quite out of the question for him to sign an agreement with a foreign organization. He was only a provincial official. Protocol insisted that any agreement with foreigners had to be negotiated at ministry level and also involve the Central Planning Organization and the Foreign Ministry. This really should have been pointed out to us earlier so we could have avoided a wasted journey to Nakhwa.

Dr Thaalib seemed to have outwitted us once more, but John did not despair. 'The title of this piece of paper does not matter. We can call it whatever you like. The important thing is that we must know if we share a common approach to implementing the national primary health care plan.' He tried to discuss matters of substance but Dr Thaalib insisted on first settling the question of nomenclature. Half an hour was wasted tossing round a series of verbose document headings and discussing how best to translate them into English.

After another masterly demonstration of culpable circum-locution we finally reached an acceptable form of words for the title page. We had barely begun the first page of the document when Dr Thaalib announced that he had an appointment with the governor. He promised to study our draft intensively and to present us with his amended version within a week. We took our leave in a disgruntled state. We decided to write to the ministry reporting the unsatisfactory conclusion to our meeting. On John's suggestion we added a deadline. Dr Thaalib had one month to sign his approval of our understanding of the national primary health care policy or BSDA's withdrawal from helping male training would be irrevocable.

Brian and John were going back to Sana'a and, after some dithering, I decided not to accompany them. We had agreed that in order to reinforce the seriousness of our decision I would not show my face in Ahad. However, it had been arranged that the British ambassador and his wife, who took a great interest in the work of all our projects, would visit Ahad and it seemed discourteous not to be present. The ambassador arrived the next morning without driver or guards. He told us he longed for these rare opportunities to get out and see Yemen, meet ordinary people, experience genuine hospitality and speak Arabic. In Sana'a he was constrained by the security authorities who vetted all visitors and deterred Yemenis from having social relations with the British other than on rare formal occasions.

The ambassador was well received in Ahad as he came bearing photos from his previous visit and copies of *Hinna London*, the BBC Arabic Service magazine which is a prized possession. By chance, he met Salah who had brought some patients down to the hospital. We talked about the continuing problems of his work, the fact he still did not have a motorbike, did not have a salary and, worst of all, had just been ordered to work six days a week in Suq as Sebt despite our agreement.

The ambassador asked what he might do to help. Would it be useful if he wrote to the Minister of Health pointing out that British money had been given to build a health post which was not being allowed to function? Salah was extremely enthusiastic and we drafted a mild letter setting out the facts, the details of the compromise reached in Nakhwa and the witnesses to the agreement. In the final draft the ambassador regretted that unless the situation was remedied the experience of Bani Salim might jeopardize the prospect of future British assistance to development in Nakhwa province.

I returned to Sana'a in the ambassadorial Range Rover. For days I kicked my heels in the Sana'a office, uncertain how to occupy my time. Helen, the deposed Kahima co-ordinator, sometimes dropped into the office in between visits to other expatriates round the city but for most of the time I was alone with Hassan. With Brian absent in London Hassan could drop the pretence of being busily occupied. He read the paper and swotted for university exams and I worked on the word processor, finalizing the glossary of colloquial Yemeni medical terms which, I was now convinced, would be the sole legacy of all my efforts. I wondered how the workaholic Brian managed to create work when there was so little that needed doing or could be done to further our programme's visionary goals.

Margaret, a midwife who had been working for our Rahbaan project for the past six months, came to Sana'a for some much needed rest. She looked shattered by the turmoil in her working life. She told me of problems with a recently recruited Egyptian colleague. BSDA had finally taken on board the persistent criticism from AFJAD that we did not recruit native Arabic speakers. Yet, rather than advertise widely in the Arab press in London, Beirut and Cairo as our funders urged, we had put one advertisement in an Egyptian newspaper. The London office had selected a doctor they said was the best of the applicants.

Bashir had been to Britain to study for a postgraduate primary health care qualification which he had failed to obtain. His English was poor, and he was given no orientation to Yemen. Nothing was done to lighten the cultural baggage of contempt for Yemenis which he, like most Egyptians, carried with him. Our ally Mujahid, the Rahbaan hospital director, could not stand our new recruit. Sarah, the third project member, tried to work with Bashir but was overwhelmed by the frightening ill-feeling which developed between him and Margaret. So great was their mutual contempt that within weeks they stopped speaking to each other, slandered each other to Yemeni counterparts and sent messages only through intermediaries. Sarah feared physical violence between the chronically unsuited pair, and hinted that BSDA should move either the Egyptian or Margaret to another project. Though aware of the complete breakdown of their relationship neither the London nor Sana'a office did anything.

As days went by and the deadline we had given Dr Thaalib grew closer I wondered whether I might as well leave Yemen for all the good I was doing. I needed a diversion from my morbid inactivity and was glad when an invitation arrived asking BSDA to attend celebrations for International Volunteer Day. The letter said that senior officials from several Yemeni ministries would attend a reception at the UN complex in Sana'a to show their gratitude for the work being done by the youth of the world. When I arrived my first impression was how middle-aged the many UN youth volunteers were. All were from the Indian sub-continent, were earning salaries which dwarfed ours and neither spoke any Arabic nor saw any need to do so. I looked round for Yemenis to talk to but could not find any.

I chatted to some Egyptian women contracted by WHO for an integrated rural development programme, centred round a group of villages ninety minutes' dusty drive from Sana'a. I learnt that they commuted to the area each day, having found they could not bear to live in the area or eat what they claimed was the dreadful Yemeni food. Initially large groups of curious local women had come along to classes to meet the Egyptians but numbers had greatly fallen off. I was not surprised, when I learnt what these highly-paid 'experts' had been teaching in the last week – how to crochet doilies and to make filo pastry.

We were called to order. Representatives of various agencies followed the pompous UN volunteer director in blandly outlining the work they were doing. The Peace Corps director raised eyebrows among the Dutch, Germans and Swedes with his insistence that 'the Peace Corps is an independent organization, not under the control of the United States government.' With raised glasses of *kanada* and fruit juice we toasted the president and hoped for continued harmonious co-operation between the international community and Yemen.

The meeting was formally thrown open to 'contributions from the floor'. A sticky silence ensued, but finally a Peace Corps volunteer spoke up. 'Mr Chairman. We have all heard a great deal of how grateful the Yemeni government is for the work our organizations have been doing. For my part, since arriving in this country I have been hospitably received by ordinary people but met with bureaucratic intolerance and deliberate frustration of our work plans. I hope my experience is not typical. But why, if co-operation with our hosts is so good, has not a single representative of the Yemeni government accepted an invitation to this reception?' He sat down to stunned silence.

I was tempted to clap and caught the eye of some cynical Dutch volunteers equally uncertain of their response. We were all too shy and were pre-empted by the embarrassed UN chief. 'I think we have had enough comments from the floor', he stammered. 'I declare this reception open. I hope our esteemed guests enjoy the humble repast we have provided.' He waved to the attendant Filipino waiters to bring on the food trucked in from the local Sheraton. The Peace Corps director was crimson with rage as he moved across the room to his insolent compatriot. I was glad not to be in the young man's shoes.

The next day the refreshingly down-to-earth British ambassador rang to tell me how his letter about Salah's closed health post had been received in the ministry. The deputy minister had invited him to a meeting, only to inform the ambassador that no communication was possible between the ministry and an embassy except through the Foreign Ministry. In any case, the matters referred to in the letter were nothing to do with the British.

The ministry rang shortly afterwards to summon us to a meeting as soon as possible. As I did not wish to be the sole victim of official wrath I rang Caroline and Susan in Ahad, and they agreed to come up to Sana'a. Hassan came back from the ministry with news that Dr Thaalib had been busy lobbying for two days, had chewed *qat* with the minister and mobilized contacts in the president's office. Hassan had chatted with him in the ministry and reluctantly told me what had passed between them. 'I told him you had not yet decided what to do and that I was sure you could solve your problems.' This interpretation of our position could not but further damage our case. Rebuking Hassan seemed pointless for Brian had permitted him to pursue his divisive conciliatory efforts.

When we took our places in his office Dr Khowlan feigned great rage. 'You are still living in the age of imperialism. Don't you know the sun has set on your damned empire! We decide things in this country. We do not need the kind of paltry help your government can give us. The 20,000 rials you provided for the Bani Salim unit is peanuts. I can go out into Tahrir Square right now and stop any *qabiili* who could reach into his pocket and give me twice as much without batting an eyelid. Who do you think you are? What a ridiculous title your organization has. British Social Development Agency! How presumptuous! What the hell does "social development" mean? It sounds absurd in Arabic.'

We heard him out. I agreed with much that he said and realized that for reasons of personal and national *amour propre* he had to have his say. It must be deeply humiliating for a highly educated man to have to go cap in hand to foreigners for help. The occasional outburst was understandable. Fortunately he soon reverted to his more usual self, and we discussed our problems more calmly.

I asked him to put himself in our shoes. We had reached a solemn agreement with Dr Thaalib concerning the Bani Salim health post. Protests against its closure had been initiated and led by local citizens, officials of the local development association and a government prefect. We had gone through all the right channels. Dr Thaalib had publicly given his word that Salah would be allowed to work five days a week in the unit the citizens had constructed. All the facts in the ambassador's letter were true. How could we not feel bitter at Dr Thaalib's reneging on our agreement? Such actions, and the construction of a great new hospital in Nakhwa were proof to us that there was absolutely no interest in primary health care on the part of senior ministry officials in Nakhwa.

Dr Khowlan shook his head sadly. 'I assure you I take no pride whatsoever in a foreign government, especially Saudi

Arabia, building such a large facility which does not accord
with the plans of my ministry.' I felt sympathy for the man,
despite his recent torrent of abuse.

Other less well-disposed officials joined us. I groaned when I
noticed amongst them a man who though he holds only a
relatively low position in the ministry hierarchy is one of the
most powerful men in Sana'a. We had learnt from UNICEF
that this man had commandeered aid donated by the United
Nations and had built several houses with his ill-gotten gains.
We had also heard a rumour that his greed had been so
extreme that the president himself had decided the man was an
embarrassment and sent him to Egypt to 'study'. His return
and his commanding role in the meeting dashed hopes of
UNICEF, BSDA and other NGOs that we had seen the last of
him.

Unlike his colleagues he made not the slightest effort to be
polite. He speaks no English and insulted us purely in Arabic.
It was out of the question for us to sign an agreement with the
ministry. All our problems had been solved. We were being
quite unreasonable, typical imperialists. We had a perfectly
acceptable project agreement. He had investigated the Bani
Salim problem. Dr Thaalib's decision to close the so-called
health post there was absolutely correct. Salah was an
'anarchist' and needed to be 'punished'.

I finally managed to break in and reply that Salah had
worked six months as an unpaid health worker and that
protests at closing his unit had been initiated not by him, or by
us, but by citizens and their democratically elected officials. I
turned to Dr Khowlan. 'We find it impossible to understand
how current reaction to our suggestions can be so different
from the comments we heard last time we met. Our draft was
described as a model for all other health projects. We were told
that encouragement of local communities to fund units and
buy drugs is in line with government policy.'

Dr Khowlan was put on the spot in front of his powerfully
connected subordinate. He switched back to English to appeal
to us. 'Look what you are demanding of us. We are being
asked to accept that there is a monster running the Nakhwa
health office.' We stared, eyeball to eyeball, for what seemed
an eternity. I understood that this humane, highly cultured

man had just indicated his own opinion of Dr Thaalib and his own fear of the predicament he was in. Dr Thaalib, though nominally a subordinate, had mobilized all the influence he could bring to bear and Dr Khowlan could not stand up to the man. No one likes to have their powerlessness revealed to the world. Any number of cathartic outbursts against meddlesome foreigners could be forgiven.

'Dr Tim, you must show more understanding of our culture. This is a very violent society – rub people up the wrong way, impose conditions on them and they turn obstinate and violent.' He reminded us that there had been a cold-blooded murder in the neighbouring office the year before. 'A man walked in here, openly carrying a pistol, and shot dead a colleague of mine as if he were shooting a dog. Just like that.' He mimed the action of pulling the trigger.

His tone was chilling. We were being warned of evil. Only the day before I had heard of a Sudanese health worker murdered for opposing powerful drug sellers. I had also heard of a sub-contractor whose life was threatened for publicizing corruption surrounding the construction of a new hospital in Sana'a. For all his urbanity and high office, Dr Khowlan was not safe from the violence thrown up by Yemen's rude capitalism. The health trade in Yemen is big and dangerous business. As competing calls to midday prayer swirled round Tahrir Square I wished I were far away.

Such thoughts seemed absurdly melodramatic when our main adversary came unannounced into the room. How could a shambling, balding, avuncular figure like Dr Thaalib be a threat to anybody? He apologized for his lateness, saying he had been meeting with the deputy minister. When he asked how far we had got in solving our little problems I said we had made no progress. My colleagues, our absent co-ordinator and our funders were united in insisting we be given written guarantees before our project could continue.

To our surprise this provoked a partial backdown. The idea of signing a document was suddenly back on the table. We decided that it would be called an 'appendix of understanding', as binding as our project agreement, but not requiring endorsement from the Central Planning Organization. Dr Khowlan then asked Dr Thaalib what he thought of our draft.

With an audaciously straight face he replied that he had not yet seen a copy. The man in effective charge of primary health care also claimed he had not had a chance to read it. We did not contradict them, but agreed to the suggestion that we meet again in a week or so to allow time for the document to be 'read'.

Just as we were taking our leave, the director of the international relations department made a very belated appearance. Had his been a diplomatic absence? We had sorely missed him. When told what had been decided he surprised us by a forceful and brave intervention. 'It is our duty to give a reply to our British friends as soon as possible. They have been in suspense for months and months. They have now produced a document which I think is in accordance with current policy on how to implement the primary health care plan. I believe we should sign it as soon as possible and finish all this nonsense.' On this encouraging note our extraordinarily draining morning, with its confusing alternation of rudeness and sympathy, threats and appeals, finally drew to an end.

The next day we learned that Salah had received word that he was to be allowed to re-open his health post. He was called up to Nakhwa, received two month's salary and was given a motorbike. The outcome seemed most satisfactory, the indignities we had had to suffer a small price to pay for getting Salah finally legitimized.

When I telephoned London there was a surprising reaction from Brian. In the course of a long expensive conversation it was made clear to us that we had exceeded our authority in allowing the British ambassador to write. We were berated for giving the impression that BSDA was associated with the British government. I replied that it was naïve to expect Yemenis to believe in our independence when we accepted funding from ODA and had deliberately included the word 'British' in our organization's Yemeni name. We agreed to discuss the matter further in a fortnight when Brian returned to Yemen. The desk person and the newly appointed general secretary of our agency would be accompanying him.

The general secretary arrived with his wife and the London desk person and they were soon whisked away on a flying tour of the country. The already cumbersome group of development tourists was joined by Hassan, by a visiting ODA-funded 'expert' and by Magda, a young Egyptian woman who had been invited to Yemen to see if she might like to work with us. Suggestions from colleagues that expecting Yemenis to provide hospitality to such a large group was an imposition went unheeded. We had insisted that the party not complicate matters by visiting Ahad and making our withdrawal seem negotiable. Several key BSDA personnel were absent on holiday and had requested, when asked for their opinion, that the visit of the general secretary and his entourage be postponed. This had not been done. Brian was undoubtedly relieved by their absence for he understandably felt threatened by those of us who had been in the country for several years and knew how to speak to, and comport ourselves among, rural Yemenis.

Under Brian's management 'Yemenization' had become the flavour of the month. On his urging, committees had been set up in Kahima and Rahbaan and BSDA workers and counterparts co-opted on to them. Yemenis constituted a majority and were to be given a controlling say in the management of the projects. The promotion of efficiency was invested with central importance. If our counterparts could be taught to 'prioritize' their tasks all would be well. Yemeni committee members would be 'trained up' to take over all the work currently done by BSDA. It would be necessary to send them abroad to study English, accountancy and management. 'Yemenization' was glowingly described in an article written for the agency's annual. Funders were assured that the primary health care programme in North Yemen had become 'firmly established' and that 'Yemenization' was being successfully implemented.

To someone of my generation the sudden fervour for 'Yemenization', the notion that our native allies would somehow pull off the victory we had so manifestly failed to achieve, had echoes of Nixon and Vietnamization. AFJAD, our funders, shared my scepticism. Two decades of experience working in a great number of developing countries and thousands of hours of in-house soul-searching had produced a much more coherent and strategic perspective on the interplay of conciliation and confrontation, of principles and pragmatism in development work. It seemed clear BSDA was imposing a technocratic blueprint of development management which, though relevant in countries where we worked with autonomous highly politicized neighbourhood and community groups, made no sense in Yemen. The Yemeni government did not permit foreigners to work directly with grass-roots associations which were, in any case, proscribed. In Yemeni circumstances a formalization of decision-making procedures was counter-productive and invited the suspicion of central authorities. In Yemen we provided all the money and, given the realities of international aid finance, it was not feasible to directly involve locals who know no English in the cumbersome process of soliciting money from governments and charities. Empowering such a committee could mean that a single powerful individual, such as the sheikh and director of health in Kahima whom AFJAD regarded with great suspicion, could railroad any proposal through the committee. No amount of training and efficiency could hide the reality that health was given a low priority by the state and that funds for rural health care were inadequate, often expropriated for irregular purposes and capriciously paid or withheld by powerful well-connected men.

In the atmosphere of renewed rivalry between our two agencies, and between Brian and John, my views were now regarded as disloyal. I was only invited to talk to the general secretary for a few hours at the end of his eight-day whistlestop tour. He showed little desire to talk about Yemen and was more interested in reminiscing about his days teaching in a seminary in central Africa. His comments on Islam and Middle Eastern politics did not indicate much knowledge of our region.

Two weeks later we received his tour report. He was fulsome in his praise of Brian. He was said to have an excellent grasp of Yemeni affairs and to be greatly respected by all his colleagues. It was wonderful to see the work he had done devolving power to capable and committed counterparts. Brian was such a vital resource that it was essential that BSDA find a Sana'a-based job for his wife to encourage him to stay in Yemen for many years. He described the Kahima project as a 'model project' and could not imagine a more successful primary health scheme anywhere in the world. His report was received with incredulity by all BSDA workers. Two colleagues were so incensed that they demanded a right of reply at the six-monthly conference we were shortly to hold.

Brian informed me that during the general secretary's tour he had called a meeting of the new committee in Rahbaan. The absence of Mujahid, the local director of health, and of Sarah, who had worked in the area for four years, had not deterred Brian from putting major decisions to a vote. I found the committee had been persuaded not to approve my transfer to Rahbaan.

After the general secretary's departure Dr Khowlan again summoned us to the ministry. This meeting was mercifully brief. He told us he had read through our proposed document of understanding and made notes. He handed us his amended copy and indicated he wished us to leave. In great suspense, we stopped in a corridor to read his comments.

We were dumb-founded. Dr Khowlan had gone through line by line conscientiously negating the meaning of almost every sentence. The effect was to produce nonsensical prose which in effect endorsed Dr Thaalib's complete freedom of action in deciding what primary health care was and how UNICEF and other foreign aid was to be used. It was a petty and insulting way to signal rejection of our proposals but we had to contain our anger. We immediately drafted a letter of reply to the minister expressing sadness that initial favourable reactions to our proposals had not led to agreement. Without such an indication of common intent our funders were not prepared to lend support to the training of male health workers. We confirmed that BSDA now employed only Caroline and Susan in Ahad.

I was tempted to announce my immediate departure from Yemen. I had been hanging round Sana'a or commuting to fruitless meetings for three months. I now despaired of having any input on BSDA policy. I observed the impending confrontation with AFJAD with a mixture of personal frustration and an anthropological fascination at the power of vain individuals to destroy well-meaning institutions. I had seen enough and thought it time to go.

At the same time I did not want to hand Brian the satisfaction of my absence at the six-monthly conference due in another few weeks. Major discussions were to take place. This was not to be an ordinary gathering. For the Yemen desk person, who had departed with the general secretary, was due to return, this time in the company of the head of the agency's overseas programme. She would brief us on London's new management policies and we would evaluate BSDA's future. The hidden agenda of her visit, which the management imagined to be concealed from BSDA workers, was to persuade John to continue recommending AFJAD funding of our three projects.

Pigheadedness prevailed and I decided to stay. I resolved to write a report and to engage in the struggles to come. I returned to Ahad for a week's visit, planning to say my farewells, to pack up and to help Caroline and Susan move out of the unvisited office for which we were paying an exorbitant rent. Disposing of the detritus accumulated in the course of the preceding four years proved time-consuming. I felt dislocated in Ahad, sleeping under the fan in the new office, without the comforts I had built about me. My cat had disappeared without trace.

In my two previous six-monthly reports I had followed official BSDA guidelines but also voiced my disquiet in the frank manner I had been led to believe was encouraged by the Eze-Vu evaluation process. Both reports had been ignored in Sana'a and London and I had received no feedback. By now I was determined to write a much longer and unconventional report, a general critique of BSDA's developmentalism which could not be disregarded. I wanted to review the whole history of our Ahad adventure and went through our voluminous project files. I found much grist for my mill. A lot I wanted to say had been said before – but then filed and forgotten. Caroline helped weed the report of its more vituperative remarks so that it would be ready to present and be read before our conference.

My reappearance in Ahad fuelled speculation as to BSDA's intentions. I was approached by those hoping to get onto the training course which was about to start or men wanting to know about construction of 'hospitals' in their areas. It was obvious that Dr Thaalib's misinformation machine had again been at work. Most men I spoke to assumed that BSDA would be paying training stipends and that UNICEF would provide for health workers after their course.

It seemed our duty to disabuse local people of these notions so the young men coming forward for the course would know the uncertain prospect they were letting themselves in for. As a strategic move to protect BSDA against the charge of bad faith it was necessary to publicize our withdrawal from male primary health care and stress our continued support for female training. We wrote a brief letter to the Nakhwa governor and to prefects and leaders of the development associations in our area. Caroline and Susan added force to their signatures by brandishing our official stamp (embossed in English and Arabic with 'Co-ordinator, British Social Development Agency') which we had inherited from Graham. I made multiple photocopies of the letter and sought out men who would deliver them to their intended recipients and relate their contents to all who were interested. I also sent a copy up to Sana'a.

I knew Brian would be upset for he seemed still not reconciled to our departure from male training and was proving sensitive to any gesture implying a threat to his authority. He was piqued that the Rahbaan project's new agreement with the ministry had been signed and stamped by Sarah on BSDA's behalf. Brian informed us that we had exceeded our authority. Caroline and Susan were told they should hand over the stamp.

Salah invited me to Bani Salam for a farewell feast. I would have liked to go with only Caroline and Susan, to share for the last time our pleasure at Salah's success. However, Brian had announced that he was bringing the party headed by Pauline, the director of the agency's overseas programme. Hassan and Magda, our possible Egyptian recruit, were also due to come. I knew they would wish to visit Bani Salam and thought it unfair that Salah be burdened with providing hospitality on two occasions. I arranged for us to descend en masse on Bani Salam.

The party arrived in Ahad. To my relief, I found Brian had, at the last minute, turned back to Sana'a from Hodeidah. The reason for his absence soon became apparent: Rosita, the newly appointed deputy administrator of AFJAD, was among the party. We made her welcome but expressed our surprise at her visit. She told us that a month previously John, her boss, had informed Brian that he wished to send her to Ahad to evaluate the situation. Brian, for whatever reason, had not told us of the date decided upon.

Our funders were not pleased that Brian had promoted the recruitment of Magda, a young Egyptian commerce graduate, to be a community health educator (CHE) in Ahad. She knew little of Yemen and development and had led a sheltered provincial life. Her sole qualification was the fact she spoke English and Arabic. John wanted to know why the job had not been advertised and a more qualified Arab recruited from the excellent health training institutes in Lebanon, the West Bank or Cairo. Hassan confided to me that, though he liked Magda, his pride as a Yemeni had been hurt. What right did BSDA have, without consulting any Yemenis, to appoint an Egyptian when a large number of Yemeni women had her skills? The Ahadi *murshidaat*, when told Magda was coming, immediately asked about her qualifications. Though all but one was too polite to say so, they were obviously surprised to hear that our new recruit was untrained.

The volunteer cycle was grinding onwards regardless of all that had gone before. As one victim got ready to leave, another was being presented for sacrifice. The project needed a trained health worker able to consolidate Susan's improbable success at promoting the *murshidaat*. The job description for Magda's post as CHE was a transparent fiction. Brian had told her how she might travel round local schools promoting health education but I knew the education authorities would never allow a foreign organization to dictate how health should be taught. Egyptian fundamentalists running the local schools would not permit an unveiled female Christian anywhere near their classrooms. Yet the more AFJAD urged BSDA to reconsider, the more determined Pauline and Brian became to assert institutional autonomy and to proclaim the correctness of the appointment.

Relations between Rosita, the AFJAD representative, and Pauline, the head of our agency's overseas programme, mirrored the tension between their two organizations. Pauline wanted to know why we had reached a decision not to support male training. Her tone was brusquely critical. She implied the decision had been premature and one we had had no right to reach unilaterally. I defended the decision and the protracted process of communicating it to the Yemeni government. Rosita, with a wealth of experience in the country and a fluent command of the dialect, spoke in our defence. Hassan, who still knew nothing of the Ahad project, insisted that we should reconsider. Nothing was resolved and our gathering broke up as the women had agreed to visit the *murshidaat* in their homes. In their absence I worked on finishing my report.

The next morning we walked to the hospital. Mercifully, important officials had yet to report to work in the old hospital, and we were able to take refuge in the mother and child annex, the part of the institution where we had achieved a measure of success. It was a delight to watch the *murshidaat* at work, to hear how they talked intelligently about their problems and to say goodbye to those with whom I had established a joking intimacy. There was still no procedure for providing health education, no facilities for rehydrating children or for demonstrating sample weaning foods to their mothers. Yet it was a time for putting aside such disgruntled thoughts of all that we had failed to achieve, of delusory expectations, of anger at lack of drugs, vaccines, and salaries. Whatever now happened to them, these were women on the move. The bounded female universe of Ahad would never be the same.

I was having my photo taken for the umpteenth time when the arrival of Ali Ahmad cast the first of several clouds over my day. I had assumed that copies of our letter of withdrawal from male training had now been received and had not expected we would receive any replies. I was thus surprised to be told all the officials of the Ahad local development association, the *mudiir an naahiya* and his armed guards had turned up at the hospital. The two Yemeni doctors had also arrived and the whole party was eagerly awaiting us.

We were totally unprepared for a meeting. After all the occasions on which we had been rebuffed while trying to set up meetings I thought we would lose face and appear weak by not asking for at least a short delay. In any case, we needed time to discuss a strategy and decide who was to speak for

BSDA. Pauline could not be swayed and insisted it would be rude not to meet at once.

The officials who had for years been consistently rude to all BSDA employees filed into the room. They epitomized courtesy, benevolence and civic concern. Caroline, Susan and Magda settled for inconspicuous places while Hassan, Rosita, Pauline and I competed for the centrally-placed seating. Rosita whispered to me that I should be our spokesperson, try to keep the meeting as brief as possible and stress that the decision process was over. Sana'a and London had decided and nothing could now be done.

Pauline had other plans and asked Hassan to present our case. Rosita nudged me but I thought it more politic to bide my time. Hassan willingly took the floor. He and the other dignitaries engaged in a narcissistic display of classical Arabic which was finally ended by a blunt question from the association president, the sheikh heir-apparent of Ahad. Why, after so many years of fruitful co-operation, had the British decided to abandon them?

I began a response but Pauline glowered and Hassan held the floor. He spoke at length without mentioning any of the issues which divided us from the Nakhwa office. He expressed a personal opinion that our problems could be solved and that 'after a while' aid could be restored. The president was delighted and broke in to ask when this would be. Hassan told him the question of financial support for the training course might be reconsidered in a few months.

Rosita was indignant and interrupted Hassan to tell him, in English, that he should let me speak. Pauline, whose Arabic was very limited, seemed to have little idea what had been said and resented the intrusion. I spoke up. I said that BSDA appreciated the sincere efforts of all local officials, would continue to support the training of women but had made a firm decision not to support a male training course. Budget and recruitment constraints meant that this decision could not be reviewed for two years. The meeting broke up with much head-shaking but had achieved its purpose.

As we milled about on the verandah watching the big men depart, we were not in good temper. I chided Hassan for misrepresenting our position but he merely shrugged and walked over to chat to the prefect. After they had been talking for a few minutes we wandered over to join in, but our approach caused the men to move apart. As the *mudiir an naahiya* drove away Hassan told us he and the prefect had been at school together and had once been 'very deep intimate friends'. Notwithstanding the fact Hassan could not now remember the name of his ex-comrade, he had decided to exploit the connection for the benefit of BSDA. He announced that he and the prefect were to meet that evening to work out a solution to our problem.

We were all agitated but it was Caroline who angrily told Hassan he was to do no such thing. He had to respect other people's opinions and appreciate the importance of solidarity in negotiations. His colleagues had met and decided they did not wish him to pursue any private initiatives. He had to grow up and learn to work as part of a team. We persuaded Pauline to deter Hassan from continuing his campaign of opposition. She told him not to go to see the prefect, an order he took with bad grace.

He was still sulking the next morning when we all set out to visit Salah. Conversation was stilted as we ground our way up the rutted track to Bani Salim. When he saw our vehicle approaching Salah immediately shut up his unit and came to meet us on the road. This was, he announced, a special day. When friends were leaving sociability had to take priority over work. I got out and began walking the few hundred yards to Salah's hamlet. Locals came up to greet me and express regret at my departure. Nasar Mohammad, the elderly sheikh, warmly shook my hand. What a shame I was leaving just as we were beginning to understand each other! He had never been able to make head or tail of anything any other *nasraani* had tried to say to him.

I was struck by what an incongruous group we made. Five Europeans and an Egyptian Christian were dressed to please the susceptibilities of Yemeni Muslims while the one Yemeni amongst us was dressed in the style of his favourite musician, Michael Jackson. We wobbled on the unsteady beds in Salah's crudely built reception room and took tea. The usually gregarious Hassan declined to converse with our hosts, preferring to chat up Magda and tell bad jokes in English.

Hassan was proving a social embarrassment. One by one my female colleagues drifted out of the room and walked over to the huts which are the female domain in Salah's household. My day was being spoiled and I saw no reason why I should put up with Hassan's unwelcome company. Salah left to look after his other guests and I took his hint, got up and also joined the women. No shame attached as I had done so many times before. Fortunately Hassan was deterred from following.

By the length of time we were waiting for lunch it was clear a major feast was being prepared. Hassan decided to take a nap and I was allowed for the last time to enjoy the engaging informality of village life, the stirring spectacle of Salah helping the men and women who stopped by for advice, the untraditional conjugal intimacy between Salah and his wife, the joy of seeing their son's continued healthy progress into an unhealthy world. Cameras were brought out and babies, women and men organized for posterity. I reached into my bag for my parting gift, a small but powerful nine-band radio economical in its consumption of batteries. I had agonized over the suitability of such a relatively expensive gift but knew how much Salah wanted to continue his education by dipping into the broadcasts of the world.

My pleasure at his pleasure turned to unease when I saw the extent of his valedictory gift – a sheep had been slaughtered in my honour. I was mortified. I had extracted a promise from Salah that he would not impoverish himself by providing *qat* for my farewell but had not reckoned on this. A poor man had gone to a much greater expense than I had, for all livestock in Yemen is exceedingly valuable. Salah laid a plastic sheet on the uneven bare-earth floor of his shabby room and carried in dish after appetizing dish. We could eat only a portion of the vast amount of food laid before us.

We were replete and barely able to move but had to be off. We had agreed to drive on to Sana'a that day for Pauline had a meeting to attend the day before our conference. We hoped to make good our escape before Salah succeeded in providing us with leaves. Though himself only a modest chewer, Salah was keen to spend the afternoon chewing *qat* with us. By dint of persuasion we managed to beat a retreat in the direction of our car. To postpone farewells we agreed to walk over for a last visit to Salah's modest health post.

Men gathered from nearby villages to say farewell. Rosita, greatly impressed by Salah's success, chatted with the local men. When they expressed a desire to build a school alongside Salah's unit Rosita said she would see if AFJAD could contribute some funding. There was much excitement at this news. It was agreed that Salah would arrange the submission of a formal request and costing estimate. It was getting late and we really had to leave. I promised I would return to see the school and to show Salah the son I hoped one day to have. Choking back tears, I embraced Salah for the last time and drove away.

We stopped in Ahad to collect our baggage and buy *qat* for the long journey ahead of us. As ever, I was warmly received by friends in the *qat* market. We haggled over the cost of our leaves and handed over a bundle of notes. I fancied we had already been given a good deal but the seller generously threw in some extra choice twigs. As shadows lengthened I crossed the dusty wastes of the Tihama for the last time. Under *qat's* mellowing influence ours seemed a friendlier party. Pauline remained silent and Hassan aloof and disapproving of our chewing, but Rosita continued to enthuse about our role in helping transform an unlikely lad and nine unknown women into respected and influential health workers. Rosita told us she would report to AFJAD that in all her years in Yemen she had never seen a man who so embodied all the ideals of preventative community health care as did Salah.

On arrival in Sana'a I was filled with restless energy, part *qat*-induced, part manic response to the tension in my life. After midnight I let myself into the AFJAD/BSDA offices to edit and print out my report on our word-processor. Once started I could not stop and found myself working for hours trying to make the report as hard as possible to ignore. At five in the morning it was done. I made photocopies and left them to be found by colleagues from both British agencies the next morning.

We had a free day before our conference and I slept in. I could not resist a brief visit to our offices in late morning. In a side room I saw Pauline poring over my report, scribbling comments in a notebook. John was reclining, chuckling to himself as he also read the report. Brian rushed past us, tight-

lipped. John made sure we were not overheard and told me my
report had come at an opportune time. It strengthened his
hand for the showdown meeting between the two agencies,
scheduled for the last day of the conference.

The conference started with unexpected drama. Brian
begged leave to depart from the planned agenda to hold an
emergency discussion of disturbing events in Kahima. Nabil
and Salwa, our two Arab colleagues working in Kahima, were
given the floor. Salwa began an incoherent tale of theft and
threats, sabotage and slander, intrigue and imprisonment. It
became clear that BSDA and AFJAD had arrived at fundamentally different interpretations of these developments. The
meeting was asked to totally reject a report on the events
written by Lucy, the water engineer employed by AFJAD.
Copies of her report were handed round to be condemned.
The meeting was about to be rushed to judgement long before
the rest of us had any idea what had really taken place.
Someone asked if our colleagues could begin at the beginning
and report the facts, leaving interpretation to later.

We already knew that some months previously Lucy's
expensively renovated house had been broken into. Little of
value had been stolen but her house had been completely
turned upside down. The amount of spiteful damage either
indicated a great amount of enmity towards her or resentment
at the work she was trying to do. Now we learned that the
previous week, as she had been working with her Yemeni
counterpart and a group of local farmers on preparing the site
for a water cistern, a group of armed men had suddenly
appeared. They ordered the work party to drop tools and leave
the area. Some of the men refused but were persuaded when
the raiders began firing. As the workers prudently retreated,
the intruders began systematically sabotaging their work and
tearing up an approach road to the site. Lucy and her party
went straight to the *mudiir an naahiya* to lodge a complaint. On
hearing the news, John had immediately driven up to Kahima
and evacuated Lucy to a safe house in Hodeidah.

We were told that shortly afterwards one of the houses
occupied by BSDA in Kahima was broken into and several
thousand pounds stolen. Though the key to the safe had been
well hidden it seemed to have been found by the thieves

without much effort. The finger of suspicion seemed to point to our counterparts, for only they knew we had a safe and had seen my colleagues taking money from it.

We also learned that the Kahima director of health, together with a group of men from the sub-district of which he is sheikh, had been arrested on the orders of the prefect. The nature of the charges against them was unclear. Such a move was unprecedented for it is extremely rare for such important men, whatever the gravity of their misdeeds, to be imprisoned. To make matters worse, the prefect had allegedly ordered that the sheikh be closely confined in chains and that he be dismissed from his post as health director.

In mountain areas such as Kahima where, unlike the Tihama, tribal loyalties remain intense, the uneasy balance of power between representatives of the state and traditional leaders is rarely upset in so confrontational a manner. It seemed to me that the prefect might have overreached himself. It was far from clear that he had the right to dismiss the director from his post. Events were still unfolding, but we were told the sheikh's prospects were improving. He had somehow induced his guards to take him to the one telephone serving the 100,000 people of Kahima. A few calls to well placed men in Sana'a had won his immediate release. He was now on his way to the capital to press home his advantage and reclaim his post.

We now came to the point of our crisis debate. Lucy's report had obviously been written in great haste and while still in a state of understandable shock. Yet its conclusion, endorsed by John, seemed to make sense: we had been completely conned by the sheikh/director. He had used his charm to persuade us he shared our objectives but had now decided he had no more use for meddlesome foreigners. To Lucy and John it was clear that the man whom BSDA had worked with for a decade, a man who had been consistently depicted as a progressive feudalist, a valued counterpart whom we planned to send abroad for management training, was a rogue. He had instigated both the shooting incident and the robbery in order to force our evacuation. Lucy urged that AFJAD and BSDA abandon all work in the area pending a thorough investigation.

Brian, together with Nabil and Salwa, asked that we approve the writing of a formal letter to AFJAD protesting at the hasty judgements and slanders contained in Lucy's report. My demurral was not popular with BSDA management, especially as my colleagues ended by refusing to condemn the rival interpretation of events before all the facts were known.

We moved on to our agenda. Pauline took the floor to brief us on the agency's new management structure decided upon at the annual three-week conference of programme co-ordinators which had just been held in London. The agency, she said, had been forced to reassess lines of command and decision-making. We should now know that the programme co-ordinator had the power to remove volunteers from his or her programme and, if matters should come to such a head, to override a majority decision of volunteers.

This was a clear redefinition of authority but not an unexpected one. Several aid agencies had been going through the same process and we knew ours was following suit. Sarah had been preparing a defence of the principle and practicality of non-hierarchy but, to my disappointment, had been suddenly called to Britain for an interview and was absent throughout the conference. I also missed the presence of her former colleagues in Kahima who had been the most forthright in reminding the co-ordinator that he was one amongst equals.

In their absence I spoke of my own surprise at the new line. I had volunteered to work for the agency precisely because it was known to have non-hierarchical principles, all its workers earned the same salary and it was implied that a structure of inner programme debate ensured that all voices were equal. Pauline interrupted to tell the meeting she was astonished that I could have ever got hold of such ideas. Eyebrows were raised all round the table. I replied that abandoning the ideal of co-operative work-practice was, in itself, sad. To do so in the name of improving efficiency and communication was even sadder for it revealed the triumph of an insidious Thatcherism even in the most unlikely of institutions.

I expected Pauline to be stung and she began a steely-eyed counterattack. My views were naïve and dangerous and to prove so she talked at length of her recent visit to Nicaragua. We were informed that only through disciplined line management had the Sandinistas saved their revolution from collapse. I seemed not to be alone in failing to appreciate the connection between the strategy of a state at war and the policy and practice of our own humble organization. In the face of Pauline's anger I said nothing. I changed tack to propose that as it was now definitely established that the Yemen programme had a director it would be naïve to continue calling him a co-ordinator, especially as this term was virtually untranslatable. We should now refer to Brian as our *mudiir*.

Sean, the London desk person, who had hitherto maintained an embarrassed silence, broke in to reassure us that our opinions would always be valued. It was most unlikely that disagreements between a group of volunteers and their co-ordinator would come to such a crisis that the views of volunteers could be vetoed by one person. All kinds of safeguards would continue to exist to minimize the chance of conflict getting so far. Colleagues pressed him to be specific and mentioned issues on which it was clear that Brian disagreed with the majority, or even of all, his colleagues. What would happen if he pressed his ultimate right of unilateral decision-making? Sean said he could not envisage such a circumstance arising.

I replied that, on the contrary, we had a clear example in front of us. At our previous conference we had mandated Brian to make efforts to recruit Sudanese health workers to fill vacancies caused by the imminent departure of Salwa and Nabil from Kahima. Our preference for Sudanese recruits had not been a frivolous one. We were not alone in noticing that Sudanese find it much easier than Egyptians to work in Yemen. For the most part they are admired for their integrity, piety and willingness to conform with Yemeni mores. Their army did not occupy large parts of Yemen throughout the 1960s nor had they broken Arab ranks by recognizing Israel. I reminded Sean that we had agreed that Nabil would fly to Khartoum, would place advertisements and make a short-list of the better candidates among those coming forward. However, at the last minute Brian had ordered the trip to be cancelled. He had unilaterally decided it would be better to recruit in Egypt and had himself gone to Cairo for a week to do so.

Brian seethed with anger and denied ever having ordered Nabil not to make the trip to Khartoum. We all knew this not to be the case, but said nothing. Nabil, normally the mildest and most diplomatic of men, looked exasperated and eventually muttered, 'Not true, not true.' We broke for lunch.

The afternoon proved equally acrimonious when we discussed the appointment of a Yemeni as assistant programme co-ordinator. It had been decided in London that every programme should appoint a national to be trained up to take over the responsibilities of programme leadership, evaluation and planning. The proposal seemed admirable but was it workable in Yemen? Our office was already obviously overstaffed. The strict surveillance of any Yemeni working for foreign organizations would make it hard for the national co-ordinator to objectively assess the prospects for development.

An obvious question mark hung over Hassan's suitability for the post. Brian had been promoting his candidature for several months and had hoped to appoint him without advertising the post. However at the previous six-monthly conference I had persuaded my colleagues to vote that we advertise for other candidates. Brian had now placed one advertisement in a Sana'a newspaper and other candidates had come forward. Brian told us a short list had been drawn up, but that Hassan was still the most favoured candidate.

Our funders were in no doubt that Hassan was an unsuitable candidate. He appeared to have no knowledge of development problems, to lack political sophistication and to possess an urbanite's disdain for his rural compatriots. This was an assessment I entirely shared. Because Hassan had been asked to leave the room during the discussion I and some colleagues were free to express this viewpoint. Brian remained determined. The debate was getting nowhere and Pauline broke in. She informed us that though our views would be taken into consideration the process of selection was the prerogative of BSDA management. We were moved on to our next item.

As the conference dragged on, other discussions were ended in this unsatisfactory manner. I came to realize that there was no place for independent opinion. The flow of debate which had characterized conferences under the egalitarian leadership of Brian's predecessor had given way to a stage-managed event. A host of contentious issues were brushed under the carpet. Margaret glowered and refused to address a word to her Egyptian colleague but the issue of their working relations was not addressed. There was no mention of the impending crisis with AFJAD. We had all heard on the grapevine that a meeting was to be held but joined the conspiracy of feigned ignorance.

Most galling was the suppression of my report. All my colleagues had now read it and spoken to me in private but Brian, Pauline and Sean still acted as if it did not exist. Some colleagues tried to raise the issue obliquely by expressing hopes that under the new management structure six-monthly reports from volunteers would still be appreciated. We were assured this would be the case. I subsequently asked if it was still policy that six-monthly reports should be submitted to Sana'a and London and that written feedback would be received. Pauline adroitly changed the subject.

That evening I learned that John had written a long letter to our management proposing an agenda for the meeting to take place the next day. He had quoted extensively from my report which he described as an invaluable, if painful, document for all development workers in Yemen. AFJAD and BSDA had to face the reality that the system of primary health care in North Yemen was in a state of collapse. Aid agencies in Yemen were faced with constraints which in other parts of the world they would not dream of accepting. He had to ask himself if he was justified in recommending funding for our projects when Yemen was such an expensive country to work in, co-operation with its government so unsatisfactory and progress so hard to measure. He said he now found it considerably easier to recommend continued funding for the Ahad project than he did for our enterprises in Kahima and Rahbaan. In Ahad BSDA had shown it could be an agency of radical development. Its workers had stood up to representatives of unprogressive vested interests. The project had not shied away from making known its disagreements with such individuals and its desire to promote the involvement of local people in providing health care. Success in promoting Salah and the *murshidaat* showed BSDA could reach out to the kind of conspirators for change which AFJAD sought to find and fund in all the developing countries they worked in.

He did not, he stressed, want his funding agency to dictate policy to BSDA which as the implementing agency had managerial autonomy. However, certain issues had to be faced if AFJAD funding was to continue. He wanted a chance to discuss BSDA's recruitment procedures, to know how Magda had been selected as a community health educator, to hear why Nabil had been stopped from going to Khartoum, to learn what BSDA understood by 'Yemenization' and why it maintained an aversion to 'interventionism'. AFJAD had made many mistakes trying to work in Yemen but was at least aware of the difficulties and encouraged a process of frank assessment. From reading my report he noticed an absence of such debate inside BSDA. He agreed with my assessment that BSDA seemed 'determined to hold on to the slice of the development action granted to it, come what may'. Institutional rivalries should not prevent BSDA from joining AFJAD in asking themselves whether they were justified in spending so much money donated by the British public.

We had just come to order for our final conference session when the phone rang and an Arab caller asked for Abdullah. I was surprised to hear the voice of the old hospital director in Ahad, but even more surprised when I learned that he was in Sana'a for he had not visited the capital for at least a decade. He told me he would wait for me and/or Brian in Tahrir Square as he wanted our support before going into the ministry. I told him it would be difficult to come as we were having a meeting and invited him to come and see us later in the day. We later learned that the reason for the trip to the ministry had nothing to do with the work of the Ahad hospital. The old man had recovered his strength and now enjoyed as much mobility as someone of his age could normally expect after a serious accident. He thought that if he played his cards right he might be given a trip to a private hospital in Frankfurt and needed our help to arrange it.' In the eyes of wealthy Gulf hypochondriacs keen to escape the worst of the summer heat West German private hospitals have become much more chic than those of Harley Street. The Yemeni middle class now wishes to emulate them. Yemenis with influence with the national airline, powerful ministries or foreign agencies have begun to seek expenses-paid trips to

Germany. The old man, though not knowing a soul in Sana'a, thought that if we backed up his request and provided guarantees he might have a chance of a free trip. He seemed to imagine Frankfurt was in Britain.

We returned to our deliberations. All the volunteers were silent and frustrated, waiting for the discussion of evaluation procedures. I expressed my anger. I had now written three reports on the work I had been sent to Yemen to do. I had put a considerable amount of work into the last report and been encouraged that others with experience of the development scene in North Yemen had found it a valuable document. I did not expect the agency's management to share my views but did expect those working for an aid organization purporting to have radical and democratic credentials would not engage in suppression of opinion. I asked why other critical reports had been removed from the files. I felt bitter that the agency seemed so convinced that its management knew best that it was once more allowing a volunteer to leave Yemen without the slightest acknowledgement of anything he had written. Pauline was stung into acknowledging the need to respond and told Brian to write a formal reply. It arrived six months later.

I saw no more of the BSDA managers until that evening. Most of the employees of the two agencies were present at a farewell party given for an American and were obviously doing their utmost to avoid each other. I found John and he told me what had happened behind closed doors that afternoon. Expecting a long parley, Rosita and John had arrived with bundles of *qat*, BSDA with an indignant letter which they immediately presented. In it Pauline stated that BSDA had no intention of discussing the topics raised by John for they were internal management concerns. She hinted that if John persisted in his unwarranted intrusion into the affairs of another agency it would be necessary for her to get the general secretary to have a chat with John's bosses and request he be reprimanded.

John replied that wherever AFJAD worked it sought to work directly with local people. He could only justify spending the greatest portion of his agency's Yemen budget on our expatriate-run projects if AFJAD knew what was happening to its money. BSDA's accountancy procedures were slipshod. The issues he had raised were legitimate concerns of any funding agency. If BSDA simply refused to engage in dialogue with AFJAD then he would have no choice but to recommend the immediate cut-off of all assistance to BSDA projects in Yemen.

As tempers mounted, John could not refrain from telling Sean that he had spent too much of his life working with the Yemen programme to be able to retain a critical perspective. It was no good living in the past, imagining circumstances and needs in Yemen had not changed in the years since he had left Kahima. Because Sean had a vested interest in justifying his past and maintaining his present job he ran away from contemplating withdrawal from Yemen or radical realignment of BSDA's work.

Pauline rushed to denounce this personal attack and a slanging match developed. John countered that he was right to personalize issues for time and time again BSDA had allowed its volunteers to burn themselves out and shown an insensitivity to their plight. BSDA's reaction to my report showed, not for the first time, that the agency was blind to criticism of any kind.

The meeting came to a premature end. BSDA announced it would look for other sources of funding and requested twelve months leeway while they did so. John granted this breathing space. Both sides then departed in a spirit of high dudgeon half an hour after they had walked in.

John told me he was not proud of what had happened. He regretted losing his temper and knew that he had deeply hurt Sean. But the truth had had to be said. He only wished it could have been said more calmly. His comments about Sean reflected my own views which I had never expressed. My sense of relief at being vindicated was tempered by the knowledge that an exceptionally kind man, already deeply hurt by the bitterness amongst the BSDA volunteers, had been unnecessarily wounded.

In the days remaining before my departure we watched, with the expectancy of pre-glasnost Kremlinologists, for news of the split to be announced. Sean and Pauline flew home and Sarah returned from London but still there was no report of the meeting we were not supposed to know about. After four days Brian issued a petulant communiqué which he photo-copied and left for every volunteer. It presented the break-up as a cathartic experience which would rejuvenate our organiza-tion. A root-and-branch divorce from AFJAD was to take place at once. We were to move out of our office and seek new lodgings far away from those who thought they knew what was best for us.

I began to unwind and enjoyed a *qat* party with friends and colleagues who came to say farewell. The next morning Sarah and Mujahid drove me to the airport where I learned that the plane I was due to catch had broken down en route to Sana'a. Stranded passengers squabbled for information in a barrage of languages. A British businessman with execrable Arabic decided if he spoke it more loudly he would command respect. At dusk a diverted, already nearly-loaded Tristar, arrived and we boarded. I had heard that the altitude and length of the runway do not make Sana'a a suitable airport for such aircraft. As the plane violently revved up, teetering on the very end of the tarmac, I wondered if I was fated to remain in Yemen.

We lumbered into the air and touched down in Amman late at night. With some persuasion Alia agreed to put me up and transport me to their airport hotel. I found myself dazzled by the glitter of a posh hotel lobby. No room was to be had and I was told to wait. I wandered into a plush lounge and went up to the counter. Muslims were everywhere, and tact obviously called for, so I whispered as I asked if the hotel could sell me a beer. An immaculate bow-tied barman cast a withering eye over my unsharp and crumpled clothes. He replied in voluble American, 'Course we got booze! Where you bin, man?' The pain of re-orientation to the West had rudely begun.

GLOSSARY

abiid	slaves, descendants of ex-slaves manumitted in late 1950s
akhdaam	'those who serve', menial 'non-Arab' caste
baladi	native, Yemeni
futa	sarong
haakim	judge
hakuuma	government
haraam	impure, condemned by Islam
kanada	soft drink
khaaraji	outside, foreign
khubaraa	'experts', foreign aid workers
kufiiya	expensive woven hat
markaz	administrative centre
mudiir	director
mudiir an naahia	centrally-appointed prefect in charge of a government district
murshidaat	'advisers', female primary health care workers
nasraani	'Nazarene', Christian
nidhaan	order, administration
qabiili	tribesman
qat	*catha edulis* shrub whose leaves are chewed as stimulant
ri'ayya as sahhiia al awliiaa	primary health care
sharshaf	all-enveloping female garment
suq	market
Tihama	plain along Red Sea coast